Spirituality in
Social Work
Practice

Spirituality In Social Work Practice

Ronald K. Bullis, Ph.D., M.Div., J.D.
Minister, First Presbyterian Church
Hopewell, Virginia

Taylor & Francis
Publishers since 1798

USA	Publishing Office:	Taylor & Francis 1101 Vermont Avenue, N.W., Suite 200 Washington, D.C. 20005-3521 Tel: (202) 289-2174 Fax: (202) 289-3665
	Distribution Center:	Taylor & Francis 1900 Frost Road, Suite 101 Bristol, PA 19007-1598 Tel: (215) 785-5800 Fax: (215) 785-5515
UK		Taylor & Francis Ltd. 1 Gunpowder Square London EC4A 3DE, UK Tel: 0171 583 0490 Fax: 0171 583 0581

SPIRITUALITY IN SOCIAL WORK PRACTICE

1 2 3 4 5 6 7 8 9 0 BRBR 9 8 7 6

This book was set in Times Roman by Brushwood Graphics, Inc. The editors were Holly Seltzer and Peter Lalos. Cover design by Michelle Fleitz. Prepress supervisor was Miriam Gonzalez. Printing and binding by Braun-Brumfield, Inc.

A CIP catalog record for this book is available from the British Library.

♾ The paper in this publication meets the requirements of the ANSI Standard Z39.48-1984 (Permanence of Paper)

Library of Congress Cataloging-in-Publication Data

Bullis, Ronald K.
    Spirituality in social work practice/Ronald K. Bullis.
        p.   cm.

    1. Social service—Religious aspects.   2. Social workers—Religious life.   3. Spiritual
life.   I. Title.
HV530.B85   1996
361.3′2—dc20   96-7063
                                                                                                        CIP
ISBN 1-56032-407-4 (case)
ISBN 1-56032-406-6 (paper)

TO:

Dr. Schoenberg Setzer, at Hartwick College, Oneonta, New York
my mentor and guide
above and below
and
Laura L. Duncan,
adventurer of mountains and of the soul

Contents

Preface

This book is divided into six chapters. The first chapter assesses the historic and current role of spirituality in social work practice. This is both an empirical and descriptive examination that includes a historic description of the role of spirituality in social work philosophy and intervention strategies. It also discusses why and how social workers have both embraced and shunned spirituality (sometimes simultaneously).

Chapter 2 addresses how social work assessments and interventions can apply spirituality. This chapter provides directions on how to take a spiritual history and how to create a clinical intake form. This chapter also describes the spiritual interventions applied to clinical social work, such as clarifying religious/spiritual values and utilizing meditation, prayer, and religious metaphors. The roles of guilt and forgiveness in healing and dysfunction are also discussed in this chapter.

Chapter 3 examines spirituality in light of social work advocacy and public policy issues. The spiritual/religious impacts issues of criminal justice, rights of children, domestic violence, abortion, and economic justice are explored. This chapter also considers the influence of religious/spiritual groups and political organizations on political processes and public policy issues.

Two spiritual issues with clear, direct social work practice implications are discussed in Chapter 3. The first issue presented is the use of sacramental peyote by the Native American Church. The chapter analyzes the landmark U.S. Supreme Court case titled *Employment Division, Department of Human Resources of Oregon v. Smith* (1990), which decided whether two Native American Church members could be suspended from their jobs as rehabilitation counselors for ingesting peyote in a worship service.

The second spiritual issue addresses the sacrificing of animals by a spiritual group called Santeria. This issue prompted another Supreme Court case, *Church of the Lukumi Babalu Aye, Inc. v. City of Hialeah* (1993), which decided whether the City of Hialeah, Florida could prohibit the group's animal sacrifice. Chapter 3 also examines the spiritual practices in light of this case and suggests implications for social work practice.

Chapter 4 explores ethical implications of spiritual assessment and interventions by social workers, describes the stages of mysticism, analyzes implications of cultic practices for social work, and recounts criteria that contraindicate the use of religious/spiritual interventions. A methodology to determine the usefulness and ethics of using spiritual interventions is proposed. Following the adage "to do no harm," the clinician needs to know when it might be dangerous to employ spiritual interventions on some clients. Social workers need to know when, with whom, and under what conditions such interventions should be used. Research indicates that the more comfortable social workers are with regard to the ethics of using spiritual interventions, the more comfortable they are using the interventions themselves. This, of course, should be the way it is because social work is an ethics-driven profession. This chapter also discusses the nature and ethics of spiritual interventions and assessment in the cult phenomena.

Chapter 5 specifically examines the variety of spiritual diversity in social work practice. This chapter introduces the concept of spiritual democratization—a process whereby spiritual traditions are adopted and adapted into new cultures and circumstances. This process tends to open up one culture's spiritual traditions to another culture and tends to alter that culture's spiritual traditions.

Chapter 5 also studies spiritual healing (both individual and communal) from two cross-cultural perspectives: shamanism and tantrism. The spiritual phenomenon of shamanism is examined as a spiritual technology and as a technique for social work assessment and intervention. Tantra is a spiritual orientation connected with Buddhism, Taoism, and Hinduism. This chapter examines tantrism as a healing orientation and as a spiritual psychosexual intervention. Additionally, ethical and practice implications of shamanism and tantrism are discussed.

Chapter 6 discusses science and the scientific method as symbol systems, as well as the spirituality of social workers, and the possibilities for professional collaboration between social workers and spiritual professionals. This chapter probes the potential for consultations with clergy, healers, and others competent in spiritual matters. The matter of spiritual competency is addressed without strict definitions. The chapter allows for wide latitudes in providing a criteria for seeking spiritual leaders. Both formal and informal structures designed to educate and encourage spiritual leadership are discussed. These structures include educational and organizational means of designating clergy and other professional religious or spiritual designations. Such professional designations are no guarantee of spiritual maturity or leadership and academic degrees are no guarantee of spiritual proficiency. Equally suspect is spiritual leadership by self-appointment—those who claim spiritual status for themselves. Spiritual leadership is both an individual and a community designation.

A series of discussion questions follows each chapter. These questions are designed to stimulate discussion and application of the concepts described. These questions should prompt students and instructors to imagine and innovate scenarios in which spiritual assessments, interventions, and considerations are applied.

Acknowledgments

The author gratefully acknowledges the people and organizations that have significantly contributed to this book. First and foremost is Schoenberg Setzer, Ph.D. who, in the early 1970s, taught meditation and other spiritual techniques. He taught classes describing mysticism, shamanism, telepathy, and comparative spirituality, and led his students on retreats to Roman Catholic and Eastern Orthodox monasteries. He was later murdered as he was conducting pastoral counseling.

The author is also grateful for the clinical supervisors who have integrated spirituality into their own practices and taught me to do the same. My supervising chaplains at Holmsburg Prison in Philadelphia and Reverend Fred Buker at the Ancora Psychiatric Hospital in Hammonton, New Jersey, and Bonnie Kerness, M.S.W., my supervisor while I worked with the Prison Visitation Project of the American Friends Service Committee in Newark, New Jersey. All inspired my pursuit of integrating spirituality in clinical practice.

The authors' special gratitude go to the people on the Fort Berthold Indian Reservation—both Native Americans and non-Indians. The staff and faculty of the Fort Berthold Community College, where I taught and was president for a short time, and all of the members of my congregation, the New Town United Church of Christ, have strengthened my spiritual life.

Chapter 1

Making Connections Between Spirituality and Social Work Practice

Spirituality and social work practice might seem like strange bedfellows. They have been estranged for so long that it might seem that they have been long divorced with irreconcilable differences. Twenty years ago, it might have seemed that the final divorce decree was issued. Today, the divorce seems neither inevitable, final, nor desirable. Social workers and other mental health professionals are willing, even eager, to discuss spirituality and to apply it to social work assessments and interventions.

This book illustrates how clinicians can integrate spirituality into their work and presents the incredible variety of cross-cultural spirituality. The empirical research discussed in this book (some for the first time) reveals that social workers are using spiritual concepts and techniques in making assessments and interventions. Recent research also demonstrates that social workers are thinking carefully about the ethical implications posed by these spiritual concepts and techniques.

In choosing to employ spiritual concepts and techniques, social workers join other mental health professions and professionals who are doing so. Psychologists, psychiatrists, licensed counselors, and pastoral counselors are all in the process of researching and developing strategies and criteria for use of spiritual assessments and interventions.

RESURGENCE OF SPIRITUALITY IN THE UNITED STATES

There is a resurgence of interest in spirituality, in all its variety, in the United States. *A Generation of Seekers* (Roof, 1993) empirically examined the religious and spiritual beliefs of the baby boomer generation. The author reported that those more exposed to the counterculture movements of the 1960s are more prone to be unconventional in their religious beliefs and practices. Indeed, they are much more likely to have more spiritual or mystical beliefs than conventionally religious or theistic leanings. Mystics tend to view God as immanent and to value feelings and experiences about God; theists tend to value cognitive and creedal knowledge about God. Roof has indicated that more active mystics and seekers were more likely to view that "God is within us, believe in reincarnation, psychic powers, ghosts, and meditation." Defining the differences between religion and spirituality is crucial in understanding both the focus of this book and the different ways in which social workers and clients understand spirituality in their practices and in their lives.

⌐ DISTINGUISHING BETWEEN RELIGION AND SPIRITUALITY: MORE THAN A DIME'S WORTH OF DIFFERENCE

Social work's history of defining spirituality mirrors the history of the use of spirituality in social work itself. One of the first social work writers to define religion was Susan Spencer (1956) who defined a religious person as one who holds beliefs about "the affirmative nature of the Universe and man's duty to do something in addition to advancing his own ends; a belief which furnishes some degree of comfort and strength to the individual" (p. 19). Building upon this notion, Joseph (1988) asserted that religion is "the external expression of faith . . . comprised of beliefs, ethical codes, and worship practices" (p. 444).

Conversely, spirituality is defined as the "human quest for personal meaning and mutually fulfilling relationships among people, the nonhuman environment, and, for some, God" (Canda, 1988, p. 243). The differences between these two definitions and modes of thought are becoming crystallized within the social work profession. Religion refers to the outward form of belief including rituals, dogmas and creeds, and denominational identity. In this sense, it is perfectly consistent to speak about one's religion as Methodist and belief in historic statements of belief such as the Apostles' Creed.

Spirituality refers to the inner feelings and experiences of the immediacy of a higher power. These feelings and experiences are rarely amenable to the political formulations of creedal statements or to theological discriminations. Spirituality, by its very nature, is eclectic and inclusive.

Spirituality is defined here as the relationship of the human person to something or someone who transcends themselves. That transcendent person or value may take a variety of forms—and this definition is intentionally broad. This broad definition is intended to include the enormous variety of transcendent values, concepts, or persons with which people identify as higher sources.

AN ECOLOGY OF CONSCIOUSNESS

The variety of spirituality is illustrated by the variety of the occasion for spiritual experiences. A November 1994 *Newsweek* poll of 756 adults, with a margin of error of plus or minus 4 percentage points, hints at such diversity (Woodward, 1994). It found that a full 50% feel a deep sense of the sacred all or most of the time during worship services. Interestingly, the research discovered that, even outside church, 45% feel a sense of the sacred during meditation, 68% feel a sense of the sacred at the birth of a child, and 26% feel a sense of the sacred during sex.

A more operational definition of spirituality is needed. This book asserts that transcendence operationally means a higher altered state of consciousness. A higher state of consciousness means an altered state of consciousness that has a divine or a sacred consciousness. In other words, spirituality is divinely focused altered states of consciousness. Figure 1.1 illustrates the nature of altered states and spirituality and describes how meditation connects with spirituality. As the figure depicts, human beings are capable of several states of consciousness. This figure describes four main states of consciousness. The first and most familiar state is called *beta*. Beta consciousness is waking consciousness. It is the consciousness that most people experience most of the time. Beta is the state people are in when they drive cars, fill out forms, conduct business, play with their children, and conduct the usual affairs of the day. Indeed, the expression of altered states means any alteration from the usual beta state of consciousness.

The next deeper state is *alpha*. In most instances, the transition between beta and alpha is slow and gradual. For example, sleep is an alpha consciousness. The transition from wakefulness to sleep is gradual. The stage of consciousness between wakefulness and sleep is called hypnopompic; the stage from sleep to wakefulness is called hypnogogic. These transitional states of consciousness can be very productive for creative thinking and imaginative problem solving.

The alpha state is a deeper level of consciousness. It connotes a less anxious state of consciousness. It is the level of consciousness associated with meditation, prayer, and dreams. In fact, the hypnogogic and hypnopompic stages illustrate the alpha state. The alpha state is the key to the spiritual consciousness. It is here that the beta consciousness characteristics of logic, analysis, and empiricism give way to the alpha consciousness of intuition, poetic thinking, and analogy. The alpha state is a two way street—where the spiritual realities meet the temporal realities, where the earth and the heavens join.

The differences between the beta and alpha states can be described as the differences between reading a newspaper and reading a poem. In reading newspa-

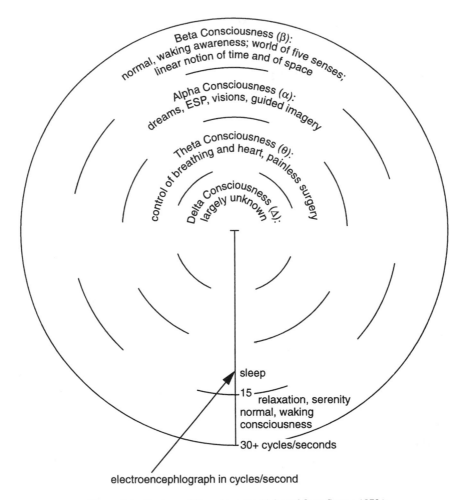

Figure 1.1   Ecology of Consciousness (Adapted from Setzer, 1973.)

pers, the analytical questions of who, what, when, how, and why are paramount. Newspapers give literal accounts of the facts. That is their job and that is what the public expects of them. In the vintage television series Dragnet, Los Angeles detective Joe Friday always tells witnesses that he wants "just the facts, ma'am, just the facts." Beta consciousness acknowledges just the literal facts.

Reading and understanding poetry, however, requires a different consciousness. It requires the alpha consciousness' facility with imagery, symbolism, simile and metaphor. In fact, understanding poetry is not the purpose of poetry. The purpose of poetry is to move and to sensitize and to change consciousness—not just to be understood intellectually. In that same way, the parables (poetic teachings) of Jesus and other spiritual leaders are designed to change consciousness, not just to teach a moral principle.

Spirituality requires the same facility as parable and poetry. Spiritual consciousness is invoked and is fed by the power of imagery to overwhelm and to initiate. It is no coincidence that the majority of most religious scripture is in the form or function of poetry. Worship requires alpha consciousness. Worship facilitates consciousness surrender into a deeper, more profound state.

It is no coincidence that sexuality and spirituality occupy common ground. The Song of Songs or the Song of Solomon is an explicitly erotic Biblical book with a long history of spiritual analogy. Neither is it any coincidence that some spirtual terminology, such as referring to being seduced by the spirit or submission (the literal term for Islam) to the will of God, conjures sexual imagery. Sexual imagery connotes the altered consciousness that is indicative of spirituality. Places of worship are, thus, more like bedrooms than classrooms. Places of worship are specifically designed to invoke the alpha, meditative state. Classrooms cater to the beta mind with bright lights, highly technical learning equipment, and students in a hierarchical position vis-a-vis the instructor. Classrooms are designed for linear, analytical, logical thinking. Places of worship, conversely, are designed to initiate alpha thought waves with dim lights, hymns, liturgical poetry, candles, chanting, praying, meditating and other consciousness-altering devices.

The two deepest states, designated *delta* and *theta,* can illustrate the most remarkable spirtual consequences. In this stage adepts can undergo painless dentistry, surgery, and childbirth. These stages, thus, manifest perhaps the most dramatic example of how spirtual exercises can influence and control physiological activities. There is, currently, little research on these states. Science is just beginning to scratch the surface of understanding such phenomena. Delta and theta states are rarely even recognized—let alone researched. Suffice to say here that, in every religious tradition there are miracle stories. The future is known, the dead are made live again, the blind are given sight, the lame are made to walk. There are stories where, seemingly, the laws of nature are contradicted. As a matter of fact, they are called miracles only because they offend the laws of the beta consciousness. Telepathy, clairvoyance, and spiritual healings all contradict logical and rational thinking. In alpha consciousness, as in dreams and trances, such miracles are commonplace.

SPIRITUALITY IN SOCIAL WORK HISTORY

Charlotte Towle in *Common Human Needs*, first published in 1945 and revised at least twice (1952 and 1957), recognized early on the significance of spirituality in social work practice. Borrowing a line from the Gospels, in a section titled "Spiritual forces are important in man's development," she asserts that "man does not live by bread alone" (Matthew 4:4, Revised Standard Version)[1]. She relates that spiritual needs "must be seen as distinct needs and they must also be seen in relation to other human needs" (p. 8). She also wrote that "through the influence of religion the purpose of human life is better understood and a sense of ethical values understood" (p. 8).

Traditionally, social work literature has reluctantly addressed religion's or spirituality's impact on clinical practice. Loewenberg (1988) has synthesized the reasons for this neglect that include the historic rift between the religious and psychoanalytic movements; the alleged atheistic orientation of social workers (Spencer, 1956); and the economic, political, and professional competition between religious professionals and secular social workers (Marty, 1980). For the most part spirituality in social work literature is conspicuous only by its absence. Loewenberg (1988) writes that "social work literature generally has ignored or dismissed the impact of religion on [social work] practice" (p. 5). In fact, he despairs over the small amount of space Towle gives to spirituality in her book. It is gratifying that she gave such a clear and cogent description of the significance of spirituality and religion. The glass can be half full, too.

Spiritual traditions incorporate potent terms that are useful for social work practice. The Hebrew words tzedakah and hesed mean, respectively, short-term giving (usually money) and a longer term relationship characterized by "loving-kindness" (Linzer, 1979). Islamic social concepts include *maslalah* (public interest) including the notions of collective good over private interest and the responsibility of the *Ummah* (Islamic community) for the common well-being of all its members (Ali, 1990). The term *karuna* (compassion) or the Sanskrit term *metta* (loving-kindness) are terms from Buddhist thought (Canda & Phaobtong, 1992). In fact, Dorothea Dix's funeral service included the Gospel passage:

> I was hungry and you gave me food; I was thirsty and you gave me drink; I was a stranger and you took me in. I was naked and you clothed me: I was sick and you visited me: I was in prison and you visited me. (Matt. 25:35-36)

Another misconception is that spirituality has more heavenly concerns whereas social work has more earthly concerns. To suggest that spirituality and religion are exclusively preoccupied with otherworldly concerns is a gross exaggeration—an exaggeration with a short memory about the history of social work.

---

[1] Note that all biblical passages quoted in this book were taken from the Revised Standard Version of the *Bible*.

The pioneers of the social work profession and its values were intimately connected with religious and spiritual traditions (Stroup, 1986). Jane Addams founded Hull House, led the settlement house movement, and is generally regarded as a seminal figure in professional social work. After graduating from Rockford Seminary (later Rockford College), she traveled to Europe and discussed social problems of the day with current leaders. After Europe, she returned home and soon became depressed. She found the social life "a waste of time" and university men "dull" (Stroup, 1986, p. 8). Then, she found both a challenge and an outlet for her humanitarian concerns. At age 25 she joined the Presbyterian Church, and while at Hull House she joined the Congregational Church (now the United Church of Christ). These faiths offered her religious inspiration and a focus for her service with the poor.

Another form of evidence refutes the otherworldly assertion. In 1978, for example, 46% of all charitable dollars and an equivalent amount of volunteer giving-in-kind were from religious organizations (Marty, 1980). Even this contribution does not adequately consider the long history of Jewish Social Services, Catholic Charities, Lutheran Social Services and any number of other religiously or spiritual motivated organizations. This also does not account for the big and small charities and programs supported by local religious or spiritual groups.

RATIONALES FOR THE USE OF CLINICAL SPIRITUALITY

This section discusses a series of reasons for using spirituality in clinical practice. These rationales flow from the preceeding section and from the data reported in the following chapter.

1. Social work, historically and philosophically, is connected to spirituality. It was noted earlier that early social work leaders were influenced by spirituality. Chapter 2 presents empirical data that indicate that spirituality is a very prevalent factor in current social work practice. Philosophically, both social work and spirituality promote common interests and self-respect.

   Social work and spirituality are natural allies in personal and social healing. Social work and spiritual professionals have similar goals. Both wish to promote the healing of personal and community strife, violence, and ignorance.

   Although the goals are similar, the means are not—nor should they be. Professionals concerned with spirituality are generally concerned with the development of the inner person. Mystics are suspicious of social progress at the expense of inner development. Yet, much of social progress has been spiritually motivated and initiated.

2. Social work and spirituality have much to learn from each other. Also, they can contribute to each other's effectiveness. Spirituality offers social work experiences and insights on personal and community levels that promote social and personal transformations. The Autobiography of Malcolm X is an excellent example of one person's spiritual journey complementing and inspiring both individual and social transformation. Indeed, it is significant that Spike Lee's popular film, based on this autobiography was released 30 years after the publication of the book. This speaks to the enduring spiritual and social relevance of Malcolm X's life and to the social and spiritual impact of his life on contemporary culture.

    The bibliography in Appendix A (at the end of this book) is full of such illustrations. Additionally, the bibliography includes numerous examples of spiritual leaders who played important social or political roles as well. An example of such a person is Pope John XXIII. Under his leadership, the Roman Catholic Church instituted major changes specified under the auspices of Vatical II—a church-wide council in the late 1960s. This council instituted major ecclesiastical changes within the Roman Church and advocated major social, political, and economic changes outside the church.

3. Knowledge of spirituality helps social workers construct spiritual cosmologies and spiritual anthropologies. Cosmologies are graphic depictions of a person's worldview. A spiritual cosmology is necessary to examine the spiritual sensitivity of the client or the social worker. To the extent that a social worker uses spirtual assessments and interventions in his or her work, the social worker will possess an implicit or explicit spiritual cosmology.

    Likewise, a spiritual anthropology is necessary for any examination of healing—whether it be personal or community. Without constructing such an anthropology, assumptions about what is healed and how it is healed are merely implied. Such assumptions need to be clearly expressed if the spiritual mechanisms of healing are to be assessed and addressed.

    A spiritual anthropology is much different from the anthropology with which much of traditional science currently operates. Most traditional science operates with a mechanical anthropology. This anthropology considers the human body as materialistic and mechanistic. Organs are analogous to car parts. When one part gets worn out with disease or malfunction, it can be repaired, replaced, or removed.

    Conversely, spiritual anthropology operates using a mystical model that holds that all creation differs only in speed of energy frequency. This model maintains that energy among organisms and among components can be exchanged, increased, and decreased. This model also holds that there are levels of energy in every organism. For example, spiritual traditions hold that the human body has several spiritual energy centers, or chakras, each with its own vibrations, sources of knowledge, and perspectives. This book explains these chakras in Chapter 3.

4. There is no reason why social workers and spirtual leaders cannot collaborate. The historical estrangement notwithstanding, social work and spiritual professionals have no ethical or philosophic barriers to such collaboration. There are no ethical mandates requiring a separation of these two professionals. In fact ethical mandates promote such collaboration. These ethical considerations come from the National Association of Social Workers' Code of Ethics (1990). These ethical considerations fall into two categories: (a) social workers' responsibility to clients, and (b) social workers' responsibility to society.

Section II (F,3) of the Code of Conduct reads:

> The social worker should not practice, condone, facilitate or collaborate with any form of discrimination on the basis of race, color, sex, sexual orientation, age, religion . . .

This provision against discrimination is broad in scope, and prohibits discrimination across a broad spectrum of classes.

This book breaks new ground for social workers, professional counselors, religious and pastoral counselors, marriage and family therapists, spiritual directors, psychologists, and others in the mental health fields. Increasingly, clients raise spiritual issues with mental health professionals. Increasing also are the numbers of professionals who want to address these issues in a professional manner.

The spiritual issues clients raise are as diverse as the clients themselves. For some, grief over the loss of a loved one, a job or career, a marriage, or a child is spiritual. For some, decisions over pregnancy, marriage, separation and divorce, disease, terminal illness, or debilitating illness are spiritual. For others, the experience of depression, alientation, isolation, or ennui evokes spiritual issues. For still others, crises of war, emmigration, child custody disputes, child abuse, or domestic violence trigger spiritual concerns. Spiritual questions deserve thoughtful, deliberate, and authentic responses. This book's role is to stimulate and instigate such responses.

Chapter 2

The Role of Spirituality
in Social Work Practice

This chapter assesses the role and function of spirituality in social work assessments and interventions. It focuses on therapy and clinical work; spirituality in advocacy and public policy is discussed in Chapter 3. This chapter empirically explores how frequently spiritual assessment and interventions are used in social work practice. It also details specific assessments (including a spiritual history) and specific interventions used by social workers.

This chapter illustrates the role of spirituality in ancient therapeutic and healing ceremonies and practices. In addition, a table compares the medical model of healing and the spiritual healing model and depicts the gradual return of spirituality to clinical social work practice through both assessments and interventions. Implications of this reemergence are described.

SPIRITUALITY IN SOCIAL WORK ASSESSMENTS

Assessment in clinical social work refers to the process of identifying the nature of internal and external stresses disrupting the group's or individual's steady state. Assessments are carried out to aid in understanding the client's situation, to establish therapeutic goals, to identify resources and strengths, and to plan appropriate interventions (Hepworth & Larson, 1986; Northen, 1982). Thus, assessments and interventions are closely linked.

Assessment, as well as intervention, has not been adequately tested or described in the social work literature. Susan Spencer (1956), an early advocate of spiritual concerns in social work, argued against the exclusive reliance on psychoanalytic theory. Other authors have studied religious/spiritual psychic phenomena as tools for assessment. Sanville (1975) has discussed assessment relative to experiences of demonic possession, exorcisms, and object relations, whereas Ikenberry (1975) has assessed human growth and development in terms of psi (telepathic) phenomena in the clinical experience of transferences and hypnotic rapport. Additionally, Berthold (1989) catalogued the most extensive list of spiritual factors in assessment to date in the social work literature. Her list includes the sources of illnesses attributed to spiritual causes, including the work of malicious spirits and malicious sorcerers.

Greif & Porembski (1988) interviewed 11 respondents related to nine different persons with AIDS. In this qualitative study, the researchers looked for the coping mechanisms of individuals, families, and friends faced with the crisis of AIDS. They found that a renewed or continued faith in God, both for themselves and the person with AIDS, was a factor, if not the most important factor, for 9 out of the 11 respondents. These authors wrote that implications from these data include an appropriate inquiry into the significant other's religious beliefs that can play a role in dealing with death and dying.

Sexuality and sexual issues related to religion/spirituality also have been addressed in the social literature. Spiritual and human development have been linked to sexual self-esteem (Helminiak, 1989). The spiritual journey of gay men and lesbian women is also addressed (Ritter & O'Neil, 1989). They describe the philosophical and moral context of both traditional religion's appraisal of issues surrounding homosexuality and ways in which spirituality can help recast the losses through death and alienation sustained by gay men and lesbian women. Bullis and Harrigan (1992) stated that fundamental differences regarding sexual issues exist between religious denominations and that social workers need to be sensitive to those differences in their clinical work.

A later survey of 328 licensed professional counselors, licensed clinical social workers, and licensed clinical psychologists in Virginia identified the importance of religion and spirituality in assessment and interventions (Sheridan, Bullis, Adcock, Berlin & Miller, 1992). A vast majority of the sample (89%) knew their clients' religious and spiritual backgrounds. The study indicated that none of the professional groups harbored biases based on their clients' religious views.

This author conducted a 1992 survey of 294 clinical social workers in Virginia and received 116 returned (44%). The respondents' personal and professional characteristics are summarized in Table 2.1.

Frequency of Use and Importance of Spirituality in Assessment

Table 2.2 presents the data reported on respondents' view of the role of religious and spiritual roles in assessment. On a 5-point scale asking how frequently religious/spiritual factors are included in assessment (1 = Not at all, 5 = Always), respondents reported a mean of 3.57 (*SD* = 1.1). Study participants were then

Table 2.1
Respondents' Personal and Professional Characteristics

Variable	Test Statistic
Gender	
% Male	29.3% ($n = 34$)
% Female	69.8% ($n = 81$)
Age	
M	48.5
SD	9.1
Race	
% African American	2.6% ($n = 3$)
% Caucasian	96.5% ($n = 111$)
% Native American	.9% ($n = 1$)
Degrees	
Masters	
% MSW/MSSW	89.3% ($n = 100$)
% Other Masters	3.6% ($n = 4$)
% Dual	7.1% ($n = 8$)
Doctoral (of those responding)	
% Ph. D.	21.4% ($n = 3$)
% D. S. W.	78.6% ($n = 11$)
Accreditations	
% ACSW	2.6% ($n = 3$)
% LCSW	10.4% ($n = 12$)
% ACSW & LCSW	27.0% ($n = 31$)
% ACSW & Other	4.3% ($n = 5$)
% LCSW & Other	10.4% ($n = 12$)
%All Three Accreditations	42.6% ($n = 49$)
Years as Clinician	
M	18.8
SD	7.7
Primary Client Age Group	
% All Ages	36.5% ($n = 42$)
% Adult	33.0% ($n = 38$)
% Child-Adolescent-Adult	12.2% ($n = 14$)
% Child-Adult	8.7% ($n = 10$)
% Adolescents	5.2% ($n = 6$)
% Older Adults	2.6% ($n = 3$)
% Child-Adolescent	1.7% ($n = 2$)
Work Setting	
% Private Practice	58.8% ($n = 67$)
% Hospital	12.3% ($n = 14$)
% Mental Health	10.5% ($n = 12$)
% Child & Family	7.9% ($n = 9$)
% Other	7.0% ($n = 8$)
% Justice	1.8% ($n = 2$)
% Educational	1.8% ($n = 2$)

(Table 2.1 *continued*)

Variable	Test Statistic
Nature of Work Setting	
% Public	23.4% (*n* = 26)
% Private	76.6% (*n* = 85)
% Sectarian	8.2% (*n* = 9)
% Nonsectarian	91.8% (*n* = 101)
Religious/Spiritual Content in Graduate School	
% Never	23.9% (*n* = 27)
% Rarely	43.4% (*n* = 49)
% Sometimes	27.4% (*n* = 31)
% Often	5.3% (*n* = 6)
Satisfaction with Religious/Spiritual Content in Graduate School[a]	
M	3.3
SD	1.2

[a]Based on a 5-point scale; 1 = Not at All Satisfied, 5 = Completely Satisfied

asked to respond to a series of eight questions asking them to state the percentage of their clients for whom religious and spiritual factors either contributed to the client's problems or situation or served as a strength or a resource. Respondents were asked to answer each question:(a) from their professional viewpoint, or (b) from their perception of their clients' viewpoint. In terms of how religious or spiritual factors contributed to clients' problems, respondents reported that, from their viewpoint, about one third of their clients had *religious* factors which played a role in their clients' current difficulties. Respondents reported a substantially higher percentage of clients who, from the practitioner's viewpoint, had *spiritual* factors related to current problems. Respondents reported that a lower percentage of their clients viewed religious or spiritual factors as contributing to current problems or situations.

The remaining set of four complementary questions asked respondents to state the percentage of their clients for whom religious and spiritual factors acted as strengths or resources. Respondents were again asked to answer each question: (a) from their professional viewpoint, or (b) from their perception of their clients' viewpoint. Respondents reported that, from their viewpoint, about one third of their clients viewed religious factors as strengths or resources. Respondents again reported a substantially higher percentage of clients who, from the practitioner's viewpoint, saw spiritual factors as strengths or resources.

As with religious/spiritual factors viewed as problems, respondents reported that a lower percentage of their clients viewed religious or spiritual factors as strengths or resources. Respondents reported an average of 31.1% of their clients

Table 2.2
Practitioners' Use of Religious and Spiritual Factors in Assessment and Views on
Religious and Spirituality as Sources of Client Problems or Strengths

Variable	Test Statistic
Frequency of Use of Religion or Spiritual Factors in Assessment[a]	$M = 3.57$ $SD = 1.1$
Importance of Religious and Spiritual Factors in Assessment[b]	$M = 3.77$ $SD = 1.1$
Religion and Spirituality Viewed as Problem	
Percentage of Clients with Religious Factors Contributing to Problems/Situations (Practitioners' Views)	$M = 29.5$ $SD = 25.2$
Percentage of Clients with Spiritual Factors Contributing to Problems/Situations (Practitioners' Views)	$M = 54.0$ $SD = 36.1$
Percentage of Clients with Religious Factors Contributing to Problems/Situations (Perception of Clients' Views)	$M = 20.5$ $SD = 19.5$
Percentage of Clients with Spiritual Factors Contributingto Problems/Situations (Perception of Clients' Views)	$M = 29.3$ $SD = 26.5$
Religion and Spirituality Viewed as Strength/Resource	
Percentage of Clients with Religious Factors as Strengths or Resources (Practitioners' Views)	$M = 33.4$ $SD = 20.3$
Percentage of Clients with Spiritual Factors as Strengths or Resources (Practitioners' Views)	$M = 52.6$ $SD = 29.1$
Percentage of Clients with Religious Factors as Strengths or Resources (Perception of Clients' Views)	$M = 31.1$ $SD = 19.0$
Percentage of Clients with Spiritual Factors as Strengths or Resources (Perception of Clients' Views)	$M = 40.3$ $SD = 22.8$

[a]Based on 5-point scale; 1 = Not at All, 5 = Always
[b]Based on a 5-point scale; 1 = Not at All Important, 5 = Extremely Important

who viewed *religious* factors as contributing to their strengths or resources. Respondents reported a slightly higher percentage of their clients who viewed *spiritual* factors as helpful. As with religious/spiritual factors viewed as problems, practitioners assess religious and spiritual factors as positive factors more often than they believe their clients do.

Spiritual Assessment in the DSM IV

The newest version of the American Psychiatric Association's *Diagnostic and Statistical Manual-IV* (1994) recognizes religious and spiritual issues as a source of assessment criteria. This new category moves spiritual assessment forward considerably and falls under the *DSM-IV* section called "Other Conditions That May Be a Focus of Clinical Attention." The section titled "V62.89 Religious or Spiritual Problem" is reproduced below.

> This category can be used when the focus of clinical attention is a religious or spiritual problem. Examples include distressing experiences that involve loss or questioning of faith, problems associated with conversion to a new faith, or questioning of spiritual values that may not necessarily be related to an organized church or religious institution.

This category merits further discussion for three reasons. It represents a major change from some prior psychiatric positions. "By recognizing religious [and spiritual] problems as a category of concern distinct from any mental disorder, the revision reflects psychiatry's steady movement away from an earlier tendency to treat religion as a delusion or as evidence of immaturity, escapism or neurosis" (Stenfels, 1994).

This *V* code uses three examples of religious or spiritual problems (see above). These examples are illustrative and not comprehensive of the types of such issues likely to be encountered in clinical practice. Clinicians, therefore, should be aware of other religious or spiritual issues.

This definition includes both religious and spiritual issues. To put some conceptual flesh on the definitional bone of these terms, the team spearheading the inclusion of this new category defined these in a working definition (Lukoff, Turner & Lu, 1992): "Psychoreligious problems are experiences that a person finds troubling or distressing and that involve the beliefs and practices of an organized church or religious institution" (p. 44). The authors illustrate this definition through examples such as the loss or change in denominational membership, conversion to a new faith, or the questioning of a deeply held faith. The authors also make a working definition for spiritual problems:

> Psychospiritual problems are experiences that a person finds troubling or distressing and that involve that person's relationship with a transcendent being or force. These problems are not necessarily related to the beliefs and practices of an organized church or religious institution. (p. 44)

The authors also offer illustrations for this definition, including near-death experiences and mystical experiences. Near-death experiences, explained in the next chapter, involve the clinical death of someone, often on the operating table. In the event of clinical death the person senses that he or she is in the presence of God, or in an ultimate reality. Upon returning from this death, the person almost always feels a renewed sense of purpose and direction in his or her life.

Mystical experiences need also be defined. They are direct, personal encounters with divine realities. Both English words *mysticism* and *mystery* come from the same Greek root word *mysterion* (Meyer, 1987). This word is derived from the Greek *myein*, meaning *to close*, and refers to the closing of the eyes and lips. The one initiated into the ancient Mysteries was not to divulge any of the secret rites. This "closing" also refers to the closing of the lips and eyes as a medium for transcendence. It is in the darkness of the Mystery rites that the eyes of the initiate are opened to the spiritual light. In this sense, mysticism refers to the opening of senses to a spiritual dimension. Underhill (1915) in *Practical Mysticism* defines mysticism as the "art of union with Reality" and a mystic is a person who has attained that union in greater or less degree; or who aims at and believes in such attainment" (p. 3). Thus, mysticism and spirituality are closely connected and are used similarly throughout this book.

SPIRITUALITY IN SOCIAL WORK INTERVENTIONS

Social workers are just beginning to define the nature of spirituality in interventions. Keefe (1986) offered an exercise in meditation as a "social work treatment." Other authors have given more direct attention to prayer as a therapeutic technique. Canda (1990) described the methodologies of prayer for social work practice and related the support system of Buddhism for Southeast Asians (Canda, 1992).

Another author who conceptualized a term usually associated with religious acts is Laird (1984), who constructed the concept ritual. Laird asserted that a primary function of ritual is to express and reflect shared meanings, and that rituals can be transformed in ways that are therapeutic. Canda (1983) and Cataldo (1979) described the use of shamanistic interventions in clinical practice and Berthold (1989) suggested the similarities and differences in Puerto Rican Spiritism and psychotherapy for treating spiritual ills. Berthold described the interventions of exorcism, persuading the spirit to quit its attacks on the human victims, and rituals designed to remove a malevolent spirit's influence. Bullis and Harrigan (1992) suggested the use of religious imagery and scripture in the intervention with sexual issues.

Brower's (1984) dissertation also addressed religious/spiritual interventions. Her study of 10 to 12 respondents showed that the spiritually sensitive clinician intervened in 97% of the spiritual needs of the 78 clients discussed by respondents. Sister Joseph's study (1988) of 61 Washington, D.C. social workers also found that her respondents very often or often collaborate with clergy on religious issues (18%) and use religious institutions for concrete services for clients (35%).

Canda (1986, 1988) telephone-interviewed 18 social work authors who have researched and written on religion/spiritual issues. He found that spiritually sensitive social workers explore the meanings of clients' life events versus imposing diagnostic categories on clients.

Krassner (1986) found that folk healers used a number of spiritual cures. These cures included giving the illness a name with an accompanying cultural myth. Another intervention was to instill in clients the belief that they would, indeed, be cured. This motivation is essentially the expectation, hope, or faith in a cure. Finally, Krassner indicated that the healers incorporated rituals into their healing practices that were specific to the illness.

Sheridan, Bullis, Adcock, Berlin and Miller (1992) found that a majority of the three professional mental health groups used religious or spiritual interventions in working with their clients and that different classes of clinicians use techniques differently. Fifty-nine percent of the total sample used religious or spiritual language or concepts, 70% helped clarify religious/spiritual values, and 88% referred clients to self-help groups.

Frequency and Use of Spiritual Interventions in Social Work Practice

Table 2.3 represents the average frequency of the use of religious/spiritual interventions reported in the author's study of Virginia clinical social workers. The four most frequently used interventions are exploring a client's spiritual background, exploring the client's religious background, clarifying the client's spiritual values, and recommending participation in spiritual programs. The three interventions used most infrequently are performing exorcisms, touching clients for healing purposes, and reading scriptures with clients.

Beside representing the most frequently and most infrequently used spiritual interventions, Table 2.3 reports a significant variety of spiritual and religious interventions. It is clear that social workers of this survey engage in an enormous amount of spiritually oriented interventions. Indeed, spiritual interventions are invariably used more often than are religious interventions.

To reveal the average use of religious/spiritual interventions in general was more difficult to calculate. To do this, it was necessary to determine whether each intervention was used by the clinician with some of their clients. If a respondent used a particular intervention with at least 10% of his or her clients, the response was coded with a "1," meaning "uses intervention." If, on the other hand, a respondent indicated that he or she used a particular intervention with less than

Table 2.3
Practitioners' Use of Religious and Spiritual Interventions in Practice

Intervention	Mean Percentage of Use
Explore Client's Religious Background	$M = 58.3$
	$SD = 35.1$
Explore Client's Spiritual Background	$M = 62.0$
	$SD = 32.8$
Use or Recommend Religious Books	$M = 7.6$
	$SD = 15.3$
Use or Recommend Spiritual Books	$M = 24.0$
	$SD = 24.8$
Teach Spiritual Meditation to Clients	$M = 7.9$
	$SD = 18.6$
Meditate Spiritually with Clients	$M = 2.8$
	$SD = 10.5$
Pray Privately *for* Client	$M = 32.0$
	$SD = 38.6$
Pray *with* Client in Session	$M = 3.1$
	$SD = 10.1$
Use Religious Language or Metaphors	$M = 12.3$
	$SD = 19.6$
Use Spiritual Language or Metaphors	$M = 32.6$
	$SD = 32.1$
Touch Client for "Healing" Purposes	$M = 1.2$
	$SD = 5.0$
Read Scripture with Client	$M = 2.2$
	$SD = 9.0$
Recommend Participation in Religious Programs (Sunday school, religious education)	$M = 15.4$
	$SD = 22.4$
Recommend Participation in Spiritual Programs (Meditation groups, 12-step programs, men's/women's groups)	$M = 41.3$
	$SD = 29.0$
Help Clients Clarify Religious Values	$M = 19.8$
	$SD = 23.5$
Help Clients Clarify Spiritual Values	$M = 45.2$
	$SD = 30.7$
Refer Clients to Religious Counselors	$M = 9.7$
	$SD = 19.3$
Refer Clients to Spiritual Counselors	$M = 9.6$
	$SD = 20.6$
Help Clients Develop Ritual as a Clinical Intervention (House blessings, visiting graves of relatives, etc.)	$M = 14.7$
	$SD = 19.7$
Participate in Client's Rituals as a Clinical Intervention	$M = 4.8$
	$SD = 13.8$
Explore Religious Elements in Dreams	$M = 10.4$
	$SD = 20.8$
Explore Spiritual Elements in Dreams	$M = 24.6$
	$SD = 31.1$

(**Table 2.3** *continued*)
Practitioners' Use of Religious and Spiritual Interventions in Practice

Intervention	Mean Percentage of Use
Recommend Religious/Spiritual Forgiveness, Penance, or Amends	$M = 16.4$ $SD = 26.7$
Perform Exorcism	$M = .14$ $SD = 1.8$
Share Your Own Religious/Spiritual Beliefs or Views	$M = 13.1$ $SD = 22.0$

10% of his or her clients, his or her response was coded "0," meaning "does not use intervention." Possible scores ranged from 0 to 25.

These data reveal how spirituality is used between social workers and their clients, and indicated the significance that social workers and their clients place on spirituality. Additionally, these data show specific ways in which spiritually is used in clinical social work practice.

Valuing spirituality did not arise spontaneously. The value attached to spirituality comes from a long tradition of spiritual healing in the Western tradition. The following section describes some ways in which spirituality was historically integrated into healing and social policy.

SPIRITUALITY IN SOCIAL POLICY AND HEALING: A HISTORICAL PERSPECTIVE

This section offers an overview of the role that spirituality has historically played in the cultures that have most influenced Western social work practices. It also describes the role that spirituality played, and continues to play, among their clients.

Social workers were not the first healers. The first sentence in *The History of Psychotherapy* (Ehrenwald, 1991) is, "If mental healers were to be summoned to the patient's bedside in the order of their appearance in history, the magician or medicine man would be the first to answer the call" (p. 17). This chapter also examines how spirituality affected personal and social healing in other Western cultures. Following this section, the relevance of these illustrations will be examined in relationship to social work practice today.

Ancient Sumer and Babylon

The following is a Sumerian hymn, possibly written in the second or third millennium B.C. to the god Ninurta (Prichard, 1975, p. 123). This god was both worshipped as the lord of vegetation and fertility and the lord of battle and destruction. It is not uncommon for deities to have seemingly contradictory attributes. The superficial paradox of Ninurta, for example, was that a lord of life and death may arise from the notion that every birth can cause a death, and every death may be an occasion for new life:

> Life-giving semen, life-giving seed,
> King whose name was pronounced by Enlil,
> Life-giving semen, life-giving seed,
> Ninurta whose name was pronounced by Enlil.
> My king, I will pronounce your name again and again,
> Ninurta, I your man, your man,
> I will pronounce your name again and again.

There are three aspects of this hymn, briefly stated here, that merit attention. First is the importance of the name of the god. In ancient Mesopotamia, and the mid-East generally, to pronounce the name of the god or goddess was to invoke the very presence of the god. The invocation of the divinity made manifest the reality of the divinity him or herself. To call upon the name of the god or goddess was to call the presence of the divinity. Second, the name of the god or goddess contained the essence of the divinity. Invoking the name invokes all the characteristics of the divinity, including its healing and destructive powers. The real name of the divinity is often jealously guarded by his or her priests and is seldom revealed. The name of the god is an important feature in spiritual healing and wholeness. A jealous god guards this dynamic power against misuse.

This jealous guarding is the real meaning of the Old Testament story of Moses' encounter with "He Who Is" on Mt. Horeb (Exodus 3). God instructed Moses to free the Hebrews from Egyptian bondage. Moses asks God to reveal His name so that Moses could respond when the Hebrews asked him, "What is his name?" God responds [recorded in Hebrew], "I Am He Who Is." Scholars still dispute the Hebrew pronunciation because it was forbidden to speak the true name of God. Even today, the Hebrew rendering is often a euphemism such as God or Lord and does not attempt a more phonetically correct version like *Jehovah* (Latinized) or *Yahweh*. The power of God resides in the name and must be carefully guarded. Playing with spiritual power can be dangerous.

Third, to know and to invoke the name of the divinity is to hold power over the divinity—or the demon. In the Old Testament story of Adam and Eve, God gave Adam the names of the animals of the earth. Because Adam knew the animals' names, he had dominion over them. The same notion is carried through in the New Testament with Jesus' (literally "God is salvation") healings. Invoking Jesus' name involved his healing presence. Healing in the New Testament is discussed later in this chapter.

The Old Testament

The Old Testament is the sacred text of Judaism. It is an enormously divergent set of literatures ranging from historically oriented books (Exodus, Judges, Chronicles), to poetry (Psalms), to law codes (Deuteronomy, Leviticus), to prophetic literature (Isaiah, Jeremiah, Jonah). The following is a brief example of the justice theology of prophetic literature, and a brief pericope (passage) from the prophet Micah (the last 25 years of the eighth century B.C.E.). The prophet himself came from the laboring class. He came from the Southern Kingdom of Judah at a time when the powerful Assyrian empire was threatening. The prophet's message linked the political and social welfare of Israel to her devotion to justice, kindness, and spirituality. Micah excoriated both political and religious hypocracy and argued for authentic spiritual development. He says sarcastically (6:7-8):

> Will the Lord be pleased with thousands of rams,
> with ten thousands of rivers of oil?
> Shall I give my first-born for my transgression,
> the fruit of my body for the sin of my soul . . .
> and what does the Lord require of you
> but to do justice and love kindness,
> and to walk humbly with your God?

Micah's admonition forms a crux of social values in the Old Testament. Justice, in Old Testament terms, means social justice—fairness and mercy for the poor and the oppressed. It meant mercy and fairness, for example, to widows who could no longer support themselves and the foreigner who had no means of support. The poor and oppressed in Micah's Southern Kingdom meant more than mere observance of outward rituals and external forms of worship. For Micah, spirituality, not mere religious conformity, was the essential ingredient to a socially and politically healthy social structure. Spirituality had a decided social impact. Helping the poor was a spiritual discipline. Social values and social welfare integrated spirituality.

Anatolia, Greece, and Rome

The Great Mother Goddess was called by many different names, in many different places, in many different times. She has been known as Cybele, Ceres, and Tellus Mater (Mother Earth). In any case, the main themes are the regeneration of earthly produce and of fertility—particularly of grain (Baring & Cashford, 1991).

The Goddess may have had her origin in Asia Minor (Anatolia) and, once this land was conquered by Alexander the Great in 336 B.C.E. and later by Rome, the Goddess was assimilated into these cultures. The following prayer to Mother Earth from third century A.D. Rome illustrates the worshipping imagination to Cybele (Vermaseren, 1977, in Baring & Cashford, 1991):

> Holy Goddess Earth, Nature's mother, who bringest all to life, and revives all from day to day. The food of life Thou grantest in eternal fidelity. And when the soul hath retired we take refuge in Thee. All that Thou grantest falls back somewhere into Thy womb. (p. 403)

This prayer is full of imagery and imagination. It acknowledges that the Goddess is the mother of all life, and that all nourishment (physical, emotional, and spiritual) comes from her. Even in death the Goddess gives life. In fact, in the wake of the Goddess, life and death are one child in her cosmic womb. Imagery and symbols speak the language of spirituality. Spirituality is both invoked and expressed by a rich variety of images and imaginings.

Rituals, as "symbols in motion," also play an important role in healing and spirituality. Rites play important roles in social health as well. The rites and rituals associated with Cybele were dramatic, solemn, and sacrificial. The Roman rites were also orgiastic and ecstatic (Baring & Cashford, 1991). This means that for part of the worship of Cybele, the worshipper engaged in trance-inducing rituals and bloody baptisms. Even a cynical Latin poet, writing in the fourth century A.D. (Vermaseren, 1977, in Meyer, 1987), relates the manner of sacrifice. The priest descends into a specially designed pit over which the sacrificial bull or ram is led. The animal is adorned with gold on the forehead and golden disks on the flanks. A sacred spear bursts the animal's arteries and a shower of blood bathes the priest:

> And on his head the priest catches the drops
> With utmost care, his vestment soiled with blood
> And all his body dabbled with the gore,
> Nay, bending back he presents his face,
> His mouth and cheeks now to the scarlet flood;
> His eyes he washes in the gory flow.
> He moistens then his palate and his tongue . . .
> A bull's inferior blood has washed him clean. (pp. 129–130)

An inscription, made in 375 A.D., states that the worshipper is *in aeternum renatus*, or "reborn for eternity" (Meyer, p. 129) through this experience. Rebirth is a powerful image for transformation and renewal of the complete self (intellectual, emotional, spiritual, and physical) as well as an image for a healthy society. Psychologically, through the ritual death of the bull or ram (both common mythological creatures) the worshipper experiences a new self—a new dimension of him or herself. *Baptism* is another term used for this transformation. The ritual washing or cleansing is a common feature in many spiritual practices.

Ancient Greece

Little is known about the origin of the worship of Asklepios, the ancient Greek god of healing. The central temple was located at Epidauros on the Adriatic Sea; however, temples were located throughout Greece (Cartlidge & Duncan, 1980). Healing was often accomplished by the patient sleeping within the confines of the temple and having a healing dream. It was the custom for those healed to leave the facts of their cases on marble plaques. The two following fourth century B.C.E. case histories are direct translations from such memorials (pp. 151–152):

> Ambrosia from Athens had one good eye. She came, a suppliant, to the god. But, as she walked around the temple of healings, she mocked some things as incredible and impossible, that the lame and blind could be healed at only seeing a dream. While lying there, she saw a vision. It seemed that God stood over her and said to her that he would make her healthy, but it was necessary that she set in the temple a silver pig as a reward, that is, as a remembrance of her stupidity. While saying these things, he cut into the place where her other eye was diseased and poured in some medicine. When it was day, she went out healthy.

Ambrosia's account reveals three illuminating themes: (a) the plaques plainly address the skeptics; (b) the dream instructed Ambrosia to make a public offering commemorating her healing (offering a gift often has the effect of solidifying and concretizing the spiritual healing); and (c) the dream appeared to diagnose and remedy a second eye problem about which Ambrosia had no knowledge.

> A man who had the fingers of the hand crippled except one came to the God as a supplicant. But seeing the tablets in the temple, he disbelieved in the healings and he sneered at the inscriptions. While sleeping he saw a vision. It seemed he was casting the bones (in the crypt) under the temple [to predict a healing or not] and as he was about to cast the bones, the God appeared and seized upon the hand and stretched out the fingers. As it turned out, he seemed to bend the hand to stretch out the fingers one by one. When he straightened all of them, the God asked if he still disbelieved the inscriptions upon the tablets of the temple. He said, "No." Asklepios replied, "Because formerly you did not believe those things which are not unbelievable, may you henceforth be named 'Unbeliever.'" When it was day, he came out, healthy.

This healing was also mediated through a dream. Again, the god appeared to the dreamer personally and used some form of touch or instrumentality to effect a healing. The god took this man's hand and stretched out his afflicted fingers. Asklepios cut Ambrosia's good eye and poured something into it. In both cases, some memorial of the healing was required—even beyond that of the marble plaque. These memorials (a silver pig for Ambrosia and a new name for the man) were reminders of previous repentance for skepticism. These memorials may have provided a warning for others against such skepticism. A more plausible rationale is that the memorials may have provided positive expectations for their own healing. The relationship between these spiritual scenarios and social work practice is described next.

ANCIENT SPIRITUALITY AND SOCIAL WORK PRACTICE

The scenarios of the spiritual experiences discussed earlier are not just ancient psychic artifacts. Ancient spiritual experiences offer the modern social worker, and other mental health clinicians, insight into the very essence of healing and health itself. Indeed, the Greek word for *holy* and the English word for *health* have the same root word. The Greek word *holos* means something that is whole or complete. Today, this word means something in English that is both sacred and healthy. Real health requires real holiness. Thus, for authentic therapy and healing to take place, the clients must have a sense of the sacred or wholeness in their lives.

Real health means the transformation of the client, not just the relief of symptoms. Clients look for a sense of renewal in their lives. Clients know that this renewal comes at a high price—the price of sacrifice, death, and rebirth. The images of sacrifice evoked by Micah and the images of death and rebirth evoked in Sumer and in the dramatic Cybele baptism are the spiritual components of psychic health and healing. Healing blindness and restoring sight at the temples of Asklepios was a prime illustration of physical and emotional healing by the use of spiritual interventions.

Mental health works in tandem with spiritual health. To the extent that spiritual health complements mental health and vice versa, the healing is more complete. These themes continue in such diverse spiritual literatures as the New Testament and the Mayan *Popol Vuh*.

The New Testament: The Gospel of Luke

A classic pericope in Luke's versions of Jesus' healing ministry was the healing of the Gerasene man afflicted by demons. Luke relates that the afflicted man wore no clothes and he lived homeless outside the city among the tombs (8:26-33). At first, the man avoided Jesus' ministrations, saying, "What have you to do with me, Jesus, Son of the Most High God?" Jesus persisted, however, and asked the name of the demon possessing the man. "Legion," replied the demons, "for many demons entered him."

This pericope commands attention. The cause of the Geresene man's illness was attributed to spirits, in this case malevolent spirits. The attribution to demons for both physical and mental illness was a widespread notion. Indeed, as you shall see in the next chapter, that notion is still widespread. Although Western medicine has dismissed the notion of spirits as a causal factor in illness, many people and culture consider spirits an integral part of a wellness ecology.

An important clinical evaluation of spirits considers exactly what a spirit is and is not. Spirit comes from the Latin word *spiritus,* meaning wind or breath. The English words *inspiration* and *inspire* come from the same root. So, spirit means something that inspires or animates. The spirit is that which gives life and breath. Thus, in the clinical sense, spirits are animating principles—the most deeply held beliefs about oneself and others. A person's animating principle has an impact on his or her purposes and practices. One's most cherished beliefs can control one's actions. This spiritual anthropology is discussed at length in Chapter 3.

Quiche Maya

The Quiche Maya flourished in what is now the Yucatán of Mexico, Guatamala, Belize, and Honduras. Their civilization achieved a high degree of technological and spiritual sophistication before 1500 A.D. The National Aeronautics and Space Administration (NASA), for example, has calculated that the Mayan calendar is accurate to within 15 seconds every thousand years. Remains of their civilization have been uncovered and are being translated and interpreted with increasing refinement. Luckily, monuments preserving and detailing this heritage still exist.

In a significant Mayan pyramid at Chichen Itza called El Castillo, there are 365 steps from the bottom to the top of the pyramid—one for each day of the year. The priests of the Maya walked up the steps symbolizing the journey from earth to heaven—from the realm of ordinary consciousness to sacred consciousness. People can enter an inside staircase to the pyramid's inner chamber. In this inner chamber, the priest ascended to the mysteries of the upper chamber where the jaguar throne is still intact.

A lesser known part of Mayan culture is the sacred book the *Popol Vuh*. The literal translation of *Popol Vuh* is *Book of the Community* (Goetz & Morley, 1950). The author favors the translation as the *Book of the Reunion*. The *Popol Vuh,* as a record of the Mayan myths, "reunites" the Maya with their cultural history and traditions and reunites them with their own spiritual traditions. The book was first written by a Quiche Mayan in the sixteenth century and was translated into Spanish in the seventeenth century. The sacred book tells the story of how human beings were created, after some faulty attempts, and how the Lords of the Underworld were defeated by magic and miracle. The *Popol Vuh* tells of how an ambitious and self-centered Lord named Vucub-Caquix (Seven-Macaws) was outwitted by two shamanic youths named Hunahpu' and Xbalanque'. The name Xbalanque' literally means *little jaguar* but most likely refers to his designation as a *little sorcerer* because the Maya equated the jaguar, with its ability to swim, run, and climb, with a being that is able to move gracefully through different worlds and different consciousness.

The following words and description of Vucub-Caquix suggests how he violated Mayan spiritual and social values and norms (Goetz & Morley, 1950, pp. 93–94):

> "So, then, I am the sun, I am the moon, for all mankind. So shall it be, because I can see very far."
> So Vucub-Caquix spoke. But he was not really the sun; he was only vainglorious of his feathers and his riches. And he could see only as far as the horizon, and he could not see over all the world.

The hubris of Vucub-Caquix speaks of an ecologically spiritual component, not just an ethical component, to Mayan social values and social behavior. He mistook his gold (the symbol for imperishability) for immortality and transcendent consciousness itself. Thus, although he thought he could see far (into the future and into the human heart), he could not. He was therefore not so much evil as deluded, not so much sinful as estranged from the real supernatural powers. The cure for hubris and twisted spiritual and social function was wrought through shamanic relationships with the spirit world. Traditional Mayan healing incorporates both a causal element attributed to spiritual causes and spiritual interventions.

THEMES IN SPIRITUALITY IN HEALTH AND WHOLENESS

The previous illustrations reveal several themes that connect spirituality with personal and social healing. Fundamental values of social workers include "the worth, dignity, and uniqueness of all persons as well as their rights and opportunities" (National Association of Social Workers, 1990). This line of the Preamble in the National Association of Social Workers' (NASW) Code of Ethics means that the entire individual is valued, including his or her spirituality. This provision also ensures that religious liberty rights are protected as well. These religious rights (guaranteed in the federal and state constitutions) include the freedom to exercise religious beliefs and the freedom from government restriction of such practices. These constitutional considerations are more fully considered in Chapter 4. The religious rights guaranteed by U.S. federal and state constitutions (and considered in the NASW Ethics Preamble), include the rights of spiritual self-determination, the right to address those beliefs with social workers, and the right to have those beliefs valued in the course of their work together.

Such themes are considered below. First, spirituality is a fundamentally new perspective on social work practice. In many respects, this perspective is at odds with the medical model of treatment. Table 2.4 depicts the differences between what this author calls the medical model and the spiritual model of social work practice.

Recognizing the distinctions made between the medical model and spiritual model is crucial for social workers. Social workers need to determine which model of practice they use themselves. Employing a model, without reflection by the clinician, pigeonholes clients into the social worker's own model—not the model that is most valued by the client. Social workers need to be aware of the model they use and reflect whether it is really meeting the needs of the client or meeting the needs of the social worker.

Second, clinicians need to consciously choose their preferred model. Adapting either model from habit or by default is insufficient. Knowing and understanding the distinctions between these models helps clinicians make a deliberate, conscious choice. Clinicians who render services based on such choices serve their clients better than services based on habit or rote. Additionally, clinicians need to be aware that using spiritual assessments and interventions mechanistically can defeat their purpose.

Table 2.4 indicates several differences between the these models. Although these models are not as dramatically dichotomous as presented here, Table 2.4 does highlight important differences between these positions. The basic differences are ones not only of techniques, but of orientation. Although the medical model values the body and its physical components, the spiritual model values the metaphysical components of the human person. In this respect, the spiritual model could be construed as more humanistic and eclectic than the medical model. Superficially, a humanistic approach means that clients' thoughts, feelings, and beliefs influence their health. The second major difference is that the spiritual model recognizes a multidimensional human anthropology. A spiritual anthropology is discussed in detail in Chapter 3. The spiritual model recognizes that human beings have physical, emotional, intellectual, intuitive, mythic, and transcendent dimensions. The medical model recognizes a limited human dimen-

Table 2.4

The Medical Model Compared with the Spiritual Model of Social Work Practice

	Medical Model	Spiritual Model
Cosmology:	Basically limited to physical world, emotional content may be included	Includes spiritual realm as well as the emotional, and physical as well
Goal:	Relief of symptoms	Personal and social transformation
Anthropology:	The physical body exclusively	A series of increasingly subtle bodies including the physical body
Symptoms:	Limited to those signs manifesting in the physical body	Includes those signs of illness manifesting in the subtle or spiritual bodies
Assessments:	Tests made for narrowly testable symptoms	Intuitions, hunches, dreams are recognized as guides in determining illness
Interventions:	Limited to those that specifically address the physical symptoms	Including all those that address the subtle or spiritual bodies
Authorities:	Testable results under the rigors of the scientific method	Open to those methods that have authority from traditional use, scripture, recognized teachers (even spiritual guides), or that can be deduced from those above
Role of Family & Community:	Very limited	Reinforce and integrate spiritual realms and healing
Research:	Limited to those projects that comport with the medical model	Research does not determine the efficacy of the treatment

sion: physical and possibly emotional or intellectual. To the extent that social workers use the medical model in their practices, they must realize that their model may be inadequate to meet the needs of their clients—especially when those clients voice spiritual concerns. The spiritual perspective both informs and influences both social work assessments and interventions.

Having emphasized the differences between the medical and spiritual models, it needs to be emphasized that the medical model has been responsible for an enormous amount of personal and social benefits. In fact, the medical model (and Western medicine in general) should always be seen as complementary partners in the healing process.

SPIRITUAL THEMES IN SOCIAL
AND CULTURAL CONTEXTS

This section describes significant themes that flow from the aforementioned mythic stories. The following themes are not intended to be comprehensive, but are intended to suggest important relationships between spirituality and social phenomena.

Myth and ritual are the primary data of spiritual social work practice. Myths, simply put, are spiritual truths. Myths embody the values and the world view of the community. Rituals act out the myths. They are myths with motion. The Greek god Asklepios created its own myth and its concomitant ritual. What the god could not do in waking consciousness, Asklepios worked in dreams.

A prevalent and useful example of both myth and ritual is the hero(ine) round or hero or heroine quest (*The Hero with a Thousand Faces,* Campbell, 1949). The main elements of this adventure round are composed of three themes: separation, initiation, and return (p. 30). These themes are present in all myths of heroes or heroines in their adventures, which contain similar themes as spiritual healings. When social workers use spiritual assessments and interventions, they are guiding their clients through their own hero or heroine adventures. Separation means pulling apart from the ordinary world of the adventurer. This separation may be the adventurer's own choice or it may be thrust or even forced on him or her. Mental or physical illness, divorce, the death of a loved one, and the loss of job or status can all act as such a separation. Initiations are rituals that memorialize the adventurer's entrance into the spirit realms. The return of the adventurer means his or her integration back into normal consciousness, usual environment, or normal circumstances. This return is also accompanied by teachings, healings, or other boons by the adventurer to the community.

This adventure round indicates the ultimate empowerment of the client. For it is not the social worker who takes the client's adventure for him or her, or even with him or her; it is the client who makes the journey. The power to initiate, endure, and complete the journey is the adventurer's power. The social worker acts as the psychopomp for this spiritual journey. The role of psychopomp was traditionally played by the ancient priests or priestesses who led sacred processions. For the purposes of social workers and spirituality, the clinician can be seen as a psychopomp—one who leads the client through this spiritual adventure. In leading the client through illness or crisis, social workers are "mental health psychopomps."

This chapter has described the role of social workers who act as mental health psychopomps, and the next chapter discusses the techniques used by social workers to engage clients in this spiritual journey.

SUMMARY AND CONCLUSION

This section defines and describes several issues which have been discussed throughout this chapter.

1. *Spirituality is an important ingredient in the beginning and development of social work practice.* For years, religion and spirituality have animated social workers to address the needs and problems of those most forgotten by society. The introduction and this chapter have reviewed some of the more notable of these social work pioneers.

   The focus of the social work profession as a religiously or spiritually oriented profession has been noted in Chapter 1. Indeed, perhaps a hallmark of this is denoting social work as a calling or profession. *Calling* connotes a vocation that is motivated or initiated for religious or spiritual reasons. *Profession* connotes a more detached and studied approach to a vocation.

   For some time the profession either looked askance or ignored the spiritual dimension of social work. This attitude basically mirrored general patters of social skepticism of spirituality. At this time spirituality is undergoing a resurgence in both society in general and in social work practice in particular.

2. *Spirituality has a social component.* Spirituality does not focus on only individual responses to the divine dimensions. It is also vitally interested in social welfare, social organization, and the quality of social organization.

   Spirituality has played, and continues to play, an integral role in social values and social norms and systems of distributing wealth. Chapter 3 discusses that spiritual values and norms have contributed to ancient community life, the monastic model of community life, and the values that have shaped values of jurisprudence and social policy in the United States.

3. *The spiritual dimension is not well understood in the social work profession.* Although this book cites the most important and useful research and conceptual literature in this field, the volume and depth of even this literature is limited relative to other social work issues.

There are many gaps, both in content and in procedure, in the volume and depth of research related to spirituality and social work practice. Issues such as the effectiveness of spiritual assessments and interventions, the use of spiritual social work advocacy, the frequency of using spiritual assessment and interventions, and the ethical comfort of using such assessment and interventions are all under-researched and under-published.

4. *Spirituality is an entirely different way of understanding cosmology and anthropology than that of traditional Western science.* This chapter has outlined the distinctions between the medical and the spiritual models of healing. How social work practitioners view their cosmology and anthropology determines how they might view their clients, their clients' problems, and their treatment interventions. Cosmologies and anthropologies can be tools for sophisticated assessments and interventions.

Table 2.4 may appear more dichotomous than is warranted. That the models are separated does not mean that the realities of the medical and the spiritual models are mutually exclusive. The goals, assessments, interventions, anthropology, cosmology, and other elements may merge with one another.

5. *Social workers, as a group, may be less religious than their clients.* This finding has several implications. As noted previously, social workers may ignore religious or spiritual issues that their clients may want addressed. This difference in assessment can undermine clinical rapport and create a rift in the effectiveness of clinical interventions and the therapeutic process.

The remedy for this difference is not to dismiss or ignore these differences but for the clinician to thoroughly discuss these differences with the client. The discussion itself helps establish rapport even if the initial differences are never resolved, and has the additional value of making possible the mutual exchange of viewpoints on spiritual and religious issues. This exchange of viewpoints allows the clinician to fully hear and appreciate the client's feelings and experiences relative to religion and spirituality. Conversely, the clinician has the opportunity to fully discuss his or her own insights and suggestions on religious and spiritual matters.

6. *Spirituality offers social workers a way of transformation for their clients.* Spiritual assessments and interventions offer more than the alleviation of symptoms. Symptoms refer to parts of the body or psyche, whereas spirituality addresses the entire person. Where most psychotherapy may address one part of the client's spiritual biopsychosocial system, spirituality addresses the deepest, most profound components of the person. Relieving of symptoms is derived from the medical model.

   A spiritual model of social work practice does not speak of curing, but of transformation. Personal and social transformation includes more than the relief of symptoms—it refers to the wholesale shifting of consciousness. In traditional terms, this transformation was known as repentance, from the Greek verb that meant *to turn around*. The client is completely and fundamentally turned around in a different direction, with corresponding transformations in consciousness and behavior.

7. *Social workers are theologians whether they like it or not.* Theologians interpret religious and spiritual experiences. Theologians, happily, have no monopoly on understanding sacred things. Anytime clinicians are placed in a position to understand or to discuss a client's religious or spiritual experience, they are doing the work of a theologian. Again, this does not mean that social workers should shy away from religious or spiritual discussions. It only means that they should educate themselves to make informed interpretations. There is no magic in interpreting experience theologically. Theologians are educated like anyone else. They take classes and write papers and put on their pants and skirts like anyone else.

   The extensive bibliography at the end of this book provides a thorough starting point for exposure to several different religious traditions. Increasingly, religion and spirituality are being offered in seminars, in-service training, and other continuing education opportunities. Asking for these continuing education programs and offering social work courses at the master's level also promote such educational opportunities.

8. *Social workers must be trained across many different disciplines because spirituality is an interdisciplinary world.* The days when professions can rely exclusively and strictly on theories promulgated for and by social workers are long gone. Disciplinary turf wars are wasteful, petty, arrogant, self-destructive, and inevitably hurt the client and the profession. Turf wars are fought merely for political purposes, power, and professional advantage. They are like the Cold War fought between the East and West. Social workers, psychologists, psychiatrists, and professional counselors erect

"Berlin Walls" when they promulgate exclusive jargon, chisel out self-proclaimed exclusive areas of expertise, and claim private economic advantage over other disciplines. These claims tend to balkanize disciplines and to set them against one other in a self-serving manner. Bigotry is not confined to racial and ethnic issues.

There is no legitimate purpose for such disciplinary warfare, particularly when addressing a client's spiritual issues. Spirituality, as we have seen, is necessarily an interdisciplinary process. For example, ever since the translation of the Bible from Greek and Latin into the language of the people, the power of translating and interpreting the Bible no longer lay in the hands of any one professional group. This decentralization of biblical translation and interpretation is the literary equivalent of a universal divine spirit pouring out universally.

As the divine spirit is not the property of any one group, neither is spiritual healing the property of any one profession. The history of spirituality is replete with leaders who are both trained and who use spiritual insights across different disciplines. At a time in Western history when interest in spirituality is reaching new and innovative proportions, it is no time to restrict the research, the assessments, and interventions to any exclusive professional group.

Chapter 3 discusses spirituality and social work assessment and intervention in depth and takes advantage of the insights of theologians, psychologists, pastoral counselors, and social workers.

DISCUSSION SCENARIOS AND QUESTIONS

The following exercises and discussion questions are intended for personal and classroom use. They are intended to provide experiential and intellectual data about personal spiritual experiences, and to initiate eclectic critical thinking about spiritual assessments and interventions that may be useful for social work clinical practice.

1. Construct a spiritual genogram (Bullis, 1990). The creation of a spiritual genogram is similar to those of family or genetic genograms. A genogram is a kind of family tree that charts ancestral roots. Similarly, spiritual genograms chart spiritual ancestry. A spiritual genogram can chart those persons, places, ideas, and experiences that have formed one's current spiritual identity (or even lack thereof!). Anything and everything spiritually formative can be included.

After constructing a spiritual genogram, you should be able to answer the following questions: Who were the most significant persons and what were the most significant events in your spiritual development? How have they affected your spiritual growth and development? How have you changed your spiritual stance in the past five years? Was there one particular experience (or experiences) that had a lasting spiritual impact on you? What are the current spiritual ideas, books, authors, persons, or events most important to you?

2. Time lines portray spiritual journeys. Draw a time line of your religious experiences, either in an elaborate or simple graph or chart that chronologically depicts your beginning spiritual experiences, principle spiritual events, and current experiences. The time line can be supplemented with photographs or a collage of pictures or drawings, and can depict the seasons of one's spiritual unfolding. Sometimes it is a spiritual summer of growth and transformation; sometimes it is a spiritual winter of dormancy and reflection. The traditional liturgical seasons of many religions incorporate times of rigorous self-reflection, celebration and renewal, and recognition of human suffering and mortality. The value of the time line is that the chronology of spiritual experiences makes it possible to place spiritual journeys in perspective over a long period of time.

Once the time line is constructed, the following questions can be answered: How long have you been on a conscious spiritual journey? Did your own spiritual journey begin from your deliberate effort or did it begin from a spontaneous, unplanned event? Have there been large gaps in your spiritual growth and development or has your spiritual growth been regular and consistent? Have you changed your spiritual outlook or position since your childhood upbringing? If so, how?

3. If you currently belong to a formal spiritual group, answer the following questions with respect to that group. If you do not belong to a formal spiritual group, answer them with respect to any informal spiritual group or affiliation. Keep in mind that spiritual groups are defined in a much larger sense than denominational or religious affiliation. Formal spiritual groups may include Alcoholics Anonymous (AA) participation, meditation groups, prayer groups, study groups, or discussion groups: What are the spiritual purposes for which your group was formed? Are these goals stated or unstated? How are leaders chosen? What are their qualifications? What are the predominant rituals, holidays, and symbols for the group? Does the group have a set of scriptures from which it draws authority or inspiration? What is the origin of such literature? How are such scriptures used during any liturgy or ritual actions of the group?

4. To which model (medical or spiritual) do you ascribe? How do your assessments and interventions reflect your model? Do you use a combination of these models? If so, how do you determine under which circumstances to use which model and which set of assessments and interventions? In your personal life, which model do you use to understand and to treat problems? Do some models more adequately address issues than others? If you combine the models, how do you use a combination of both medical and spiritual assessments and interventions?

Chapter 3

Integrating Spirituality
Into Clinical Social Work Practice

This chapter integrates the theory and the practice of spirituality into clinical social work practice. It is divided into several different sections, including spiritual cosmology, anthropology, assessment, interventions, and ethics.

Spiritual cosmology refers to a world view from which the client understands his or her place in the universe. An example of such a cosmology is depicted in Figure 3.1 (see page 39). The cosmology might also be represented by abstract symbolism. Spiritual cosmology often depicts the origin of human beings, seminal spiritual places, the world of spirits, the place of human beings, and where and how healing can be accomplished. These depictions are highly symbolic and their meanings can change over time. Spiritual cosmology, in the form of a world, is also a symbol of the formation, homeostasis, and expansion of consciousness. As such cosmologies depict consciousness, cosmologies themselves point to important clues for healing.

Anthropologies flow from cosmologies. A spiritual anthropology represents the ways in which human beings are made and function. This chapter explores several different anthropologies that incorporate the spiritual dimension into human functioning and behavior. Spiritual assessment and interventions flow from spiritual anthropologies. This chapter also provides specific resources for spiritual assessments, including how to take a spiritual history of the client.

Interventions are the specific techniques of therapy. Later sections describe spiritual interventions that are most broadly applicable to social work clinicians and have been shown by research to be most prevalent among practitioners. The interventions include how to explore a client's spiritual background, how to clarify a client's spiritual values, how to recommend participation in spiritual groups, how to explore spiritual elements in dreams, and how to use spiritual meditation with clients.

The ethics of spiritual assessments and interventions is an extremely important consideration when deciding whether to use such techniques. Some clinicians avoid the use of spiritual assessments or interventions out of a misconstruction of ethical values. Except for contraindications otherwise present (as discussed in Chapter 6), there is no ethical mandate prohibiting spiritual assessments or interventions. Moreover, it is unethical to avoid such discussions when client needs or wishes so dictate them.

CONSTRUCTING A SPIRITUAL COSMOLOGY

Figure 3.1 is a depiction of the ancient Norse cosmology. This cosmology illustrates points already discussed and serves to concretize spiritual concepts. The cosmology is more deeply discussed in Chapter 7. Salient features of this cosmology are the layers of the universe, the relationship between the levels and layers, and the conflicts inherent in the cosmology.

The Norse cosmos has three layers divided into three tiers each. Thus, this cosmology shows a total of nine different levels. These levels represent different planes or layers of existence. This means that human beings and other creatures do not live within the structure of time and place alone, but within nine levels of existence. These levels or planes connote a multidimensional understanding of reality and an intricate and complex life for human beings.

The Norse cosmology recognizes a relationship between these layers of existence. The central subject of this relationship is the magic tree Yggdrasill. This magic tree has its roots in the lowest layers of existence and its branches in the highest layers. Yggdrasill represents the nature and the subject of the Norse multidimensional reality and the relationships of all types of life to each other. First, just as a tree is organic and dynamic, so life and reality is changing and active. The Norse universe was not static and unchanging, but dynamic and alive. Second, the tree is not only organic, but conscious. The Norse universe was a conscious universe. It thought; it felt pity; and it felt pain. So too, Norse reality itself was conscious of human beings, their strivings, and their plights.

A conscious, relational universe has important implications for social workers. Such a universe means that individuals and communities can interact with their world to *make* their lives. It is possible to break bad behavioral habits; it is possible to change lifestyles and lives; it is possible to change fate and luck; it is possible to deepen and broaden consciousness itself. If social workers intentionally use spirituality to help clients change how they feel about themselves, others and their world, this cosmology (as well as others) offers a conceptual model from which to start.

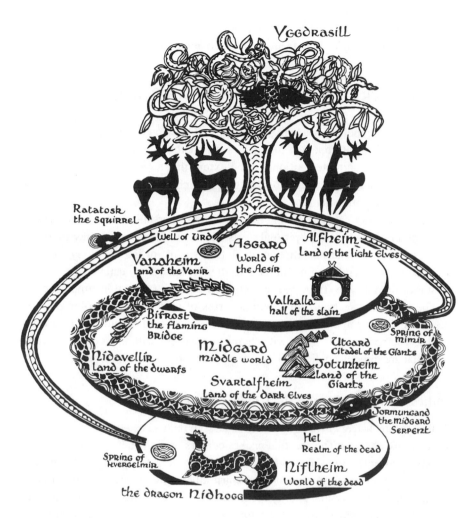

Figure 3.1 Norse Cosmology (From *The Norse myths* by Kevin Crossley-Holland © 1980 Kevin Crossley-Holland. Reprinted by permission of Pantheon Books, a division of Random House, Inc.)

The Norse cosmology also recognizes the universe with conflict in which destruction and renewal are important factors. The voracious squirrel Ratatosk knaws at Yggdrasill's roots. Other mythological animals eat its leaves. At the end of an age, Yggdrasill will die and be reborn. Time itself is a living, growing, and dying thing. Thus, the cosmos mirrors the human processes of tension, conflict, death, and rebirth. It also can be said that human conflict mirrors the conflict inherent in the cosmos.

Cosmologies construe consciousness. No matter what cosmology is used, it is symbolic, a map that provides ways to help individuals understand who they are, where they came from, what they are here for, and where they may be going. Spiritual anthropologies flow from spiritual cosmologies.

CONSTRUCTING A SPIRITUAL ANTHROPOLOGY

A spiritual anthropology needs to precede any discussion of spiritual social work practice. It is the anthropology that drives the methodology of a spiritual social work assessment and intervention. To the extent that a spiritual anthropology is authentically and competently constructed, clinicians may responsibly employ spiritual social work practices.

If a practitioner's understanding of the nature of persons is strictly biological, physical and social, then a spiritual assessment and intervention may make no sense. Even if clinicians attempt spiritual assessments or interventions, they are likely to be inept and even patronizing to their clients. They cannot offer clients what they do not have. Training is a useful antidote for spiritual incompetence.

The following section begins with a series of spiritual anthropologies from ancient and contemporary Hinduism and a mystical arm of Judaism (the Kabbalah). The section concludes with themes consistent with each of these traditions that are directly applicable to contemporary social work practice.

Bodies within Bodies and the Chakra Systems

Chakra means *wheel of energy.* Each successive body sheath is more subtle and more highly charged. The spiritual chakra centers are key factors in understanding spiritual anthropologies and are both a map of anthropology and of consciousness. The transformation of these spiritual energies changes consciousness.

The centers of spiritual energy are a "Jacob's Ladder" from increasing duality and materialism to increasing unity and subtle energy. The symbol of Jacob's Ladder is expressed because the chakras are a series of powerful spiritual centers that are analogous to a series of organs along the human spine. These spiritual centers, although formed from energy not directly corresponding to human organs, are analogous to joints, glands, and ganglia. Indeed, one's entire body is a wellspring of energy centers of which one is largely unaware. An easy way to experience such energy centers follows: Stand erect and extend your hands with the palms facing each other. Feel nothing between the hands. Now vigorously rub both hands together. Feel the energy—like a subtle ball of electricity—awakened between the hands. This is a form of the energy which permeates the entire body and is more powerful in certain joints, particularly along the spinal column.

In fact, the images of Jacob's Ladder, the Ladder of Judgment, and the Ladder of Divine Ascent described by St. John Climax in the seventh century to symbolize the system of spiritual energy centers are both accurate and useful. There are two sides of a ladder that hold the rungs together, just as there are two sides or channels in the spiritual energy centers through which the spiritual energy flows. One side of the spiritual energy ladder is known as *ida*—the side connected with the moon. The other side of the ladder is known as *pingala*—connected with the sun (Campbell, 1974). It is important to note that with the solar and lunar symbolism, the human being (both male and female) is a unity of these elements.

Continuing with this ladder symbolism, each rung of the ladder is a spiritual center. The number of these circles or rungs varies, but seven is the most common number. They run along the length of the spine and are connected with anatomic features and glands. It should be remembered, however, that the spiritual circles are energies associated with, but are not derived from such physical organs. In fact, these physical organs derive their power from the spiritual energy centers.

The spiritual energy itself is described as *kundalin*, meaning circular, coiled, or winding. The image of this kundalin energy is, therefore, often symbolized by a coiled serpent. This energy is coiled at the base of the spine and can spring upward toward the increasingly powerful centers. This spiritual energy is also called *shakti* in the East. There is no precise Western equivalent for this term, but it is the sum of the body's spiritual energy. Eastern writers consider this a feminine energy. A symbol for the relationship of the human body to the shakti might be the Madonna (feminine energy) and the Christ child.

The Old Testament relates the shakti symbol in the story of Moses and the bronze serpent (Numbers 21:4-9). The Israelites beseeched Moses to ask the Lord to protect them from snakes. Moses prayed to the Lord and the Lord told Moses to make a poisonous or fiery serpent and set it on a pole. Moses made a bronze snake and all the victims of snake-bite were to look at it to be healed.

Commentators usually interpret the snake on the pole as simply a means of easier visibility. This reduces the symbol to mere sympathetic magic and reduces God to a mere magician. After all, it was God who told Moses to make the serpent and the pole in the first place! The serpent-pole is the kundalin and the shakti. The healing takes place on the physical level when the kundalin ascends through the chakra centers. Healing takes place on the physical level after the healing on the spiritual level. The serpent ascending the staff, or caduceus, is the symbol of medicine and healing.

The first center, located at the base of the spine, is the *root support (muladhara)*. This is the center that values material possessions and drives hard to possess them. This center hangs onto life, but without vigor, enthusiasm, or warmth.

The second ascending center is called *her special abode (svadhisthana)*. This is the center of compulsive, even ignorant, sexuality. Sexuality in this center is seen as a possession—a goal to be achieved or won. In this center, sexuality is also a metaphor for seeing the world in contradictions, in the duality of either/or. This center could also be called the adolescent hormone center. The goal of the energy springing to life at this center is to begin to see life less in terms of opposites and to possess another through sexuality, but to set another free by means of sexuality.

The third center is the *city of the shining jewel (manipura)*. This is the center driven by power, and is depicted by the devil's temptation of Christ in the desert (Luke 4:1-13). The devil tempts Jesus with both material and spiritual power. The goal of this energy is to transform personal power into community love. This is exactly what Jesus did when he refused the devil's temptations.

It is no wonder that the fourth energy center is called the heart chakra. The Sanskrit name is *not struck (anahata)*, because it is the place where the sound of God is heard without anything being struck together. This description may sound obscure, but it means that this energy center is accessed when the essential unity of the cosmos is appreciated rather than its apparent dualities. A sound of God for the Hindu is the *OM* or *AUM*, for the Christian it may be *Kyrie eliason* (Lord have mercy). This is the voice of God speaking within, the voice of God calling to the voice of God—the divine speaking to the divine within oneself. It is the beginning and end of mercy. God does not need another to make one hear God's voice. The term *unstruck* has particular connections with the theology of St. Paul's writings. In Paul's famous love chapter (1 Corinthians 13) he uses two symbols, the noisy gong and the clanging cymbal, which employ the necessity of being struck:

> If I speak in the tongues of mortals and of angels, but do not have love, I am a noisy gong or a clanging cymbal. And if I have prophetic powers, and understand all mysteries and all knowledge, and if I have all faith, so as to remove mountains, but do not have love, I am nothing.

The goal of the fourth chakra is not to possess life, or possess another sexually, economically, politically, or socially, but to liberate oneself. The first three energy centers are concerned with the external world; the fourth energy center inaugurates an inward journey. This is a journey preoccupied with the conquest of inner fears, anxieties, and demons in order to realize an inner ecstasy. The fourth chakra is the entrance to ecstasy.

The fifth energy center is called *purified (vishuddha)*. This center is a threshold to great spiritual awakening. However, this awakening is a pearl of great price. The cost for this inner ecstasy is everything—all one is that is not of God. The fifth chakra inaugurates a cleansing of all that is not of God. This cleansing is not seen as a duty, but as a desire to be close to the divine Beloved. If there is a speck of dust on the mirror, the image is distorted. This does not mean that the image itself is flawed, but the perception of the image is flawed. The English mystic poet William Blake (Huxley, 1954) wrote, "If the doors of perception were cleansed, everything would appear to me as it is, infinite" (p. 3). The fifth chakra opens material phenomena to the light of transcendence.

This spiritual center is also characterized by a sense of spiritual unity—where all there is, is God. The purified energy of the fifth chakra means that there is less and less distinction between who one is and who God is. As Christ said, "I and the father are one." The goal of the shakti at the fifth chakra is to purify the self to the point at which the self and God are one.

The sixth chakra has a spacial location between the brows and is known as *command* or *third eye (ajna)*. In Eastern symbolism, the third eye is often painted on figures and statues to indicate that a third sight is now available to those who have reached this stage of spiritual growth. It means that they and the world are seen with an inner vision that pierces the world of form.

In Egyptian symbolism, the cobra and the vulture appear between the brows of queens and pharaohs. On one level, these represent the unity of the northern kingdom goddess Wadjet and the southern kingdom goddess Nekhbet (Wilkinson, 1994). On a deeper spiritual level, they represent the unity of the sixth spiritual center and the unity of the lower and upper chakras. As the embodiment of the living god, the pharaoh personifies the cosmic human. The pharaoh is not a special human, but the personification of the highest spiritual attainment. The symbols of the vulture and cobra represent the unity of the upper and lower world, the physical and spiritual realms within any person. They represent the incarnation of the divine in and among the human person. For Christians, the sign of the sixth chakra are Paul's words, "It is no longer I who live, but Christ who lives in me" (Galatians 2:20).

The seventh chakra *(sahasvara)* has no physical counterpart in the human person. It is symbolically located above the head or at the crown of the head. In the West crowns indicate the presence of God or the lifting up of humanity to God. The seventh chakra indicates a resurrection or a transcendence—even an extinguishing of the individual self into God (nirvana).

The symbol of the Tree of Jesse is the Christian symbol related to the seven spiritual centers. Although the images are different, the symbolism is consistent. The shakti (serpent) power is likened to sap of a tree growing from the loins of Jesse. For Jews, the shoot of Jesse means the spirit of the Lord.

> There shall come forth a shoot from the stump of Jesse, and a branch shall grow out of his roots. And the spirit of the Lord shall rest upon him, the spirit of wisdom and understanding, the spirit of counsel and might, the spirit of knowledge and the fear of the Lord . . . In that day the root of Jesse shall stand as an ensign to the peoples." (Isaiah 11:1-2,10)

For Christians, it signifies the genealogy of Christ, but means so much more. The shakti runs through the tree instead of the ida and the pingala. It is also significant that, like the chakra system, the tree of Jesse has seven stages. Indeed, the Isaiah passage above denotes three spirits: the spirit of wisdom and understanding, the spirit of counsel and might, the spirit of knowledge and the fear of the Lord.

The first stage of the Jesse tree is the roots of the tree. It depicts a sleeping Jesse, the reputed father of King David, with a tree growing out of either his loins or abdomen. The sleeping Jesse is a perfect analog to the sleeping shakti energy. The sleeping Jesse is lethargic and unconscious and his spiritual power is unaware, even of itself. The second stage of the Jesse Tree is King David. David, of course, was sexually preoccupied with Bathsheba. This means, of course, that he was stuck at the second level chakra. The symbols of patriarchs occupy positions of the third, fourth, and fifth energy centers.

The sixth level is occupied by the Virgin Mary, who represents the birth of the spiritual being and the unity of heaven and earth. The mother of God represents the birth of the spiritual person. The seventh level of the Jesse Tree, of course, is Jesus Christ. This is the inauguration of the messianic chakra.

The Human Microcosm and Macrocosm

The final consideration of a spiritual treatment in this chapter consists in the construction of the human microcosm and macrocosm of the Kabbalah. The Kabbalah, translated as *instruction*, is a mystical system known mostly in Judaism. Once again, this mystical system is widely divergent and eclectic. Kabbalah is practiced differently across both Judaism around the world among other systems of mystical thought as well.

A primary principal behind Kabbalah is that human beings and the universe are reflections of each other. They are inextricably and organically connected. The operative quote is the ancient mystical formula, "as above, so below" (Hoffman, 1989, p. 45). This is the same formula incorporated into the Christian "Lord's Prayer" (Matt. 6: 9-10).

> Our Father who art in heaven,
> Hallowed be thy name.
> Thy kingdom come,
> Thy will be done,
> On earth as it is in heaven.

This central, but often overlooked, section of the Lord's Prayer reflects the ancient dictum "as above, so below." This section states that earth reflects the will and structure of heaven and heaven can reflect the will and structure of earth. The dictum reflects the organic unity of the cosmos. What affects one affects the other. This is an ancient cosmic ecology that at times takes the symbolic form of a human being.

What concerns this chapter is the concept traditionally known as *Adam Kadmon*—a universal cosmic person. This person, depicted as both male and female, is the microcosm of the universe. The Kabbalah cosmology closely reflects the order and structure of the human body and vice versa. Conversely, the universe is a macrocosm of the human body, as the human body is the universe writ small.

The Tree of Life is also an analogy for the anatomy of God. This tree is unusual in that it grows upside down. Of course, the directions of up or down are symbolic and should not be considered literally. Its roots are in heaven and its fruit is in the earth. These images symbolize the anatomy both of human beings and God. These *sefirot* (singular form—*sefirah*) are almost like spiritual antennae materializing the will and power of God.

There are 10 specific sefirot, the symbolism of which is deliberate and traditional. Each sefirah enjoys its own function and has an organic relationship to all other sefirah (Scholem, 1991). The root three sefirot closest to heaven are the crown (*keter*), wisdom (*hokhmah*), and insight or wisdom (*binah*). The trunk next three sefirot are loving kindness (*hesed*), judgment (*gevurah*), and beauty (*tifereth*). The fruit final three sefirot are endurance (*netzah*), splendor (*hod*), and the foundation (*yesod*). The 10th sefirah is called foundation (*malkuth* or *shekhinah*). God's creative energies flow from the upper sefirot into the material world by means of this sefirah. This is why it is called the foundation. This sefirah is the means by which heaven is reflected on earth. The foundation makes it possible for the above dictum "as above, so below."

This sefirah is also called shekhinah for a specific reason. Shekhinah is the feminine principle of God and God's immanent presence (Epstein, 1988). The feminine image for the incarnational aspect of God is especially apt. After all, it is only through the woman that the man's seed comes to fruition. The woman's body is the living image of the immanent presence of God. Indeed, the earthly home of the Shekhinah is the tabernacle, or the "holy of holies" in the synagogue (Cooper, 1978).

There are several components of this universe microcosm and the human macrocosm. The first is the concept of the sefirot. Sefirot are "concentric circles of bioenergy" (Hoffman, 1989, p. 57) or "primordial energies" (p. 53). These energy centers are aligned at various points of the body but are not connected to any physical organ.

The sefirot are similar to the chakras (Blank, 1991). Both chakras (or centers) and sefirot (or spheres) are realms of energy. These centers or spheres vibrate at different levels, signifying different relationships and experiences of God or the divine. The difference between them is their respective teleological emphases, or respective goals. Sefirot emphasize the connection with the transcendent and divine outside the individual. Spiritual growth up the sefirot connects the upper worlds to the lower worlds, thus connecting human beings with the divine. The sefirot have a greater social and communal emphasis than the chakras because an individual's movement toward God raises the entire community and the community's spiritual movement up the sefirot lifts the individual.

Thus, the sefirot anthropology represents a model of individual and corporate healing. Conversely, the movement up the chakras emphasizes the individual's relationship to his or her own divine self with less emphasis on community. Indeed, marriage and family life are religious obligations for the Jewish Kabbalist. The highest aspiration of the Hindu adept at chakra transformation is often the solitary phase in later life. The adept retires into the forest for solitary contemplation. Although ashrams or community spiritual workshops are part of the chakra development and realization, the difference is one of emphasis, not of quality.

Synopses of Spiritual Anthropologies

Several themes flow from the spiritual anthropologies presented. First, human beings are multidimensional, the levels of whom include the physical and emotional dimensions but are not limited to them. The current biopsychosocial model, currently in widespread use among social workers, is inadequate to include these spiritual anthropologies. A spiritual-biopsychosocial model is more compelling and able to do so (Nelson, 1984).

Second, healing begins at the spiritual level and proceeds to the physical level. Kabbalah proceeds from a right relationship with God or the sacred at the highest levels to the lowest levels. In the chakra formulations, real healing must begin at all levels for the healing to last. Otherwise, the social worker is just treating symptoms. Ameliorating symptoms is not a cure. The symptoms will only appear elsewhere with as much, if not more, vengeance.

The spiritual anthropologies compel one to view symptoms not as something to eliminate, but as something from which to learn. Symptoms are teachers. Physical or emotional symptoms signify that something is wrong, or that one's many bodies (chakras or sefirot) are not in synch with one another or with the divine. Thus, symptoms are spiritual reflections and warning signs (Hay, 1984), revealing through the body what the soul needs to say. In this way, symptoms are the soul's diagnostic hieroglyphics.

The spiritually sensitive and spiritually trained social worker interprets these signs. As discussed in the first chapter, one important difference between the medical and the spiritual models is that the medical model relieves symptoms whereas the spiritual model promotes transformation. Only a spiritual cure out- lasts the variety of physical symptoms. The next section describes the spiritual nature of assessments.

ASSESSMENTS

Spiritual assessments gauge the client's health from a spiritual perspective, and require testing the person's spiritual centers. No matter what model of spiritual anthropology is used, the spiritual components of the anthropology must be tested and examined for health or disease. This section illustrates such tests and opportunities for such discernment.

Three principles of such assessment should be noted. First, assessment is an organic process that has three main aspects. As discussed earlier, spiritual anthro- pologies all assert that the body is intimately connected with the spirit. Above all else, an organic assessment means a connected assessment. Whether the connec- tion lies in "bodies within bodies," chakras, or sefirot, the connection is an inti- mate one. The second aspect of this organic assessment is that the connection changes as people grow and change. A spiritual assessment is, thus, an ongoing assessment. Assessing a person's spiritual relationships at one time is insufficient for claiming an overall assessment. Thus, assessment is a dynamic process. This is the second theme—that assessments of a spiritual nature may be quite different depending on the time and circumstance. It is an organic process.

Third, assessing a client spiritually is an eclectic process that excludes psy- chological or medical assessments. Indeed, spiritual assessment is cognizant of all data useful in describing the client's situation. The usefulness, however, of these eclectic and interdisciplinary assessments is in the service of gaining a clear picture of the complete human being.

The following are specific suggestions for making spiritual suggestions, including taking a spiritual history, making spiritual genograms, and drawing spirit bodies.

Taking a Spiritual History

Appendix B, at the end of this book, provides a spiritual history. It is designed as an assessment tool and covers three significant areas of spiritual impact: (a) parents or parental figures, (b) spouses or significant others, and (c) one's own history.

The questions are designed to elicit much more information than the client's denominational affiliation. Religious affiliations alone are almost useless in gleaning the central elements of a client's spiritual orientation. There are significant differences among members of the same religion and even denomination and, conversely, there are significant similarities among those of widely different religious or spiritual backgrounds. For example, not all Roman Catholics accept the religion's official position on abortion, nor do all Presbyterians accept (or even know about) their historic position on predestination. By the same token, the similar spiritual rationale for abortion and other social policy positions runs across religious and denominational lines. Belief in astrology, extrasensory perception, and mystical experiences also run across denominational lines (Roof, 1993).

Useful information is gleaned by examining how the client is spiritual, and not what religious label is attached to the spirituality. Additional information can be gleaned when clients can describe how their spirituality affects their lives today; what ideas, book, people, etc., influence their current spiritual attitudes; how they have changed from their spiritual orientations as children or young adults; and what spiritual conflicts they now address. These are the issues that the spiritual history in Appendix B addresses.

There is more to taking a spiritual history than simply gleaning information. Taking a spiritual history is also an opportunity to establish rapport with the client. How a spiritual history is taken is more important than what information is gained. If the history is taken in a routine, obligatory, or patronizing manner, the client may feel like the social worker views spirituality (and perhaps even the client) in the same manner.

Conversely, the social worker who is interested, or even fascinated, with their clients' spiritual lives are likely to be seen as being fascinated with their clients and their clients' situations as well. Such interest is sure to deepen and broaden the clients' interests in their own spiritual journeys. Clients often need only slight affirmation from their clinicians that spirituality is an important factor in their treatment outcome in order for clients to initiate rather deep (if not profound) spiritual insights. These insights can bear directly on clients' speed and completeness of compliance to treatment and recovery. Such interest is sure, in turn, to reciprocate the interest in the therapeutic interventions by the social worker. A word must also be said about how the spiritual histories should and should not be used. They are first and foremost, living, breathing documents that will grow and change as clients get more experience and insight into their spiritual developments and situations. Put in legal terminology, spiritual history is a piece of evidence that proves who the client is, but is not the client's final judgment. Thus, spiritual history should not be used to pigeonhole the client with any strict categories nor as a means of reductionism (to reduce the client's assessment to purely biological or psychological causes). On the other hand, the spiritual history can be used legitimately as a springboard for mutual discussion, as evidence for ongoing assessments, and as a means for making mutual, therapeutic goals.

Making Spiritual Genograms and Spiritual Maps

Spiritual genograms and maps of spiritual journeys were introduced at the end of Chapter 1. Spiritual genograms are diagrams of spiritual ancestors and influences. Such maps are depictions of the spiritual territory the client has traveled. Both depict the client's spiritual biopsychosocial geography.

Although spiritual genograms were described in the previous chapter, a more complete description is offered here. They are the spiritual equivalent of family genograms (Bullis, 1991), which are frequently used to depict the emotional and psychological attachments and stresses within the family system (Compton & Galaway, 1979). Similarly, spiritual genograms chart a spiritual family tree. Some genograms depict spiritual ancestors only, including significant books, experiences, lectures, and events that have shaped the client's spiritual orientation or outlook. Other such spiritual family trees may feature relatives and friends that have contributed to the client's spiritual orientation. Other spiritual family trees show both.

Whatever style a genogram or spiritual family tree may take, it is imperative to detemine how the spiritual family has contributed to the client's spiritual outlook through significant ideas, experiences, events, travel, or conflicts. Note particularly how these ideas and events have changed, modified, or negated earlier spiritual positions. Likewise, spiritual journey maps depict the contours, the small and large pathways, the highways and the byways of the spiritual life. They accomplish in geographic analogy what spiritual genograms accomplish in genetic analogy, and can be as varied as those depicting their journeys. Most maps will include a time line or a space line of their spiritual journey showing important events and places of the journey. Sometimes the journey will begin at an early age; sometimes it will begin with some crucial spiritual event. Some maps include photographs of significant events and people, and others even include mementos, tokens, or remembrances of the spiritual journey. This map, as well as the genogram, can also serve as a spiritual travelogue or testament of the client's spiritual journey. For example, a client's first communion, adult baptism, experience of being born again, or other intense and significant spiritual awakening can be charted.

Drawing Spirit Bodies

Drawing spirit bodies is a useful and creative way to provide spiritual assessments. Participants begin by outlining their bodies on large sheets of paper. With this outline as a focus for meditation, the client meditates and visualizes body disease or discomfort. In the meditation, the client locates problems located at various parts of the body. The meditation, however, does not stop there. It continues with visualization exercises designed to uncover symbolic pictures for each of the bodily diseases. After the meditation exercise is concluded, participants draw these symbolic images on their respective locations on the spirit body.

For example, one such exercise depicts a symbolic representation of heartburn. The symbol reveals more than the medical diagnosis. The symbol reveals both the cause and the cure. The symbol of the fire breathing volcano is a potent symbol representing both the expressed and unexpressed passion of a volcano. The truth of the assessment is embodied in the symbol itself.

Symbols disclose the body's own wisdom. A volcano is created by intense, internal pressures that build up in the earth's surface. Without a means to otherwise release this pressure, the molten rock explodes from its funnel and suffocates or burns anything in its path. Conversely, the cooled ash is enormously fertile. The lush and fertile Hawaiian island chain, for example, is composed almost entirely of volcanic ash.

This meditation-induced symbol of the volcano offers clues to the nature of the author's illness as well as its cure. The illness stems from unreleased and unresolved tensions. Without adequately releasing the tensions, the stomach acid explodes up the esophagus. As a matter of fact, when this drawing was rendered, the author of the spirit body was working a full-time job, writing two books, completing a dissertation, and considering a marriage separation. The volcano symbol evokes the intervention as well.

This indicates much more than washing the volcano with cold water. The water symbolism is rich and deep. It means that the roots of the stress itself must be resolved. The water symbol means that the reaction to stressful events must be expressed in other less harmful ways. Even the stressors themselves should be reduced. Indeed, a whole lifetime of learning to internalize stress and emotions needs to be radically altered. This is a lifetime of work.

The importance of this exercise is to help interpret the clients' situations, including any problems they are currently experiencing. The spiritual nature of this interpretation begins with a spiritual methodology of assessment, emphasizes the root causes of difficulties, and can foster creative solutions.

The spirit cannot be assessed indirectly, but it is possible, however, to assess the spirit indirectly. As diseases of the spirit manifest themselves in the body, the body's ailments can reflect the state of the soul. Hay (1984) in her book *You Can Heal Your Life* has an entire section relating physical illness to emotional and spiritual diseases.

Creating Spirit Masks

Masks have always represented spirits or even images of divinity. In fact, Joseph Campbell wrote a monumental set of four books titled *The Masks of God* (1964).

These volumes discuss the incredible diversity of images (masks) used to portray a wide array of divine images. Masks embody spiritual images.

Making spirit masks is another way for clients to express spiritual factors in assessment. It externalizes the spiritual intuitions, insights, and instincts. Clients making their own spirit masks is both a therapeutic and a revelatory act. It is therapeutic in what they disclose to the client and to the clinician. Spirit masks disclose the clients' hidden spirits and uncover previously hidden strengths and powers. They are a vehicle through which the client self-discloses fears and anxieties as well. Spirit masks disclose to the clinician all the strengths and fears revealed to the client, plus the client's motivations, drives, and strength of will. These are the issues that the social worker must discern.

There are two steps involved in constructing spirit masks. The first involves meditation, without which the masks cannot be properly constructed. The meditation is a simple exercise in sacred imagination, and is necessary to truly reveal what was previously hidden or obscured. Although meditation is examined more thoroughly in the next section, a brief explanation is included here.

The meditation exercise is designed to reveal an image for the mask itself. It is one way to allow unconscious images to surface to consciousness. Once conscious, the mask images are made by a simple drawing or actual mask itself. The meditation begins with simple breathing exercises or with muscle relaxation exercises. The client sits, comfortably but erectly, or lies flat on a firm mattress. Breathing slowly and deeply tends to relax the muscles, although tightening and loosening muscle groups is another way to relax. When the client is deeply relaxed, the social worker should suggest a visualization.

Visualization exercises can be adjusted to meet their intended purposes. A mask visualization might begin with clients imagining a guided tour of their hearts or souls. The clinician can suggest a meditation or a visualization that their hearts or souls are places to explore. The meditation or visualization can make the heart a place of infinite accessibility, a place feelings can be found and recognized. They can also make the soul a place of discoverable and understandable memories, a place where past sorrows and joys are visited and revisited.

The clinician acts as the tour guide. The tour guide marks the trail, points out the rough places and the smooth territory, demonstrates safe passage through the heights and the depths, and shows the beauty and the terror of the terrain. From this guided tour, the client finds the images (faces) for the spirit masks. Opportunities for such masks are infinite. The tour guide can assist in translating the images expressed as masks.

Clients can then either make masks for themselves or draw them on paper. This mask can depict the "holiest of holies" within the client or the "unholiest of unholies" within. Additionally, clients may sense that they or others are sacred images—that they are holy icons of each other and for each other. The clinician helps the client participate in the reality of the mask. How does the mask make the client feel? What feelings or impressions does it initiate? Does the mask help the client get in touch with divinity or a higher self? If so, how? These questions, and others like them, are designed to elicit spiritual data. The following section more directly addresses clinical interventions with such data.

INTERVENTIONS

Interventions are the techniques used to effect therapy. Table 2.3 sums research data on other data summed earlier in this chapter. This table represents frequencies of the use of spiritual interventions by clinical social workers in Virginia.

The following section discusses the most prevalent interventions used as reported in Chapter 2. These include how to explore a client's spiritual background, how to clarify a client's spiritual values, how to recommend participation in spiritual groups, how to explore spiritual elements in dreams, and how to use spiritual meditation with clients.

Exploring a Client's Spiritual Background and Clarifying Spiritual Values

Exploring a client's spiritual background and clarifying spiritual values are both high on the user list of interventions. Both have similar goals and methodologies for reaching those goals. First, exploring a client's spiritual background and clarifying spiritual values are both consistent with a spiritual anthropology because spiritual anthropologies require spiritual assessments. Second, both probe deeply into the client's spiritual life and thought, their values and backgrounds. Superficial questions about the client's spiritual life yield superficial responses, whereas deeper inquiries get deeper insights. Third, both exploring and clarifying offer opportunities for a more thorough examination of the totality of the client's situation. Discussing spiritual issues with the client can often blaze the way into the social, emotional, and physical aspects of the client's situation. Taking a spiritual history, as discussed earlier in this chapter, begins this process.

Spiritual Genograms. Spiritual genograms provide one of several ways to explore a client's spiritual background (Bullis, 1990). The genograms exercise, described in this chapter, provide a systematic way to explore spiritual ancestors and antecedents. These roots can be persons, places, things, or ideas. The structure of the spiritual genograms themselves connects these roots into a coherent relationships.

Table 2.3

Practitioners' Use of Religious and Spiritual Interventions in Practice *(From Chapter 2)*

Intervention	Mean Percentage of Use
Explore Client's Religious Background	*M* = 58.3
	SD = 35.1
Explore Client's Spiritual Background	*M* = 62.0
	SD = 32.8
Use or Recommend Religious Books	*M* = 7.6
	SD = 15.3
Use or Recommend Spiritual Books	*M* = 24.0
	SD = 24.8
Teach Spiritual Meditation to Clients	*M* = 7.9
	SD = 18.6
Meditate Spiritually with Clients	*M* = 2.8
	SD = 10.5
Pray Privately *for* Client	*M* = 32.0
	SD = 38.6
Pray *with* Client in Session	*M* = 3.1
	SD = 10.1
Use Religious Language Metaphors	*M* = 12.3
	SD = 19.6
Use Spiritual Language or Metaphors	*M* = 32.6
	SD = 32.1
Touch Client for "Healing" Purposes	*M* = 1.2
	SD = 5.0
Read Scripture with Client	*M* = 2.2
	SD = 9.0
Recommend Participation in Religious Programs (Sunday school, religious education)	*M* = 15.4
	SD = 22.4
Recommend Participation in Spiritual Programs (Meditation groups, 12-step programs, men's/women's groups)	*M* = 41.3
	SD = 29.0
Help Clients Clarify Religious Values	*M* = 19.8
	SD = 23.5
Help Clients Clarify Spiritual Values	*M* = 45.2
	SD = 30.7
Refer Clients to Religious Counselors	*M* = 9.7
	SD = 19.3
Refer Clients to Spiritual Counselors	*M* = 9.6
	SD = 20.6
Help Clients Develop Ritual as a Clinical Intervention (House blessings, visiting graves of relatives, etc.)	*M* = 14.7
	SD = 19.7
Participate in Client's Rituals as a Clinical Intervention	*M* = 4.8
	SD = 13.8
Explore Religious Elements in Dreams	*M* = 10.4
	SD = 20.8
Explore Spiritual Elements in Dreams	*M* = 24.6
	SD = 31.1

(**Table 2.3** *continued*)
Practitioners' Use of Religious and Spiritual Interventions in Practice

Intervention	Mean Percentage of Use
Recommend Religious/Spiritual Forgiveness, Penance, or Amends	$M = 16.4$ $SD = 26.7$
Perform Exorcism	$M = .14$ $SD = 1.8$
Share Your Own Religious/Spiritual Beliefs or Views	$M = 13.1$ $SD = 22.0$

This exercise is designed for, and is especially effective with, small groups of up to approximately eight people. The spiritual genograms exercise is well-adapted to explore the roots of a person's spiritual development. Sometimes facts and feelings of a personal and sensitive nature are disclosed and uncovered, and a group of this size group allows for some measure of intimacy and security. Additionally, it is necessary for the leader to carefully and competently respond to any upsetting moments. Group members or individuals may respond to one of the genograms, and upsetting comments or memories can accompany the creation of spiritual genograms.

Cherry Tree. A similar exercise also explores and clarifies the client's spiritual history and values. The focus of the following exercise, which was developed by Reverend Ann D. Cherry from Richmond, Virginia, is the potent symbol of the tree noted earlier in the sefirot of the Kabbalah. The participants begin by drawing the Cherry Tree, complete with roots, trunk, and branches, on a large newsprint paper or erasable chalkboard. The roots represent what anchors participants in their spiritual development. These anchors could be people, books, events, or anything or anyone that established or nourished their spiritual lives.

On the trunk of the tree, participants write adjectives describing the spiritual life. They serve to describe the present state of participants' spiritual quests just as the roots present the past, and also represent turning points in their spiritual lives.

The branches of the Cherry Tree consist of the hopes and aspirations for the participants' spiritual journey, including the goals for their own spiritual growth and development. The branches also include barriers and impediments to reaching those spiritual goals, and an inventory of the both the hopes and the obstacles to a deeper and more intimate spiritual life.

An additional function of the Cherry Tree involves its fruit. After all, what use is the Cherry Tree without cherries? The fruit of the Cherry Tree are the outward expressions of the spiritual life. These outward expressions are not exactly like results or consequences, which can mistakenly be interpreted as good deeds out of a sense of rote obligation or dry duty. Conversely, outward expressions of spirituality are authentic responses to the spiritual life. These responses are different than religion, and can be acts of spontaneous worship or prayer, countless acts of volunteerism, unplanned feelings, or unintended acts of mercy.

The Cherry Tree, unlike the spiritual genograms, is more appropriate for larger groups. This exercise is less likely to initiate the strong emotional feelings that spiritual genograms would. Strong, competent leadership promoting mutual respect and tolerance and the capacity to express empathy for others are necessary in both exercises.

Recommending Participation in Spiritual Groups

Today, there are almost as many spiritual groups available as there are spiritual seekers. Before examining these spiritual groups, it is important to discuss the clinical criteria for recommending participation in spiritual groups. In the survey of Virginia clinical social workers, this included meditation groups, 12-step programs (Alcoholics Anonymous, etc.) and men's and women's groups. Spiritual groups also include churches, mosques, temples, synagogues and other formal religious organizations. Whether or not a client participates in such groups is basically a Constitutionally protected right that is safeguarded by the First Amendment. The religious clause of the First Amendment provides that " . . . Congress shall make no law respecting an establishment of religion or prohibiting the free exercise thereof . . . ." It is improper, and possibly unconstitutional, to suggest that someone not attend a religious or spiritual group of his or her own choosing. Such admonitions also run afoul of the NASW Code of Ethics (1990) that states, "The social worker should make every effort to foster maximum self-determination on the part of clients."

Conversely, this section seeks to both maximize client self-determination and avoid prohibiting client freedom of religious exercise. It does so by encouraging self-reflection and self-disclosure, thus heightening the awareness of spiritual insights and longings, and helping to address spiritual fears and doubts.

It is often the case that the clinician's method of encouraging spiritual self-reflection and self-disclosure is more important than what is actually said. Accordingly, this section provides an attitude for exploring and clarifying spiritual issues and offering specific protocols of questions.

The cornerstone of maximizing spiritual self-determination is nonjudgmentalism. It would be obvious and superficial to define this word as meaning an avoidance of prejudgment or an undermining of another's faith or spiritual orientation. Non-judgmentalism goes deeper than this. It is often misunderstood, for example, by those who see it as the act of demeaning or degrading their own spiritual orientation in favor of another's orientation. This is in fact reverse judgmentalism—a prejudice against one's own origins. Discounting one's own spiritual orientation in favor of another's undermines the client's ability to understand and to discriminate against his or her own spiritual values and histories. Additionally, reverse judgmentalism precludes the authentic disclosure of both the client and the clinician, which is a prerequisite for rapport.

The following are suggestions for specific questions. These questions themselves should be asked in a respectful manner, and perhaps even a celebratory way. It is not the role of the clinician to find chinks in the client's belief, for they are professionally and constitutionally incompetent to make such determinations. More to the point, the clinician's goal of learning to appreciate the value that the clients themselves attach to their own spiritual experiences. Any questioning or critiquing of clients' spiritual experiences or orientations should come from the clients themselves—not from the clinician.

1. *Can the clinician understand and explain his or her own spiritual orientation?* Without self-understanding about their own spiritual lives and histories, clinicians cannot hope to address such issues with their clients. The script on the ancient Greek Delphic Oracle to "Know Thyself" is as pertinent to contemporary social work clinicians as it was for earlier healers. This dictum recognizes that knowing yourself protects clients from instilling in clients the clinician's own emotional content, theoretical orientation, professional biases, let or spiritual orientation.

   Self-understanding is not for the faint-hearted. It requires disciplined, un-self-conscious, unsentimental self-examination. Self-understanding is not just a matter of taking tests, it is a matter of testing oneself. In spiritual terms, this testing means an initiation—ritual of passage and transformation.

   A vision quest is a deliberate ritual of self-understanding. Young people leave their homes and enter the wilderness of mountains. Then, often after a cleansing sweat bath, they engage in 3 days of fasting and praying. The purpose is not self-denial but rather, by facing fear and hardship, to open up to spiritual insight and power. In exposing themselves to their own vulnerability, they open themselves up to higher powers.

   An outward expression of this spiritual transformation is the taking of a spirit name. The famed Lakota leaders Crazy Horse and Sitting Bull received these names from their vision quest experiences. Essentially, these names reflect their personal transformation in conjunction with the appearance of their spirit guides or spirit helpers. Similarly, the Old Testament patriarch Abram was renamed Abraham after an encounter with God, and the New Testament apostle Paul changed his name from Saul after an experience with God on the road to Damascus. Name changes signify personal transformations.

Social workers who engage in systematic spiritual self-examination adopt the social work values of client self-determination and non-judgmentalism not just because these values are imposed from without, but because they are responses to a vibrant spiritual life within. Those who go through the process of spiritual self-examination (that is, those who have walked the walk of spiritual trials) are probably less likely to pass quick judgments on the spiritual walk of others.

2. *What are the benefits of, or draws to, the client's current spiritual group?* This exercise is designed to examine benefits of the client's spiritual affiliation. No judgments by the clinician are involved, only those of the client. However, the clinician can facilitate this process through professional questions that may ask what social, economic, or political benefits are gained by the spirtual orientation. These questions explore how consistent clients' religious or spiritual participations are with their social, economic, political, or ethical values. It is likely, though not necessary, that the client's spiritual affiliation is very consistent with these other values.

Additionally, the client may discover other benefits including a link with a close friend in the group, or a close family connection with the spiritual orientation. Another benefit of this discussion could be a frank assessment, by the client, of the cost of participation in the spiritual group. When clients begin a free and open discussion of the benefits of participation, it is likely that they will begin a discussion of the costs of participation as well. These costs can include the hindrances inherent in the group that make full spiritual growth more difficult. Costs may also include client values that may conflict with the spiritual group. The clinician should not actively solicit such a critique, but it is permissible to create the atmosphere in which such a discussion can safely and respectfully take place.

3. *What are the client's aspirations and hopes for his or her participation in the group?* The clinician can also provide the atmosphere wherein the client can speculate, dream, freely associate, or visualize about their spiritual aspirations. The word *aspirations* is used deliberately. It comes from the same word as *respire,* meaning to *breathe;* the client's spiritual aspirations, therefore, are those imaginations that give him or her breath or purpose in life. After articulating spiritual aspirations, the clinician can help the client plan and organize his or her spiritual aspirations in relation to the client's mental health aspirations. As previously noted, mental health and spirituality go hand in hand.

Exploring Spiritual Elements in Dreams

Remembering and interpreting dreams is an important facet in most religious traditions. The use of dreams in ancient Greek spiritual healing was explored earlier in this chapter. Biblical literature is replete with references to dreams and their interpretation.

The Old Testament patriarch Joseph was a master at dream interpretation (Genesis 40 & 41). He came to the Pharaoh's notice by interpreting the dreams of two of his servants. Then the Pharaoh himself dreamt of seven fat cows and seven lean cows, and later that seven fat ears of corn grew on one stem followed by seven blighted ears. Joseph interpreted this dream to mean that 7 years of good harvests would be followed by 7 lean years. This came to pass, and the Pharaoh promoted Joseph to official Egyptian upper-management.

The New Testament Gospel of Matthew records four dreams in the first two chapters. Joseph decided not to bring shame to his new, pregnant wife, and thus divorced Mary. An angel appeared to Joseph in a dream and said, "Joseph, son of David, do not fear to take Mary your wife, for that which she conceived in her is of the holy spirit . . . " (1:20-21). The three wise men (Persian astrologers), having presented the infant Jesus with gifts of gold, frankincense, and myrrh, were also warned in a dream not to return to King Herod, who was jealous of the child-king (2:12). However, King Herod discovered the child and, wanting to the kill him, dispatched troops. Joseph was again warned in a dream to leave Bethlehem and flee to Egypt (2:13). Later, Joseph had another dream telling him it was safe to return to Judea (2:19). These references amount to a biblical mandate to examine and interpret dreams. Of course, many religious traditions accept dreams as a part of their religious heritage (Campbell, 1970; Fromm, 1951; Kelsey, 1978; Kelsey, 1974). Among religious adherents, however, there will be a wide variety of opinion about the use and value of dreams.

Spiritual dreams constitute a continuum of purposes. As discussed earlier, they include precognitive dreams, clairvoyant dreams, and healing dreams. Joseph's dreams were both highly symbolic and precognitive. Sometimes spiritual dreams are rather straightforward. Angels, prophetic figures, or even gods and goddesses give the dreamer direct information or render boons. The ancient Greek Asklepios dreams are good examples. Other dreams are more symbolic, and in some cases the gods or goddesses use symbols to express themselves. Spirituality speaks through symbols. In Jungian terms, symbols form the syntax of the collective unconscious (Edinger, 1972; Jung, 1965; Singer, 1972).

Symbols are divine gifts to humankind. They do not belong to any religion, sect, denomination, cultural group, or spiritual group, but instead are universal property. There is no cultural copyright to the collective unconscious. In fact, these images come every night. Proper training can unlock the keys to the language of symbols, and following are several ideas and exercises for doing so.

1. *Let the symbols speak for themselves.* It is not as important to understand the spiritual meaning of dreams as it is to experience the images themselves. The dream images need to effect their own impact in their own way.

   This book makes a strong case for the extravagant use of cross-cultural spiritual material, including images, symbols, myths, poetry, and metaphors. The bibliography at the end of the text contains a full panoply of such material. This book asserts that social workers addressing spiritual issues should be extremely well acquainted with a full range of such symbolism. Dream images are cross-cultural and eclectic.

   The dream symbols can speak most deeply when they speak for themselves. The power of the image is in the power of the imagination. The symbols themselves are perfectly suited to carry the necessary message. The metaphor itself is magic; that is to say, it is empowering and transformative—even painful. Riding in the wake of the sacred can be a rough trip.

   The therapeutic key is for the social worker to get out of the way and let the symbol or myth do its work. This means suspending the social worker's own spiritual presumptions and even his or her training in clinical diagnoses and methods of intervention long enough to allow the client to feel the impact fully and completely. Intellectualization and analysis tend to dilute this vitality. This does not mean, however, that the social worker does nothing. Allowing the image to work (creating an atmosphere in which the image can function best) is much different than doing nothing. The social worker should always protect clients from hurting themselves or others.

2. *Treat dream images like living beings.* This means allowing the dreamer to experience the symbols, not just interpret them. Carl Jung (1965) was dissatisfied with knowing God only through hearsay. Jung's *knowledge* of God was transformed into the *experience* that "God alone was real—an annihilating fire and an indescribable grace" (p. 56). Believing is not the same as knowing. Believing in something or someone on an intellectual plane does not constitute the full range of knowing another. A potently symbolic word for knowing in the Bible is *ya'dah*. It is a word beyond mere intellectual knowledge, connoting even an intimate, sexual knowing such as in the birth of Cain where "Adam knew Eve his wife and she conceived . . . " (Genesis 4:1).

   First-year medical students are given their first cadaver, which results in varying degrees of enthusiasm. Every nook and cranny of the human body is explored, yet this does not mean that the students have exhausted the knowledge of the human *person*. This is only physical knowledge and cannot tell the whole story.

   Similarly, merely knowing the rote meanings of symbols is just superficial knowledge of dream image. In order to have a deeper knowledge, the images themselves must live and breathe. The images must be able to create their own content within the human context. The dream images will, like any live organism, adapt to and adopt its environment and will transmute in order to transform the dreamer. This means creating an environment where the client can fully comprehend the power of the dream. The following are specific suggestions that flow from the care of any living being.

First, the entire dream is important. Just as a person cannot be reduced to mere parts, a dream must be considered in its entirety. Listen to the entire context of the dream and the dream images. For example, all symbols of the dream are important. Symbols are not like statistics. Symbols may be statistically insignificant, but they may be spiritually significant. The setting, time, and even minor characters of the dream can reveal significant things. Let the images speak for themselves, in their own voices.

What is undone can be far more important than what is done. Do not translate the images, interpret the voices, or clarify the images. Face the images directly. Imagine being face-to-face with a great work of art. Sit down and just admire it. Breathe in its essence. Dream images should be honored in the same way. Just sit with them, without interpretation or equivocation, and let them speak. How do the images make you feel? What associations do they suggest? What do the colors, shapes, events, or characters intimate?

Second, feed the images with generous amounts of psychic food. This means giving the images attention. Anyone knows that ignoring someone weakens them; similarly, ignoring dream images weakens their impact, at least for a time. Dreams are able to get the dreamer's attention as their symbols and myths accommodate themselves to his or her interests. However, ignoring a dream may incur a nightmare. If the dream cannot get the dreamer's attention, the dreams become more intrusive and more intense.

Third, exercise the images. Even if exercise hurts a little, it builds up the voices and the strength of the dream images. There are several ways to nourish dream images, all of which require expending energy in conscious ways. Exercising images means to paint, draw, sculpt, act, and write them. Concretizing the images on paper, in a sculpting medium, in drama, or in other media enhances their ability to teach, challenge, and inspire the dreamer. Again, exercising of dream images does not include interpreting or evaluating them. The term inspire is used deliberately. As discussed earlier, its root is the same word as respire. Inspiration is that which gives one breath—that which gives one life. Looking up dream images in art books, museums, and literature exercises the images.

Fourth, give the images rest and recreation. Play with the images and let them play. After exercising images, get emotional distance from them, and let them breathe. Leave the images alone for some time to get emotional room between the images and the dreamer. Dream images provide reciprocal relationships with the dreamer. The following paragraphs provide practical illustrations of this ecological relationship.

3. *Interact with dreams.* Once clients interact with their dreams, their dreams will interact with them. Dreams are natural, organic, interactive images. They are ancient, yet they relate and adapt to new situations and to new environments. In this regard, dream images constitute a living, psychic ecosystem, for they evolve and change with changing conditions.

Dream images, as psychic ecosystems, have practical applications. The first application is intercessory interaction. This means that the dreamer may ask dreams to intercede on their behalf. The dreamer may ask, or pray for, a dream that offers insight into a particular problem, inspiration about a particular issue, or creative solutions to particular dilemmas.

Second, the dreamer may ask for additional images and insight to supplement earlier dream images. When one dream image opens new therapeutic ground or new therapeutic issues, another subsequent dream may heighten or deepen the previous dream's impact.

Third, the dreamer may ask a dream to reframe the nature of the dreamer's questions, possibly to preclude or to limit the answers they get in dreams. The dreamer needs clear, accurate questions to get clear, accurate answers. A client may believe he or she has to choose between remaining married or getting a divorce. In point of fact, the real issue may be a consistent pattern of people-pleasing on the part of the client, or that the client has a personality disorder of some kind. Asking dreams to clarify the true nature of the problem or issue can aid in both assessing the client's situation and in developing strategy for the proper interventions. For example, a parent may ask whether his or her behavior may be hurtful to his or her child. A dream may help put the parents "in the shoes" of their children.

A set of actual dreams illustrates these points. A clergywoman was bringing charges against a male minister for sexual misconduct. During this process the clergywoman had two dreams. In the first dream she was in a bus accident. Broken bodies were everywhere, people passed by in cars without offering to help, and the accident victims had to tend to their own wounds. The dream's message was that the victim had to effect her own healing. The clergywoman had to discover the wellsprings of healing for herself.

In the second dream, the woman examined a map. She wanted to travel from one location to another but, even with the map, she could not find her way. This second dream supplemented the first. In the two dreams, the woman was told not only to save herself, but to do so without roadmaps to follow. She could not rely on others to effect her healing, nor could she rely on others to give her directions. She had to learn to heal herself and to find the way to healing herself.

These dreams offer complementary insights into the nature of the issues facing the dreamer in reality. The dreams present the true nature of therapeutic and spiritual issues in creative and dramatic ways. Once the dreams gave insight, the therapeutic task for this client involved facing the ambivalence toward exposing harm by a former lover, dealing with the harsh quasi-judicial process, and creating a strategy for self-healing.

Conducting Spiritual Meditation With Clients

This chapter has already discussed meditation (deep prayer) and will now fully address the nature of meditation and its use in social work interventions. Prayer and mediation are, here, synonymous terms. A humorous anecdote may help to define exactly what prayer is. Many years ago, a chaplain at a large New Jersey psychiatric hospital conducted a prayer group with six or seven of the residents. After some preliminary discussion, the chaplain asked, "Who would like to begin?" One man said that he would begin and started to speak directly to his mother. Another resident interrupted him and said, "This is supposed to be prayer, not a seance!" Although the author recognizes wide diversities among the definitions of meditation and prayer, there are also limits in this regard.

The broad definition of prayer and meditation states that they provide a means of communicating and communing with God, a transcendent reality, or the divine self. Meditation is a way of altering consciousness and, properly used, meditation or deep prayer is a safe, fun, and effective way to access the spiritual dimensions. The following is a description of five phases of meditation or deep prayer emphasized by the author.

1. *Relaxation.* The body and the mind exist in unity with one another. What affects the mind affects the body, and vice versa. Relaxation for the body is relaxation for the mind, and meditation begins with relaxation. Relaxation of the mind is often most effective when it begins with relaxation of the body. In meditation, body relaxation means taking a relaxed, but firm sitting or prone position. The spine should be aligned so that the spinal vertebrae are resting comfortably on one another. The traditional *lotus* meditation position creates this posture; however, sitting in a firm chair or lying prone on a firm mattress can be just as effective.

   Meditation begins with a variety of specific relaxation exercises, including the systematic tightening and loosening of muscle groups throughout the body. Alternately squeezing leg or pelvic muscles and letting them go loose gradually relaxes the entire muscular system. One might also try a visualization relaxation. Such a visualization might include systematically seeing the muscles relax "with the mind's eye." Clients may imagine that their feet are resting on a pillow of light and that this light is radiating up their feet and into their their bodies. Clinicians may want to say to their clients "where the light is, there is warmth, security, and comfort."

2. *Visualization.* Once clients are relaxed, they can more easily proceed to the visualization stages of meditation. A commonly used visualization involves a secure place of peace and creativity, often a place of natural beauty such as a seashore, forest, or mountaintop; however, the visualization could be anywhere that suits the client. Calling it a "holy place" suggests a place to encounter the divine or to experience the sacred within. To a Sikh this holy place might be known as the Golden Temple; to a Hindu it might be known as Rishikesh or Hardwar; to a Moslem, the Mount of the Rock; to a Jew, Mount Horeb or Mount Moriah; or to a Christian, the Garden of Gethsemane or Mount of Olives. In any case, these places express both a historical sacred place and a personal site of sanctuary and grace. The visualization sets the spiritual stage for sacred affirmations.

3. *Affirmation.* Affirmations are declarations or assertions that arise out of prayer or meditation. They are extremely useful in replacing negative thoughts and thought patterns with spiritually effective and motivating thoughts and thought patterns. Shinn (1925) predated many current writers who use affirmations as part of healing work. She asserted that words have enormous power to impress upon the mind the ability to accomplish divine tasks, writing, "All the good that is to be made manifest in man's life is already an accomplished fact in divine mind, and is released through man's recognition, or spoken word, so he must be careful to decree that only the Divine Idea be made manifest, for often he decrees, through his 'idle words,' failure or misfortune" (p. 85).

Shinn's assertion reflects the spiritual truths from ancient Egypt, the Bible, and other traditions suggesting that words have creative power in their own right. This power can have positive and negative consequences. A modern practitioner of affirmations is Sondra Ray (1976) who writes, "The repetitive use of the affirmation will simultaneously make its impression on your mind and will erase the old thought pattern, producing permanent desirable changes in your life" (p. 21).

Some clients may have spoken idle words to themselves for years about how bad, stupid, fat, unworthy, or ugly they are. Some clients may think that they are unworthy of happy, healthy lives. Affirmations are antidotes

for such anger, outrage, and disappointment. Affirmations can be components of prayer or they can be the essence of the prayer itself and are most
effective when they arise in altered states of consciousness. It is during
these altered states that they are closest to the inner self. Sometimes these
affirmations arise from suggestions made by meditators themselves; sometimes they spontaneously arise from the nature of the meditation itself.

Affirmations can be formulated in any number of ways. They can come
in the form of words, feelings, touch, colors, shapes, or any combination of
these. There are as many modalities of affirmations as there are human
needs. All affirmations, however, validate the essence of the meditator
while at the same time challenging it. An archetypal affirmation is the
angelic appearance to the shepherds announcing the birth of Jesus of
Nazareth. Luke is the only Gospel that records the story of the shepherds
"watching their flocks by night" when the angel of the Lord appears to
them (Luke 2:8-14). They become terrified:

> But the angel said to them, "Do not be afraid; for see—I am bringing you
> good news of great joy for all the people: to you this day in the City of David
> a Savior is the Christ the Lord."

The angel (which means *messenger*) sends the archetypical message "Do
not be afraid . . . " and brings news of cosmic joy. Affirmations usually have
both a personal message and a community message, for they are rarely the
sole property of any one individual or any one class of individuals. Divine
affirmations are normally community property; that is, affirmations have a
message of hope and renewal for all persons even though the agency of that
redemption may be through one individual or a class of individuals.

4. *Confirmation.* Confirmations are acts or words that substantiate or ratify
affirmations. They concretize affirmations in the unconscious and the conscious minds. A classic illustration of a confirmation is the story of Jesus
healing a man blind from birth (John 9:1-12). Jesus mixed spit with clay
and "spread the mud on the man's eyes." He then told the man to wash it
off in the Pool of Siloam. Washing at the Pool was not just a convenient
sink; rather, a historical examination of the Pool of Siloam reveals that it
had important spiritual implications in Jesus' time. Washing in the Pool of
Siloam was an act designed to confirm the healing.

The Pool of Siloam, before the time of King Hezekiah, was a major
source of water for Jerusalem. During the siege of Jerusalem by the Assyr-
ians, King Hezekiah stopped external water supplies and had to redirect the
Pool of Siloam. Given the scarcity and necessity of fresh water sources
near Jerusalem, such pools were highly prized. In fact, Jesus may have
referred to the Pool of Siloam when John's gospel has him referring to "liv-

ing water" (Mare, 1992). The Pool of Siloam was, in effect, a reminder of God's living healing presence.

The Pool was a physical symbol of the power of God to provide for His people. Jesus used this symbol, well-known to the people of his time, to confirm his healing of the blind man. There are few better ways to confirm a healing than to cleanse oneself in a healing, life-giving symbol.

5. *Appreciation.* Appreciation is an act of gratitude. In the spiritual sense, acts of gratitude are not mere social conventions, but serve important spiritual functions. Appreciation serves to both reinforce and integrate the meditative or prayer affirmations. Gratitude preserves the affirmations and confirmations discovered in prayer and meditation. The acts of gratitude may be brief or extended; they may be simple or they may be elaborate. Each expression of gratitude, however, should be clear and specific.

6. *Conclusion.* The most important goal of the conclusion is to return the meditator safely to the normal state of consciousness (Heikkinen, 1989). A safe and secure return to normal consciousness is an ethical duty of the clinician. Any precipitous, unprepared return to normal living (driving, operating machinery, etc.) could result in danger to the meditator or to others.

The last phase of the prayer meditation is debriefing. Debriefing accomplishes two tasks. First, like the conclusion, it provides for the meditator's safe return to normal consciousness. These few minutes are important to ensure that he or she can safely return to activities such as driving. Debriefing also allows participants to talk about their experiences. The clinician, thus, should solicit information about how the imagery affected the client. This information is especially necessary should the meditation prayer touch on sensitive issues in the client's life. Additionally, the clinician can solicit valuable data on the ability of meditators to use their imaginations, to relax, and to integrate prayer insight into their daily lives. If you do not ask the right questions, you cannot get useful answers.

Appendix C, found at the end of this book, illustrates a healing prayer meditation. It is roughly divided into the phases described above, and provides a framework for a variety of different prayer meditation experiences.

CONCLUSION

This chapter introduced the theory and practice of spiritual social work assessment and interventions. It offered empirical and descriptive examples of how social workers can apply spiritually oriented assessments and interventions with their clients. The remainder of this chapter contains individual or class exercises, discussion scenarios, and the text of a meditation or guided imagery exercise.

INDIVIDUAL OR CLASS EXERCISES

1. Create your own cosmology. Your cosmology is a key to your consciousness, spiritual orientation, and therapeutic orientation. As you understand your cosmos, so you understand your clients. Draw or otherwise depict a map of your universe. Include maps of any spiritual domains and characters that play roles in your day-to-day living. Remember, cosmologies are maps of consciousness. If you conceive separate and distinct levels of transcendent awareness, depict them as different worlds, levels, or parts of some whole. The more creative the better. Share your depictions with classmates and discuss the meaning behind your creations.
2. Create your own anthropology. Anthropologies, especially spiritual anthropologies, are maps of human beings. Follow the same procedure you used to create cosmologies. To the extent that you allow spiritual, emotional, intellectual, and physical components of the human person, depict those in any manner which makes sense to you. Again, share your creations with your classmates.

DISCUSSION SCENARIOS AND QUESTIONS

The following scenarios are taken from real-life situations. Pertinent parts have been changed to preserve anonymity. Case studies are presented here to provide the readers and students with clinical examples to apply to the concepts presented in this chapter.

1. A Jewish woman in her thirties had an upsetting dream. She dreamt that she was in a runaway car that was going to explode. Just before impact, a figure appeared to her, placed his hand upon hers, and said, "Do not be afraid." The car stopped and the crash was averted. The troubling aspect of this dream was that the figure appearing to her was Jesus Christ. She felt guilty and confused. As a young person, she was taught that even saying the word "Jesus Christ" was wrong. What are the therapeutic issues here? Should you discuss the Christ image with this client? Why or why not?

2. A woman in her late sixties was emotionally estranged from her husband and very unhappy. She had contemplated divorce, but feared that she would not be able to support herself without her husband. She entered counseling, seeking spiritual support and insight for her dilemma. What spiritual techniques of assessment or intervention would you use? How might you test them to evaluate their effectiveness?

3. A couple that was considering divorce sought counseling because of a potential custody issue dispute over their infant son. The husband was Roman Catholic and the wife was Baptist. Neither partner was particularly religious and the issue of which religious faith in which the child would be raised was not discussed.

   The husband, after an abrupt growth in religious conviction, wanted his son to be raised a Roman Catholic. The wife objected. Before the dispute escalated into a courtroom drama, though, the couple decided to try counseling. Assess the role of religion or spirituality in this couple's situation. What are the crucial spiritual issues for them? An excellent survey article is Wah, C. (1994). "Religion in child custody cases and visitation cases: Presenting the advantage of religious participation." *Family Law Quarterly*, *28*(2), 269–288.

4. A woman in her thirties suffered from multiple sclerosis that had gone undiagnosed for many years. During that time, she had severe headaches and stomach problems. Her stomach ulcerated and once, during an operation to remove half of her stomach, she had a near-death experience. She had a vision of being out of her body, which was very troubling to her. Yet, at the same time, it was incredibly beautiful. For the first time she felt a profound sense of timelessness. She felt physically drawn into the universe and was as one with it. The woman sensed a calm and peace that was very striking to her. At times she felt blessed; at others, she felt cursed. She came to counseling for help in understanding this experience. What are the conflicts that this client may feel? How would you intervene? What is the spiritual psychosocial impact of this issue on the client?

Chapter 4

Spirituality and Public
Policy Issues

This chapter discusses spirituality in the context of public policy issues. Both spirituality and religion are factors in politics, law, and public opinion, all of which are the constituents of public policy. It is no secret that religious factors have played major roles in former President Ronald Reagan's massive national electoral victory in 1980 and the Christian Coalition's work in the 1994 national and state elections that gave a majority of seats in Congress to the Republican Party (Birnbaum, 1995). Nor is it any secret that religion plays a significant role in case law and in national and state statutes.

The first section of this chapter provides an example of how spirituality and religion have historically contributed to Western social welfare policy. This section also gives an example of the early influence of monastic Christian ethical culture on the values and ideologies of Western social policy, including the concepts of charity and community through the English Poor Laws and the Enlightenment. Additionally, this section integrates these religious and spiritual values into the current social policy jurisprudence of the right to travel, the right to social security benefits, and the right to medical care. This chapter then discusses spirituality through law cases that address social issues. These cases address the limitations placed on ingesting sacred hallucinogens, the role of sacred sexuality, and the right to make animal sacrifices as part of religious ritual.

RELIGIOUS ORIGINS OF WESTERN CHARITY:
COMPETING VALUES AND IDEOLOGIES

Context of Early Western Social Welfare

Elements of the Western social welfare system have been traced as far back as ancient Mesopotamian and Egyptian cultures (Day, 1989; Popple & Leighninger,

1991; Trattner, 1984). Indeed, in the latest edition of the *Social Work Dictionary* (1987), the first two entries of the section titled "Milestones in the Development of Social Work and Social Welfare" discuss the role of charity in the Babylonian Code of Hammurabi and the Israelite covenant with God to aid the poor and disadvantaged. These early historical ideologies and values did not arise in a cultural vacuum. Nor did they pass the historical scene without leaving their mark on later charitable organizations, public policy, and law. These ideologies had an impact far beyond the cultures in which they originally arose and left their ethical and ideological imprints on the Western charitable impulse.

This section presents a conceptualization of three historic values and ideologies characterizing the Western charitable impulse within an early historical time frame and cultural milieu. Three historic documents form the raw material for this study. These documents present only some of the historic roots of Western charity; after all, Western charity is a big tree.

Figure 4.1 illustrates some of the laws that may have influenced American attitudes and legal principles currently at work in social welfare policy and practices. This diagram is illustrative but not exhaustive, and is shown to demonstrate both the diversity and interrelatedness of various legal sources at work in American jurisprudence. This chapter discusses a part of this historical corpus.

These historical materials include the Dead Sea Scrolls of the Qumran religious community in the 200-year period between the first century B.C.E. and the first century A.D., as well as during the first two Christian monastic rules. These historic documents establish an historical record for early social welfare institutions as well as values and ideologies for later Western social welfare organizations. These values and ideologies are charity and community, which can serve as organizing principles for students of welfare policy and the history of welfare systems.

The Qumran Community and the Dead Sea Scrolls. The Dead Sea Scrolls, discovered in 1947, are among the most important archeological discoveries of this century. They got their name because they were found in caves near the ancient settlement of Qumran on the northwestern shore of the Dead Sea, about 10 miles east of Jerusalem. These documents, written in both Hebrew and Aramaic between the second and third centuries B.C.E., offer insight into Jewish and Christian thought around the time of the destruction of the Jerusalem temple in 70 A.D.

For example, these scrolls are the earliest manuscripts of Jewish sacred scriptures in existence. The Dead Sea Scrolls also offer an intriguing glimpse into Jewish thought during the lifetime of Jesus of Nazareth. For example, the religious organization of early Christianity may have been modeled after that of Qumran, not ancient Greece as earlier supposed. Additionally, the Messianic

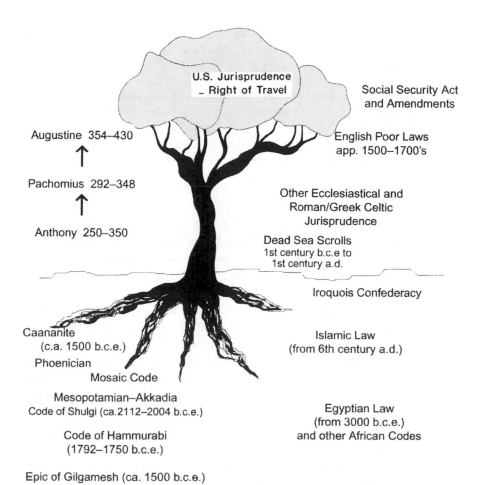

U.S. Jurisprudence
_ Right of Travel

Social Security Act
and Amendments

Augustine 354–430
↑
Pachomius 292–348
↑
Anthony 250–350

English Poor Laws
app. 1500–1700's

Other Ecclesiastical and
Roman/Greek Celtic
Jurisprudence

Dead Sea Scrolls
1st century b.c.e to
1st century a.d.

Iroquois Confederacy

Caananite
(c.a. 1500 b.c.e.)
Phoenician
Mosaic Code

Islamic Law
(from 6th century a.d.)

Mesopotamian–Akkadia
Code of Shulgi (ca.2112–2004 b.c.e.)

Code of Hammurabi
(1792–1750 b.c.e.)

Egyptian Law
(from 3000 b.c.e.)
and other African Codes

Epic of Gilgamesh (ca. 1500 b.c.e.)

Figure 4.1   Tentative Graph of Roots and Result of Religious Influence Upon Western Social Welfare

expectation, so prominent in Jesus' time, was also evidenced at Qumran (Danielou, 1958).

The authors of the Scrolls are unknown. Some scholars maintain that a group of Jewish ascetics (Essenes, to which some believe Jesus of Nazareth belonged) wrote the scrolls; others believe that other Jewish authorities were trying to hide their most precious writings from the imminent collapse of the Temple (Specter, 1989). Some scholars maintain that the Qumran building included a library and scribal area as well as a large communal dining room, whereas others think that Qumran was more of a resort area for the wealthy. Although much of the ideology inherent in the Dead Sea Scrolls is unclear, it is certain that they describe elements of a social welfare ethic, including charity and community.

It is clear that charity was a primary ethic of the authors of the Dead Sea Scrolls. The Community Scroll (Vermes, 1968) states the premise for the charitable life, saying that the Rule is written

> . . . that they may seek God with a whole heart and soul, and do what is good and right before Him as He commanded by the hand of Moses and all His servants and prophets; that they may love all that He has chosen and hate all that He has rejected; that they may abstain from all evil and hold fast to all good; that they may practice truth, righteousness, and justice upon earth no longer follow a sinful heart and lustful eyes committing all manner of evil.

This rule stresses charity so that people will practice "truth, righteousness, and justice." In these times it was common for such charity to be extended to those who had no means to support themselves, including widows, orphans, and foreigners. In ancient Israel, as in other deserts in the Mideast, charity and hospitality could mean the difference between life and death.

The Rule of Pachomius. The history and content of the Rule of Pachomius is stated in one of the few English translations from the original Ethiopic (Schodde, 1885). Pachomius, who lived from 292 A.D. to 348 A.D., established the first rule for monastic life. The Rule had such an enormous impact on monastic and religious life in general that St. Jerome was asked to prepare a Latin version from the Greek in 404 A.D. because so many Latin-speaking monastics joined Pachomian communities (Quasten, 1960).

Monastic comes from the Latin word *monas,* meaning singular or solitary. At the time of Pachomius, solitary monks (called anchorites) lived in lone huts or caves called cells in the lower Egyptian, Syrian, Judean, or Arabian deserts. These *cells* were often grouped together in loosely knit communities called *lauras.* Although Pachomius was the first to write a rule for these loosely organized and essentially solitary monks (both men and women), he was well-taught by his teacher Palaemon, who himself was taught by St. Anthony (traditionally, the first Christian monk). Thus, the Rule set down by Pachomius can be viewed as a continuation of at least two generations of anchorites.

The Rule of Pachomius, written in the southern part of Upper Egypt (Canning, 1986), asserts itself to be both divinely inspired and divinely written. The first sentence of the Rule says, "In the name of the holy Trinity" and the first paragraph states that Pachomius "lived a clean life, and there was given to him knowledge and also vision of angels." Indeed, the Rule is said to have been handed to Pachomius by an angel.

The Rule extols community and charity. Community refers to the nature and exhibited forms fellowship and charity became the operationalization of a community ethic. The importance of community in the Pachomian Rule is evidenced by its emphasis on self-sufficiency and poverty.

The theme of community is expressed in the Pachomian Rule through its organization of monks and nuns. Pachomius taught that those who gathered in their cells consisted of two types of associations: good and bad (good and bad are the translator's terms). The bad types of monks and nuns consisted of five associations of hyenas, dogs, wolves, shakals (jackals), and goats. Likewise, the good monks and nuns consisted of five associations of sheep, doves, turtle-doves, bees, and deer. Each association, good or bad, had qualities attached to it.

It is significant to note, however, that these associations were totally moral in nature and had no corresponding organizational structure. In other words, Pachomius did not organize monks and nuns into such associations and did not withhold community assets according to any classification. Such an innovation would have to await later Western political orders.

Charity was the ethical expression of community. For the Pachomians, as well as in the Augustinians, the interior life of reflection and contemplation was valued over the exterior life of travel or the accumulation of things. The prayerful life was a solitary and stationary affair.

Pachomian poverty meant more than an absence of material goods. It meant sharing a lifestyle of both inner and outer seclusion. The story is told of a monk asking Abbot Moses of Egypt for advice about the interior life. The older monk replied, "Go, sit in your cell, and your cell will teach you everything" (Merton, 1960). This brief story was remembered through the centuries because it told volumes about the ethic of sharing—sharing silence as well as words. The story is designed to speak extensively about sharing an ethical environment with others who are struggling to form an ethical, spiritual community.

This story teaches another lesson and another set of values, and reinforces personal autonomy and individual freedom. The younger monk is never given direct advice and is never told the answer to his question. This is no inadvertence. Abbot Moses deliberately allowed the younger monk to find his own way so that his path to God would be disclosed in a way unique to the individual monk. The monastic life of Pachomius allowed, even encouraged, autonomy and individuality. Living the communal and charitable life did not mean living an obsequious life.

The Rule of Augustine. Although the Rule of Pachomius was the oldest monastic rule of the East, the Rule of Augustine was the oldest monastic rule of the West. Western monasticism is somewhat different from Eastern monasticism in that it became more organized around single, larger, central buildings. Traditional Eastern monasticism is more autonomous in nature (Chitty, 1966). Augustine of Hippo, who later became Bishop of Milan, is a primary historical figure in Roman Catholic theology and a canonized saint. His monastic leadership was established when he established a monastery for lay brothers in 391 A.D. in Augustine's North African hometown of Hippo. He also set up a monastery in 395 A.D. and wrote in his Rule 2 years later.

A remarkable feature of Augustine's Rule is that it establishes identical codes both for men and women. A key component of Augustine's Rule is the community. The first two rules deal directly with community relations (Canning, 1986):

> Before all, live together in harmony, being of one mind and one heart on the way to God.
> Among you there can be no question of personal property.
> Rather, take care that you share everything.

The premise of these rules is that the community is based on the remedy of mutual needs. This remedy of common need is satisfied by the community itself. This community responsibility includes the norm of sharing personal property with those in need within the order and those outside the order. The needs of the community must be met by the community itself.

Common Components of this Early Literature

As indicated earlier, the Dead Sea Scrolls, the Rule of Pachomius, and the Rule of Augustine have two common components that influenced later Western organized social welfare: charity and community. These components are useful in conceptualizing the culturally and religiously diverse origins of the aforementioned literature. These components are treated in order below.

Charity. Charity comes from the Greek *charis* (Latin, *caritas*) meaning a love based on self-giving and benevolence (Muller, 1985). This unearned grace can be likened to the experience of being freed from a captor by the hand of an oppressor, like the Israelites freed from Pharaoh. This charis is a component in the previously mentioned literature. The charity expressed by this literature was a response to this God's divine gift. Likewise, charity as expressed in the literature of Qumran, Pachomius, and Augustine did not distinguish between those who deserved charity and those who did not. Charity arose from a religious/spiritual response, not a lawful obligation.

For example, the Dead Sea Scrolls indicate that their followers should feed the poor and protect the fatherless—not because it is a nice thing to do, but because such acts are part of communities' mutual covenant obligations to their Creator.

Of course, the orphans and the needy have no obligation to the sect of the Dead Sea Scrolls. Those engaged in such acts of charity have an obligation to their Creator and their Creator has a covenant obligation to them.

In the same manner, the Rule of Augustine demonstrated an ethical dependency on charity. Charity was the glue that bound the community together. Community possession and distribution of good as well as the service for the sick and the needy were hallmarks of Augustinian charitable acts. In addition to these outward acts of charity, the Rule also promotes humility, compassion, obedience, love, and chastity.

Community. The Dead Sea Scrolls and the Rule of Augustine are used to specifically note the ethical component of community. For these two pieces of literature, and the groups who revere them, community is theologically or ideologically defined. For the Scroll community, the covenant between the members not only ordained acts, but defined membership. The covenant relationship was defined by their divine relationship to their god. This relationship was marked by the maintenance of a sacred past, a sacred present, and the expectation of a sacred future.

The covenant relationship also provides a legal-ethical basis for the social worker–client relationship (Bullis, 1995). This relationship provides a workable, effective concept and helps the social worker avoid legal liability or the appearance of misconduct.

The sacred present was characterized by community rituals and was made sacred by sacred acts on a daily basis. These acts included such sacred acts as initiation, the community meal, ritual washing, and assemblies.

Community, Charity, and Other Conflicting Values. The literature of the Rule of Pachomius and the Rule of Augustine illustrate the ethic of community and charity. These values, however, have no monopoly on the ethical landscape. Individual autonomy and individual freedom have also competed for expression in social policy.

For the Pachomian monks and nuns, the center of life was the interior, contemplative life. The emphasis on the contemplative life expresses itself both in preserving personal autonomy and the community. At the same time, the rule presupposes freedom to travel and a large amount of personal discretion. The English Poor Laws also embody these competing values.

EARLY WELFARE ETHIC AND THE ENGLISH POOR LAWS

The early ethics of charity and community significantly influenced the ideology of Western social welfare. The 1536 Act for the Punishment of Sturdy

Vagabonds and Beggars, the 1601 Elizabethan Poor Laws, and the 1662 Law of Settlements illustrate these laws. These three ethical principles will be serially considered, along with the continued ambivalence of the alternative ethical imperatives of personal autonomy and individualism. Personal autonomy values personal independence, whereas freedom and individualism value the person over the community.

Charity

The ethical principle of charity is dramatically illustrated by the 1349 Statute of Laborers and the 1601 Elizabethan Poor Laws. The thirteenth and fourteenth centuries saw catastrophic changes in the social, economic, and religious structures of Europe (Trattner, 1984). These centuries also undermined the nature of the charitable ethic.

The feudal economic and theological system was failing. In 1517 Martin Luther, a Dominican monk, nailed his 57 theses on a Wittenberg church door and began the Protestant Reformation. At nearly the same time the monastic system of parish charities was dissolving, sending thousands of former clerics and other ecclesiastical workers into wandering unemployment. The year the Statute of Laborers was enacted, Europe was in the grips of the Black (Bubonic) Plague, which killed one-third of its population. The Plague severely reduced the supply of available workers, and employers were met with demands for higher wages.

The Statute of Laborers filled this ecclesiastic and social vacuum to limit wages, to force the able-bodied to work, and to exclude the able-bodied from receiving charity (Trattner, 1984). This Act, as well as the Act of 1572 (Henry VIII), went even further in stripping ecclesiastical authority and power from the charitable impulse. The Act of 1572 punished those who offered charity to any "rogue, vagabonds, or sturdy beggars" with a fine. Sturdy beggars were branded on the shoulder as a convenient way of identifying those to whom charity should not be extended (Aschrott, 1902). Thus, charity extended by the state's right hand was taken away by its left.

A primary reason for the Poor Laws was to keep paupers (and others needing assistance) from travelling from parish to parish. The fear prompting the legislation was that the wealthy would be besieged by paupers gravitating to the parishes with the deepest pockets. Beyond this attitude, the Poor Laws also evidenced the ethical imperatives of autonomy and individualism. They enforced the social ethic valuing individualism, property rights, and personal wealth.

Aschrott's (1902, p. 9) crisp critique of this Act asserts that it "was pushed through all the stages of legislation without affording either Parliament or public opinion time for discussion, merely because the representatives of London and a few wealthy landlords were desirous of lessening the burden of their own poor rates." The Act of Charles II was called the "Settlement Act" precisely because it required that paupers settle in one parish and move only under threat of penalty.

Community

The nature of community was also altered with the advent of the poor laws. Community as described in the Dead Sea Scrolls and the monastic orders in theological terms saw charity as a spiritual or religious organizing principle. Conversely, community was described in the Poor Laws in economic terms and saw charity as a way of maintaining an economic order. One of the hallmarks of the Poor Law system was a system of categorizing the entire community into the worthy and unworthy poor. For example, the Elizabethan Poor Laws considered the lame, impotent, blind, and those unable to work as worthy poor (Aschrott, 1902), thus denoting that they deserved public help. The unworthy poor were so labeled because they were thought to be lazy, shiftless, and irresponsible. The worthy poor made for an economic burden that the government was willing to carry, whereas the unworthy poor did not.

Classifying persons into the worthy and unworthy poor also shows the ambivalence of ethical imperatives. Without the proof of property and material wealth, persons were suspect of being less industrious, imaginative, or even morally righteous than those with the badges of prosperity. As discussed earlier, the opposite was true in Pachomian and Augustinian ethical mandates. There, ethical mandates of community and charity valued persons for their intrinsic value, not for their worth as autonomous consumers or for individual acquisition of wealth. The Poor Laws embody the competing ethical imperatives of individualism and autonomy versus community and charity. This ambivalence and conflict continues to the present.

RELIGIOUS IDEOLOGY IN UNITED STATES WELFARE POLICY

The early religious and spiritual ideologies (described above) are relatively consistent with United States welfare policy since its inception (Day, 1989; Hagen, 1982). The ideologies of community, charity, autonomy, and individualism remained consistent in current U.S. social policy until the early 1990s. This policy is illustrated below in regard to residency requirements for receiving welfare benefits, social security benefits, and nonemergency medical care at county expense. In the 1990s, federal and state legislators have rethought the value and practice of welfare policy. Major restructuring of the welfare system may well flow from major shifts toward the ideologies of personal responsibility and individual autonomy.

Public Assistance Benefits and the Right to Travel

In 1969, the Supreme Court struck down statutes in Connecticut, Pennsylvania, and the District of Columbia that restricted welfare benefits to those who have resided in those jurisdictions for at least 1 year (*Shapiro v. Thompson*, 1969). Ironically, the goal of these statutes was similar to that of the English Poor Laws; that is, to preserve the financial status of state public assistance programs. The states and the District asserted that those who require state assistance within the first year of residence are likely to become continuing burdens to the state. Thus, denying benefits to recent arrivals was designed to preserve benefits for long-term residents.

The Supreme Court was not persuaded by such reasoning and found the statutes unconstitutional. It ruled that the state-created distinctions between those new arrivals and long-standing residents violated the due process guarantee of the Fourteenth Amendment. The due process clause requires that U.S. citizens of any state origin must be treated similarly in receiving government benefits. Setting up a classification based on the length of stay in a state is an impermissible way of deciding who can receive state aid. Stated differently, the Court said that U.S. citizens may freely move from state to state without jeopardizing their rights to receive state public assistance.

Medical Care

The Supreme Court has also ruled on permissible residence requirements for medical care. The Court overturned an Arizona statute that required a 1-year residency in the country in order to receive non-emergency medical or hospitalization services (*Memorial Hospital v. Maricopa County*, 1974). The Court ruled that such a residency requirement for these necessities of life was such an severe imposition on travel that the state needed to justify its law with a compelling state interest.

Although the Supreme Court will not invalidate all restrictions on travel on constitutional grounds, the due process and equal protection clauses of the Fourteenth Amendment can be used to invalidate statutes that penalize citizens for moving from state to state or for not meeting residency requirements for essential services. Thus, the locality component of the English Poor Laws has seemingly reached current American social welfare policy in regard to the Constitutional constraint on equal protection and due process. The Court struck the ideological balance in favor of community driven charity. A Supreme Court decision in the 1990s, given similar facts, might decide differently.

Ethical Coherence and Conflict

The religious values of Western welfare are dynamic. The values of community and charity have been transformed through the social alchemy of individualism and personal autonomy.

The Nature of Charity. It is evident that the values of community and charity, expressed in the practice of the communities previously mentioned, have maintained the ambivalence and conflict among the competing ethical considerations. The meaning of charity in the ancient literatures competes with the social contract between autonomous individuals. The Poor Laws embody both personal property rights and self-giving benevolence. The English Poor Laws embody this change in their view of charity as a social contract between the haves and the have-nots.

The Nature of Community. The ancient religious ideologies created sacred communities, which were established as an expression of their spiritual identity. The Dead Sea Scrolls were found in the sacred geography of the promised land. Qumran became a sacred community within this sacred land—a sacred microcosm within a sacred macrocosm. Christian monastic communities also created sacred cosmologies within their precincts and written precepts.

A Constitutional Welfare Ideology. The current ideology invests community with national, political principles. This constitutional ideology, including the demands of due process and local, financial considerations are modern expressions of individual freedoms and autonomy. In a sense, this new constitutional welfare ideology has substantially replaced the tradition of the religious ethics of community and charity. The value of constitutional welfare means that the Supreme Court has the duty to follow the rubric of constitutional practice and policy in formulating its decisions on social welfare issues. Constitutional welfare codifies ideology and underpins it with national law. As noted earlier, however, what constitutional law giveth, constitutional law can taketh away.

This constitutional welfare ideology seeks to balance the interests of the national community and the charitable impulse with the interests of personal autonomy and individual freedoms. As shown earlier, the Supreme Court has maintained the autonomy of citizens by championing individual due process rights to welfare over local fiscal autonomy of public assistance programs. Also, the Supreme Court has upheld the rights of states to limit benefits so long as such limitations are not arbitrary.

The U.S. Supreme Court, as the final arbiter of Constitutional interests, seeks to ensure an equitable distribution of such interests. In some cases the Court tips this balance in favor of individual autonomy or local fiscal interests, or in some instances in favor of a national community and a federal charity. This Constitutional welfare ideology does not resolve these competing values, it only subjects them to public and legal scrutiny. This scrutiny can be expected to only intensify into the next millenium. This scrutiny is likely to include the moral, religious, and spiritual issues related to public welfare policy.

SPIRITUAL JURISPRUDENCE

Public policy is most potently expressed in lawcases and in statutes. The laws of the land are the operational public expression of public policy and provide useful and current case studies for studying spiritual applications in public policy issues. This section examines specific spiritual behavior in the framework of American jurisprudence. Two important Supreme Court cases serve to illustrate legal proceedings investigating, understanding, and determining the rights and obligations of participants engaged in spiritual practices.

This discussion is important for social workers because it explains the way American jurisprudence balances the respective rights and obligations of spiritual groups. Although it is one thing to extol self-determination and nonjudgmentalism as a professional ethic, it must be understood that the law does not make either ethic paramount. The constitutional principles of religion, codified in the First Amendment and previous Supreme Court decisions, are the paramount ideologies. Social workers who do not know and understand spiritual jurisprudence cannot hope to assess and to intervene competently with those clients who are addressing the nature and meaning of their own spiritual behaviors. Conversely, social workers who are aware of, and who understand, spiritual jurisprudence have additional and important tools with which to relate to the client's spiritual situation.

Law and jurisprudence are not usually seen as important in social work assessment and interventions, let alone in spiritual assessment and interventions. The new era in social work practice, however, recognizes the important connections between spirituality and social work practice as well as those between spiritual jurisprudence and social work practice. There is a strong and vital relationship among law, spirituality, and social work practice. The following section illustrates this connection.

Cults, Liturgy, and Public Policy

Distinctions must be made between religion and public policy and spirituality and public policy. Religion and public policy involve the practice of religious behavior, known as cultic or liturgical practices. Because cults are addressed in Chapter 5, the following paragraphs will be devoted to a fuller explanation of this term and its relationship to spirituality and public policy.

Cult is a technical term meaning overt religious behavior, but it can also mean *labor.* Cult, in fact, is the root of the English term *cultivate*—to work soil and make it produce. In effect, cultic activity is the work of cultivating the spiritual life. It is the behavior—the outward activity—of the spiritual life. For much of Christianity, cultic behavior revolves around sacraments or preaching. Sacraments are often described as outward signs of an inward grace or symbols of the presence of God. There are seven sacraments in the Roman Catholic Church: baptism, confession, first communion, holy communion, marriage, ordination of priests, and extreme unction or last rites. Other Christian denominations have fewer sacraments, but they are similar. Church services revolve around such cultic activities.

Cultic activity of any type is distinguishable from spiritual activity. Where cultic activity is an outward expression of inward grace or transcendence, spirituality is the inward expression of inward grace. Issues surrounding spirituality and public policy are seldom overtly discussed as public policy issues because of their inward, invisible character.

Most often it is the religious or cultic behaviors that are the subjects of public policy discussion and controversy. These behaviors include school prayer; the use of nativity creches on government property; the protection of tribal land from government or private use; religious reasons for missing work for holidays; wearing religious hairstyles or clothing (like a Rastafarian braids or a yarmulke) that may be prohibited in the military, prisons, or the work place; or conducting religious ceremonies otherwise not allowed.

Constitutional Spiritual Behavior and Spiritual Social Work

The following is a description of a major U.S. Supreme Court decision *Employment Division, Department of Human Resources of Oregon v. Smith* (1990). The

Smith decision is an extremely important one made by the Supreme Court. It fundamentally changed the interpretation of the free exercise clause and caused a public and congressional furor. Responding to popular criticism of the *Smith* case, Congress passed the Religious Freedom Restoration Act (RFRA), which President Clinton signed into law in 1993.

The rather mundane facts of this case did not portend the importance of its conclusion. Alfred Smith and Galen Black were fired from their posts in a private rehabilitation center because they ingested peyote as part of the religious ceremonies in their Native American Church. Oregon lists peyote (*lophophora williamsii Lemaire*) as a controlled substance, and its use is a felony. They applied for unemployment compensation from the state employment division, but were denied on the grounds that they were fired for misconduct. Smith and Black filed suit, claiming that the denial of benefits unconstitutionally prohibited them from freely exercising their religion. The First Amendment reads, in part: "Congress shall make no law respecting an establishment of religion, or prohibiting the free exercise thereof . . . ."

The Supreme Court decided against Smith and Black, holding that a neutral and generally applicable criminal law does not implicate the free exercise clause of the First Amendment (*Smith*, p. 1,603). This means that, where a law does not discriminate against particular spiritual groups or practices, it does not require the strict scrutiny the Court reserves to strike down such laws.

The *Smith* ruling was a radical departure from established legal precedent interpreting the free exercise clause. Before *Smith*, any law that substantially burdened a person's religious practice was subject to strict constitutional scrutiny. Such a law could stand only if (a) the law substantially furthers a compelling government interest, and (b) it uses the least restrictive means of promoting the compelling government interest (*Sherbert v. Verner*, 1963). This strict scrutiny made it much more difficult for government interference or intrusion into spiritual practices. The *Smith* decision shortcircuited this scrutiny. The holding required only that the law be neutral for it to stand.

The public outcry against the *Smith* decision propelled Congress to pass the RFRA. Essentially, the RFRA restored the legal test of *Sherbert v. Werner*. With the RFRA, Congress essentially reversed the *Smith* decision; however, the legal impact of the RFRA is unclear. To date, no legal decision has challenged the RFRA, nor has the RFRA been used as a interpretive scheme to decide a free exercise of religion case. An examination of the RFRA's legal impact on the free exercise of religion must wait, although the same need not be said of an analysis of the *Smith* decision's spiritual content. This section has considered the jurisprudence of the *Smith* decision. The next few paragraphs consider the spiritual jurisprudence of this decision.

Spiritual Dimensions of the Smith Decision. An analysis of the *Smith* case begins with how its decision affects spirituality. For this analysis, it must be noted that the *Smith* decision was a plurality decision. This means that, although the basic decision was reached by a majority (at least five) of the nine Supreme Court justices, the justices did not all agree on the reasoning for the holding. The majority opinion was written by Justice Scalia and joined by Chief Justice Rehnquist and Justices White, Stevens, and Kennedy. A concurring opinion was written by Justice O'Connor. Justices Brennan, Marshall, and Blackmun dissented while joining into parts of the concurring opinion. This range of opinion reflects the diversity of spiritual jurisprudence and well as that of spiritual practices in contemporary America.

Indeed, the spiritual jurisprudence of the *Smith* decision hinged on the nature and role of spiritual diversity. The majority opinion was prepared to allow the religious practices of the majority to dominate the spiritual practices of the minority. Justice Scalia wrote in the final substantive sentence of the opinion:

> It may fairly be said that leaving accommodation to the political process will place at a relative disadvantage those religious practices that are not widely engaged in; but that unavoidable consequence of democratic government must be preferred to a system in which each conscience is a law unto itself or in which judges weigh the social importance of all laws against the centrality of all religious beliefs. (*Smith*, p. 890)

This single sentence sums up the spiritual jurisprudence of the case. There are three significant themes in this case's spiritual jurisprudence. First, the Court did not dispute that peyote use was central to the Native American Church. In fact, the Court did not dispute either the centrality or sacramentality of peyote use in the Native American Church. The dissenting opinion noted:

> Respondents believe, and their sincerity has never been at issue, that the peyote plant embodies their deity, and eating it is an act of worship and communion. Without peyote, they could not enact the essential ritual of their religion. (*Smith*, p. 919)

As already mentioned, "sacramental" refers to the tangible, outward expression of an inward grace. Ingesting peyote is analogous to the Christian sacrament of holy communion or the Lord's supper. Peyote is sacramental because it is both a vehicle for, and an expression of, spiritual experience. The sacramental use of peyote among American Indian Nations is widely noted and recognized (Bullis, 1990; Huxley, 1974; Pahnke, 1972).

The peyote ceremony is conducted on sacred ground, which is depicted in Figure 4.2. The center of the tepee is made sacred by the consecration of sacred elements. Tobacco, sage, ashes, the lightning stick, and the fire itself all serve as

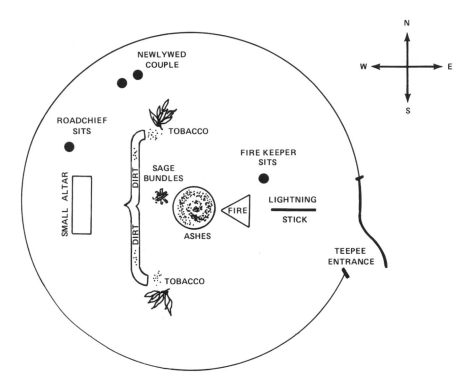

Figure 4.2 Ceremonial Floor Plan (This figure appeared in the *Journal of Psychoactive Drugs*, Volume 22, Number 3, © 1990. Reprinted with permission. All rights reserved.)

sacramental elements. The small altar contains peyote buttons and peyote tea. The purpose of the ceremony is to honor the Great Spirit. The ceremonies can be theologically eclectic, sometimes incorporating both Christian and traditional Native American elements.

Although the Supreme Court recognized the central and sacramental role of peyote in the Native American Church, it concluded that even this role is almost irrelevant to its legal determination. Precisely put, the Court ruled that sometimes an unavoidable consequence of lawmaking is the concession of unusual, peripheral, or little-known spiritual practices to majority spiritual needs or wishes. The majority opinion in *Smith* viewed such sublimation as part and parcel to the democratic process.

The concurring opinion disagreed. Speaking about the initial purpose of the First Amendment, Justice O'Connor wrote:

> . . . the First Amendment was enacted precisely to protect the rights of those whose religious practices are not shared by the majority and may be viewed with hostility. The history of our free exercise doctrine amply demonstrates the harsh impact of majoritarian rule has been on unpopular or emerging religious groups . . . (*Smith*, p. 902)

In legal terms, Justice O'Connor explains the spiritual dilemma presented by the *Smith* decision. The harsh impact of any legislation limiting the practice of a central and sacramental act is described by the justices in its legal context. The *Smith* case necessitates a discussion of just such an impact. Sacraments are not just spiritual windowdressing. Even the dissenting opinion recognizes the power of sacramental peyote. Justice Blackmun quoted the *amici curiae* brief of the Association of American Indian Affairs (p. 5-6), writing:

> To the members, peyote is consecrated with powers to heal body, mind, and spirit. It is a teacher; it teaches the way to spiritual life through living in harmony and balance with the forces of the Creation. The rituals are an integral part of the life process. They embody a form of worship in which the sacrament Peyote is the means for communicating with the Great Spirit. (p. 919)

The above brief rightly places the peyote sacrament in its healing, spiritual context. Without the vehicle of sacraments to commune with the Great Spirit, the member's spirit dries up like a leaf severed from its branch.

The second significant theme of spiritual jurisprudence involves the importance of sacraments as a form of healing mythology. Sacraments, including the peyote sacrament, have important healing elements for the participants. This healing has both personal and communal dimensions. The following story of peyote healing was told to this author in North Dakota by a Native American Church member and was first reproduced in Bullis (1990):

> A woman had a young son. On a trip one day, the woman lost sight of him. She looked high and low, but could not find him and became frantic. She went into the wilderness, but still could not find him. Finally, she lay down in complete exhaustion one night near some peyote and had a dream. God spoke to her in the dream, pointed to the peyote and said, "This is your medicine. This will be your food and water." In the dream God told her where she could find her child. The woman awoke and found her child, but the child was dead.

This story contains the mythic elements of transformation and death, the search for the soul, and of discovery.

The third significant theme of spiritual jurisprudence involves myth. The peyote ritual contains a healing myth. The healing is personal in the sense that the woman had a transcendent experience and joined with the divine. Why does the story, then, connect the tragic death of the child with the discovery of peyote? It is because the death of the child represents the initiation from egoistic ignorance into transcendent experience. One has to let one's child die its death before one can live as an adult and enter the spiritual dimensions. Death is an analogy for spiritual transformation.

The community healing is more embedded in the story. The death of the child is the wound in the community and is a deep loss to family, clan, and nation. This community loss is the community's sacred wound, which is transformed into community healing by the transcending vehicle of peyote. Peyote is a healer of communities as well as that of persons.

An enduring issue in the *Smith* case's spiritual jurisprudence is the impact and effect of parental or guardian sacramental peyote use on children or other minors. Sacramental drug use by bona fide members of a Native American Church may be successfully argued. However, the impact of such drug use in the presence of minors is an unresolved issue, as is the issue of adults who are under the influence of sacramental drugs when taking care of children. These issues are unresolved as a result of legislative action or court decisions. They do, however, make good class discussions.

Peyote use and social work practice have a stake in healing. Personal and community healing constitute the province of both peyote spirituality and social work practice. The next section further explores this connection.

Tantrism and Marijuana Use

This brief section discusses a pair of state court cases that also deal with drug use for spiritual purposes. Tantrism is a form of spirituality most closely connected with Taoism, Hinduism, and Buddhism. Although tantrism is explained at some length in Chapter 5, a brief summary is included here. Tantrism is a form of spirituality that emphasizes the direct experience of God through the expansion of consciousness. It also is a form of sacred sexuality—a spirituality expressed in and through sexuality. Techniques of such consciousness expansion have a long and venerable history in several different cross-cultural spiritualities.

This section concerns an extension of the more traditional ways of expanding consciousness. These cases test whether smoking marijuana can be sanctioned under First Amendment protections when used for tantric purposes. Two cases consider this issue with the same result.

The first case considers the appeal of a defendant convicted of unlawful possession of marijuana (*State v. Rocheleau,* 1982). He appealed his conviction on the grounds that he used marijuana to "facilitate the perception of samadhi," a form of enlightenment (p. 1,149). The Supreme Court of Vermont assumed that tantrism was a genuine religion and that use of marijuana was a legitimate part of tantric practices. Even with such assumptions, the Court ruled that the use of marijuana was not an indispensable part of tantric practices. As marijuana use was not an integral part of tantrism, then, the Court ruled that the state's compelling interest in controlling illicit drug use overrode the defendant's freedom of religion claims.

The second case also involved marijuana use in tantric spirituality. The defendant in this case also was convicted for the illegal possession of marijuana. He also appealed his conviction on the grounds that it violated his First Amendment rights of free exercise of religion. He claimed that smoking marijuana was an important element in his spiritual practice of Hindu tantrism.

Similar to the *Rocheleau* case, the Intermediate Court of Appeals of Hawaii assumed that Hindu tantrism is a legitimate religion where the First Amendment was concerned. The Hawaiian court additionally found that marijuana was neither a necessary nor indispensable element of Hindu tantrism. It found, however, that the defendant's marijuana use was an optional spiritual practice and that it was his personal desire to do so—not a spiritually required one. As such, the Court refused to protect the defendant's marijuana use under the aegis of the First Amendment (*State v. Blake*, 1985).

The *Blake* court wrote more extensively about the nature of tantrism than did the *Rocheleau* court, and the *Blake* court outlined some principles of tantrism from which it drew its legal conclusions.

> A portion of the Hindu Tantras deals with a practice known as *kundalini* (serpent power) yoga which is based on the belief that unmanifested divine energy remains within a person like a coiled serpent as the base of the spine. Through certain prescribed exercises such as meditation, chanting of *mantras,* and prayer, the *kundalini* or divine energy rises through six centers of consciousness until it reaches the seventh located in the brain where a mystic union with the Supreme Lord occurs. (p. 339)

The Court obviously took time to consider elements of Hindu tantrism and the purported place of marijuana in it. It found that the defendant's references noted only that the use of marijuana in tantrism was optional, not required, in this spiritual practice.

The next section discusses the spirituality of these cases and the *Smith* decision in the context of social work practice. The spirituality of law decisions is here referred to as spiritual jurisprudence.

Constitutionally Sacred Sexuality and its Limitations with Children

The sacredness of sexuality is expressed in the constitution through the right of privacy. Privacy became a right when, in *Griswold v. State of Connecticut* (1965), the U.S. Supreme Court struck down a state law prohibiting counseling for and the use of contraceptives. Justice Douglas, in establishing a right to privacy for contraceptive use among married persons, described marriage as being sacred.

The Supreme Court expanded the privacy right, and the right of unmarried individuals, to using contraceptives in *Eisenstadt v. Baird* (1972).

The right to privacy and sexuality among families has constitutional limits, however. This limitation is demonstrated in the case of a child, younger than 14 years old, who asked his mother how babies were made. The mother responded to the boy's question by performing sexual intercourse with her husband in front of the boy. She was arrested for lewd and lascivious behavior. Her appeal was based on the right to privacy and was denied in *Chesebrough v. State* (1971). Although the right to privacy confers constitutional sanctity on marriage, that sanctity, as the *Smith* case illustrated, is restricted by state action.

Thus, while courts give credence to tantra, and may even acknowledge the spirituality of sexuality, they will draw limits on spiritual practices when harm is shown to minors or to the public at large. Tantra is a term now widely used to describe a type of cross-cultural sacred sexuality. Chapter 6, in a section titled "Tantra, Ecstatic Sexuality, and Spirituality," more deeply discusses sacred sexuality.

SPIRITUAL JURISPRUDENCE AND SOCIAL WORK PRACTICE

This section discusses the spirituality of the *Smith* decision with respect to social work practice. Three themes present themselves in this relationship, and they will be discussed serially.

First, social workers need to know the legal and social consequences of spiritual behavior. Imagine how social workers might respond to the situation of Smith and Black, or the defendants in the tantric decisions. The threshold question for them is the extent to which they intended to provide the fact pattern for a landmark Supreme Court case or state court decision. Social workers, who are sophisticated in such matters, could help them lay out their options and render educated guesses as to the outcomes of such options. An obvious issue was whether to tell anyone in authority that they used sacramental peyote in the first place!

Another issue involves the determination of the legal status of sacramental peyote use. This determination requires some legal knowledge and forensic sophistication. It is public knowledge that the federal government exempts the religious use of peyote under proscribed circumstances (Code of Federal Regulations, 1989). The Code of Federal Regulations provides:

> The listing of peyote as a controlled substance in Schedule I does not apply to the non-drug use of peyote in bona fide religious ceremonies of the Native American Church, and members of the Native American Church so using peyote are exempt

from registration. Any person who manufactures peyote for or distributes peyote to the Native American Church, however, is required to obtain registration annually and to comply with all other requirements of law.

Social workers could also discover that 23 states, many with significant Native American populations, have statutorily or judicially created exemptions for sacramental peyote use (*Smith,* 1990, p. 912). Knowing about such exemptions provides the competence with which to address these social and spiritual issues. In recognizing these exemptions, the social worker can provide valuable counsel regarding if and when to contact legal counsel. For example, this little statute contains a wealth of information. It notes that there are exemptions to the exemption from use—namely, that distributors must be registered and comply with other laws.

Social workers can also foster insight about the relative merits of the social disclosure of sacramental peyote use or tantric marijuana use as opposed to the relative merits of social nondisclosure. Self-determination, as stated previously, requires knowledge about the probable consequences of actions. In order to aid in such self-determination, social workers should be able to address the consequences of divulging spiritual behaviors.

Second, social workers need to know the mythology connected to spirituality. The social and spiritual importance of spiritual practices is a direct consequence of its attendant underlying mythology. For example, sacramental peyote use did not arise spontaneously, nor was it chosen randomly. It was chosen because of its mythological history, illustrated by the story told earlier.

Sacraments and ritual acts are always deliberately chosen from mythological sources. The elements of the Jewish seder meal (including horseradish, a bitter herb, lamb shank, unleavened bread, wine, etc.) are taken directly from the Old Testament accounts of the freedom of the Hebrew slaves under Pharaoh. The selection of bread and wine for the Christian communion was directly linked to the last supper stories in the New Testament Gospels as well as the images of wine and vines in John's Gospel, as noted previously. Mythology and sacraments are dynamically related.

Third, social workers need to know the mythology connected to cultural and personal healing. Sacramental elements and rituals are not just ceremonial. They are designed to provide both personal and communal healing. Spiritually competent social workers will distinguish between and validate both personal and corporate healing mythologies.

Spiritual Expression and Animal Sacrifice

A major U.S. Supreme Court decision, *Church or the Lukumi Babalu Aye v. City of Hialeah* (1993), hereinafter referred to as the *Lukumi* case, tested whether the

City of Hialeah, Florida could outlaw the unauthorized killing of animals. Such a prohibition meant that the Santeria religion could not accomplish a spiritual practice central to its faith. The city ordinances prohibited the ritual killing of an animal, except by any licensed establishment otherwise permitted by law. The Supreme Court struck down the city ordinance.

Justice Thomas Kennedy's majority opinion began with a history of the Santeria faith. When Yoruba slaves were shipped to Cuba, their traditional African spirituality was fused with Cuban Roman Catholic spirituality. The result was a synthesis of African and Western spirituality. A fundamental belief in Santeria is in *orishas*—powerful but mortal spirits that guide and develop a person to his or her divinely inspired potential. Gonzales-Wippler (1987) portrays the synthesis of the Santeria faith with the African orishas and Roman Catholic saints. A partial list is provided below.

Yoruba god	*Catholic saint*
Olorun-Olofi	The crucified Christ
Obatala-Father of the gods	Our Lady of Mercy (Las Mercedes)
Oddudua-Mother of the gods	Saint Claire
Ochumare-Goddess of the rainbow	Our Lady of Hope
Oggun-God of iron and war	Saint Peter
Babalu-Aye-God of the sick	Saint Lazarus
Ifa-God of impossible things	Saint Anthony of Padua

In Santeria theology, healing, nurturing, and relating to the divine are all possible only through close relationships with the orishas. The orishas are analogous to Roman Catholic saints. The term Santeria itself means *the way of the saints*. In fact, one of the main purposes of Santeria is to discover and fulfill personal and corporate life—the life enabled by worship of the orishas.

The goal of Santeria—that of union with the divine life—makes the role of the orishas indispensable. The Yoruba cosmos is represented by two interpenetrable spheres (Drewal, Pemberton & Abiodun, 1989). The *aye* is the world of the living, of matter, of the material world, the world that one's five senses can perceive. The *orun,* conversely, is the world of the spirits, of the intangible world. This cosmos is often depicted by a gord, or a calabash, where the top and bottom fit neatly with each other. This is the great symbolism of the Yoruba cosmic calabash—that the world of the aye and the world of the orun are intimately connected and interrelated. Mediums, divinization, and orishas are vehicles where these worlds intersect. These points of intersection are known as *orita meta* ("where heaven meets earth"). In traditional Yoruba spirituality the orishas could be either deified ancestors or personified natural forces. Gods and goddesses regularly enter into the aye through the orita meta.

The human connection with the orishas is an important means of connection with the aye, as well as attendant health, happiness, and human fulfillment. Thus, connection with the orishas serves a sacramental function.

The orishas depend on the sacrifice of live animals for their survival, because the energy rendered at the sacrifice gives them life and sustenance. Animal sacrifices are made at significant moments including birth, death, marriage, curing of the sick, the ordination of Santeria priests, and the initiation of new members to the faith. The animals sacrificed include chickens, pigeons, pigs, doves, ducks, goats, sheep, and turtles. The sacrifice—performed by cutting their carotid arteries—is later cooked and eaten, except during healing and death ceremonies.

Members of the Santeria faith faced persecution in Cuba and so practiced their faith in secret. Many of the Santeria followers came to America during Cuban expatriation during the 1960s. In the United States, they continue to practice Santeria in relative secrecy.

The present case arose when a Santeria organization announced plans in 1987 to build a house of worship, a school, a cultural center, and a museum in Hialeah. The president of this Santeria Church, Ernesto Pichardo, also held the title of both Santeria priest and *Italero*—the second highest position in the Santeria organization.

The reception of the Santeria Church in Hialeah was, at best, mixed. The city council held an emergency public meeting and passed a number of ordinances that restricted Santeria worship.

In ruling that the ordinances violated the free exercise clause, the Court first determined that the city ordinances were neither neutral nor equally applicable. This means that, unlike the peyote prohibitions in the *Smith* case, the Hialeah ordinances specifically disapproved of a particular spiritual practice and that they targeted a particular faith. The Court found the ordinances to not be neutral laws of equal applicability. Thus, a strict scrutiny of such laws was required to determine whether they furthered a compelling governmental interest with the least amount of religious restriction.

Hialeah claimed that its ordinances properly protected the public health and safety and prevented cruelty to animals. The Court did not accept that argument. It found that the ordinances were overbroad or underinclusive. The ordinances either did not pursue their stated objectives in analogous nonreligious conduct or were not narrowly tailored to achieve legitimate public purposes. The ordinances failed, in other words, because the city failed to require nonreligious animal killing to comply with the same rules as required by killing at Lukumi sacrifices. They also failed because the ordinances did not gear their prohibitions toward serving only those legitimate ends of public health and safety of animals.

Although this case helps to clarify the Court's interpretation of the free exercise clause, it also delves into important spiritual issues. The next section discusses the spiritual nature and consequences of this case.

The Spiritual Jurisprudence of the Lukumi Case

The *Lukumi* case illustrates two important spiritual issues. The first is that the Court allowed that even unusual or popularly distasteful spiritual practices are sometimes afforded First Amendment protection. Constitutionally, the issue is that the content of spirituality is never the main focus. If the spiritual content were primary, this content would determine the extent of its constitutional protection. An example can be found in what the majority opinion called religious gerrymandering (*Lukumi*, p. 2,227), but the author shall refer to this as spiritual gerrymandering, which is the metaphysical analogy to political gerrymandering (political gerrymandering is the process whereby voters are arbitrarily separated along artificially drawn social boundaries). For example, some states have created very unusual and arbitrary political boundaries to ensure greater minority representation in their state legislatures. Such political gerrymandering is currently under review at the Supreme Court.

Spiritual gerrymandering, likewise, makes arbitrary distinctions between permissible and impermissible spiritual or ritual behavior. Spiritual gerrymandering is either the capricious prohibition or encouragement of spiritual acts otherwise allowed or prohibited in other sectors of society. The Court noted that although Hialeah prohibited the Santeria manner of killing, it permitted the kosher killing of animals. The Court also found Santeria seemed to be the exclusive legislative target of the Hialeah ordinances. Singling out any spiritual ritual for praise or prohibition is unconstitutional.

But a spiritual jurisprudence analysis pursues the matter deeper. Spiritual gerrymandering tends to chill spiritual exploration. *Chilling* is a quasi-legal term of art that refers to unofficially prohibiting certain acts that cannot be officially prohibited. What is not done overtly sometimes is done covertly. For example, where federal legislators could not limit what they call pornography by directly censuring it, they have attempted to pass laws holding the manufacturers and producers of such literature liable for harm done to third parties. These laws were never passed, but served to chill the production of erotic literature (Bullis, 1995b). The threat of holding erotic producers liable was likely designed to have the rippling effect of chilling the producing and distribution of erotic material.

Similarly, laws that restrict or promote particular spiritual activity may chill related spiritual activity. The Hialeah ordinances not only limited Santeria rituals, but by the rippling effect could have limited other spiritual traditions as well.

Other spiritual traditions may feel coerced into limiting their rituals by the threats posed to the Santeria faith. Thus, the liberty exercised on behalf of one spiritual tradition can embolden others to pursue their own religious freedoms.

Second, increasing religious diversity is a value in its own right. Increased spiritual diversity is analogous to increased ecological diversity. The more diverse an ecosystem is the more possibilities there are to nourish it. The more variety of life there is to a barrier reef, for example, the more chances it has to survive if environmental conditions change. Ecological diversity makes the ecosystem stronger, more adaptable, and more resilient.

Similarly, the more diverse the spiritual ecosystem is, the more it can withstand changes. If anything in the United States has changed since its founding, its spiritual landscape has. From the great diversity of Native American spiritualities to the coming of Spanish and French Roman Catholics, Puritans, and other Protestant groups, to waves of Italian and Irish Roman Catholics and Jewish immigrants from Eastern Europe, numerous spiritual traditions and traditions within those traditions have come to America. In this century, Buddhists from Cambodia and Vietnam; Rastafarians from the Caribbean; Hindus and Sikhs from India; Copts from Egypt; Eastern Orthodox followers from the former Soviet Union Republics and Greece; and Moslems from the Middle East, Africa, and Asia have diversified the American spiritual ecosystem.

Such spiritual diversity makes for important work for the Supreme Court, because a large percentage of cases every year are based on the First Amendment's religion clause. Most spiritual assumptions no longer go unchallenged, for there is no longer a national spiritual consensus. Certainly, if the *Lukumi* case was brought to trial even 30 years ago, the outcome may well have been much different.

The American spiritual ecosystem is becoming increasingly diverse and is not dependent on any one ideology or tradition; one tradition cross-fertilizes another, and the Santeria case is an excellent example. This cross-fertilization makes American spirituality adaptable and resilient. The ingenuity of the First Amendment is that it encourages religious tolerance and diversity.

The spiritual jurisprudence of the *Lukumi* case exemplifies this spiritual ecology. The Court took pains to note that animal sacrifice might be unpopular, upsetting, and even abhorrent to the citizens of Hialeah. Those sentiments, however, cannot be expressed by arbitrary laws singling out one particular group. The spiritual ecology must be organically balanced.

The question may rightly be asked about how the ecological balance was struck with the *Smith* case. It might seem that the *Smith* decision was struck in favor of popular sentiment, and that may well be. It is important to note, though, that the Supreme Court distinguished between these cases because *Smith* addressed a neutral law of general applicability and the *Lukumi* case addressed a law specially designed to curb specific spiritual rituals. The next section discusses the *Lukumi* spiritual jurisprudence in the light of social work practice.

The Lukumi Case and Spiritual Social Work Practice

As with the *Smith* decision, spiritual jurisprudence of the *Lukumi* case is intimately connected with the practice of spiritual social work. The *Lukumi* case poses its own brand of spiritual jurisprudence and its own kind of usefulness to social work practice. This section describes the primary dynamic of spiritual jurisprudence—namely, the dynamics of a spiritual ecosystem.

A spiritual jurisprudence ecosystem is analogous to an environmental ecosystem, which is constituted of several components interacting with one another in marvelous intricacy. In the ocean, from tiny algae to giant whales to crashing sea waves, ecological components are intimately connected. When one component is affected, such as by an oil spill, all components are affected. In fact, the entire ecosystem may be destroyed.

Similarly, a spiritual jurisprudence ecosystem involves interactive components. They are legal, personal, social, and spiritual in nature, and are important in understanding the spiritual jurisprudence of the *Lukumi* case for the practice of social work. In the *Lukumi* case, these four components are interconnected. The legal component consists in the the case's decision and its legal consequences.

The social components involve the impact of this case on social institutions, values, and norms. The most important social impact of the *Lukumi* case is that it leaves the social organization and social norms of the Hialeah Santeria followers undisturbed. Just as the Court disapproved of what this author calls "spiritual gerrymandering," this case disapproved of "social gerrymandering" as well. Here, social gerrymandering refers to the arbitrary and capricious separating of groups of persons for social or political ends. The Court said, "The net result of the gerrymander is that few if any killings of animals are prohibited other than Santeria sacrifice, which is proscribed because it occurs during a ritual or ceremony and its primary purpose is to make an offering to the *orishas*, not food consumption" (*Lukimi*, p. 2,227).

The *Lukumi* case leaves the social organization of the Hialeah Santeria followers intact and preserves their social fabric and connections. The connection of the social fabric is important because Santeria followers, like other spiritual groups, are a social group and spiritual group alike. Spirituality and healing are expressed in a social, community context.

The personal component consists of the impact of the case on individual behavior. The *Lukumi* case also preserves the personal dimension of the Hialeah Santeria followers, as the Supreme Court safeguarded their personal devotional and spiritual practices. The Court refused to force any change in the Santeria followers' personal spiritual practices. In Santeria, there is not spiritual substitute for personal devotion.

The Court particularly noted the animosity evidenced among community members, members of the Hialeah City Council, and other officials. Counselman Cardozo said that Santeria members "were in violation of everything this country stands for" (p. 2,230). The chaplain for the Hialeah Police Department said that the Santeria sacrifice was a sin, an "abomination to the Lord," and the worship of demons, saying, "I would exhort you . . . not to permit this Church to exist" (p. 2,230). In such an atmosphere of disapproval, the Court ruling stepped in to judicially preserve an integral sacramental act. It is the very nature of the religion clause of the First Amendment to protect even those spiritual rituals that seem most abhorrent to the community.

The spiritual component is represented by impacts on individual relations with the divine. The Supreme Court clearly believed that Santeria animal sacrifice was a central ritual act of spiritual importance, noting that neither Hialeah nor the lower courts questioned the religious sincerity of the Santeria members (p. 2,225). This discussion, however, goes beyond the holding of the *Lukumi* decision and explores the implications of this decision for the Santeria spirituality.

The *Lukumi* decision leaves undisturbed the connecting link between the divine and the human levels. As previously described, Santeria sacrifice is a connecting link to the orishas. This connection is a mediating and connecting point of the orun with the aye. The connection between these two worlds (or world views) has a beneficial, cross-fertilizing effect on human life. Without such a connection, human life is unproductive, meaningless, and futile. Contact with the orishas through the use of sacrifices enriches and preserves human life and healing.

Like an environmental ecosystem, these four components relate intimately with one another. The Santeria ritual sacrifice of animals, therefore, holds personal, social, legal, and spiritual consequences.

CONCLUSION

This chapter addressed the public expressions of spiritual social work practice. These specific expressions are addressed because they are highly relevant for social workers. A history is included that represents the spiritual and religious values significant to contemporary social work practice and public policy issues. Supreme Court cases and related legal material specifically explain the state of the law on spiritual jurisprudence, just as legal materials specifically illustrate the kinds of spiritual issues that social workers are likely to address in their practices.

DISCUSSION SCENARIOS AND QUESTIONS

Following are four discussion questions that are suitable for personal reflection, classroom use, or seminar discussion flow from the issues raised in this chapter. The questions are designed to integrate class participation with the information provided in this chapter.

1. You are a child protective services social worker in the county in which the city of Hialeah is located. Someone calls in a child abuse complaint against Santeria parents because they allowed their child to witness the ritual slaughter of a pig. The complainant asserts that this event traumatized the child. Your supervisor deems that this complaint is a *prima facie* case of emotional abuse and asks you to investigate and determine whether to prosecute. You investigate and conclude that the child was upset by the experience, but did not experience any type of trauma. Prosecution may be warranted, but you are also cognizant of the freedom of religion and spiritual issues involved. Your supervisor asks you to brief him or her on such matters. What do you say? How do your comments bear on the possible prosecution of the parents?

2. You are a social worker associated with the state of Oregon within the jurisdiction where Galen Black and Alfred Smith formerly worked. Due to their litigation, state officials have launched an investigation into the care and health of their children. State officials are concerned that their use of peyote was limited strictly to bona fide religious ceremonies and that no emotional harm came to the children. You are part of an interdisciplinary team consisting of a state prosecutor, a state police investigator, and yourself. How do you define your role and what are the principle issues or questions that you need to address?

3. You are working in a social work position in a community where a voodoo organization is being formed. You become aware of virulent and vociferous opposition to this organization. In fact, several community members have spoken to you personally about their fears—even antagonism—about this prospect. You are fearful of community splintering, divisiveness, and perhaps even violence against voodoo members. What is your role? How do you proceed?

4. You are a private clinician who gets a call from a mother who is distressed over the mental status of her 5-year-old child. In your first interview with the mother and child, you learn that the child had some friends at school who belong to the Santeria organization. They had told her that their group sacrifices animals as part of their practices. This knowledge has severely

upset your child client, who has a pet herself. She has nightmares, eating difficulties, and is visibly agitated when she thinks about the sacrifice of other animals. What is your treatment? How would your answer be different if your child client, him or herself, was a member of the Santeria spiritual group?

5. You are a hospital social worker, and a nurse approaches you with a dilemma. A patient has requested that his or her spiritual advisor conduct a healing ceremony in his or her hospital room. The advisor and patient follow the Haitian voodoo tradition, and the nurse is afraid that such a ceremony might disturb the other patients. The nurse herself is apprehensive about the ceremony, although she says that she does not know what the voodoo priest would do at the ceremony. What is your response to the nurse and the other concerned hospital staff? What is your approach, if any, to the patient? Would your response differ if some of the patient's family members, themselves, were uncomfortable with the ceremony?

6. You are a social worker for the local Young Women's Christian Association (YWCA). You are working with newly arrived Russian immigrants who are evangelical Christians. They are eager to find jobs and to be self-supporting, although several immigrants have taken jobs where Sunday work is required by their employers. They find this contrary to their religious practices and approach you for help. What do you plan to do? What is your approach, if any, to the employers? What is your approach to your clients? Would your approaches differ if you were working for Jewish Social Services and Jewish Russian immigrants approached you with the same concerns about their Saturday Sabbath?

Chapter 5

Ethics, Mysticism, Cults, and Contraindications for Use

Chapter 5 explores ethical considerations, cultic behavior, and contraindications to the use of spirituality in social work practice. This chapter also examines the use of spiritual assessments and interventions in light of ethics, cultic behavior, and contraindications for use. These specialized issues are important considerations, for they may spell the difference between a spiritual social work practice that is done effectively and a practice that is done incompetently, causing harm to clients.

The previous three chapters have tried to reignite spiritual interest in social work practice. Clients are more than just biopsychosocial beings; they are, in fact, beings with a spiritual cosmology, a spiritual anthropology, and a spiritual hierarchy of needs. Thus, remystifying social work practice is a reasonable and logical result. This means consciously reintroducing a spiritual, even mystical, element into social work practice. Social workers have a moral imperative to protect their clients (and the cosmos) from destructive spiritual practices.

This chapter reverses this practice and demystifies this process, which means that, in recognizing the spirtual nature of clients, it is also necessary to recognize the nonspiritual elements in addressing social work spiritual practice. It is especially important to take into consideration other dynamics involved, which are important for two reasons. First, spirituality does not exist in a vacuum, but instead is central to all other human experience and consciousness. Spirituality alone cannot justify the use of all spiritual assessments on interventions. Other dynamics influence the nature and the intensity of spirituality, among them personal culture, history, social and economic environment, and psychological matters.

Second, social workers need language and practice methods specifically designed to integrate spirituality and social work theory. An integrated approach without practice methods is a cup half full. Of course, not all such considerations are discussed in the space of this chapter. Chapter 5 deals only with ethics, cults, and contraindications for using spiritual factors in practice. A discussion of other dynamics must wait for future writings.

ETHICS AND SPIRITUAL SOCIAL WORK PRACTICE

This section discusses ethics with respect to spiritual social work practice. Here, ethics are used to establish appropriate norms of behavior for clinical social work (Nelson & Wilson, 1984). These authors examined the ethical dimensions of discussing religion in psychotherapy, and asserted that both spirituality and religion can be ethically discussed in treatment. The authors offer three reasons for encouraging the proper use of religious/spiritual interventions. First, the empirical evidence demonstrates a positive relationship between religion and health. Second, because empirical evidence shows that most Americans have religious affiliation, sharing religious views is neither an unexpected nor an unwelcome disclosure. Third, addressing values is an important part of therapy, and such an examination of religious values should be no exception. They concluded that it is ethical for clinicians to share religious beliefs with clients if the client's issues were helped thereby, if the discussions were held within the client's own belief systems, and if such sharing was defined within the treatment contract.

Moreover, Bullis (1991) asserted that neither the Code of Ethics for the Association of Sex Educators, Counselors and Therapists nor the much-touted wall between church and state are impediments to religious or spiritual discussions with clients, particularly because the federal government now allows grants for such purposes. A careful conception of ethical issues involved in addressing religious/spiritual concerns or clients was offered by Lowenberg (1988). This conceptual framework offers a range of clinical options, including refusal to offer clinical services, favoritism of one option over another, avoidance of such issues, or referral.

Indeed, some of the rare discussions of ethical considerations come in literature discussing whether religious or spiritual content should be addressed in social work curricula. Spencer (1961) asserted that a humanistic philosophy alone is insufficient to address the entire spectrum of client needs and suggested that social work curricula include content sufficient enough to understand clients' spiritual and religious concerns. Without mentioning ethics per se, Spencer implied that social work practice inevitably addresses religion and that "it is appropriate" for social work schools to include such course content. Twenty-eight years later Canda (1989) asserted that the social work profession and the general public recognize that religion is an important facet of human behavior and should be included in social work curricula. Again, without entering into an explicit discussion of ethics, Canda argued that social work faculty seeking to address cultural issues and values among students need to address comparative religious perspectives that honor both students' and teachers' religious/spiritual commitments. These arguments, although not posed strictly as ethical considerations, consider this issue with care.

Dudley and Helfgott (1990) surveyed 53 social work faculty members from four universities to ascertain how amenable they were to religion or spiritual elements in the curriculum. Most were in favor of such elements in the course work. For those who were not in favor, ethical considerations played a role. The researchers found that respondents were more likely to oppose such a course if they thought it would conflict with the social work's mission, or interfere with the "separation of church and state" or their own beliefs. While such cautions are laudable, they misconstrue church/state law, the NASW code, and recent research on social work and spirituality. These reasons do not preclude discussions of spirituality as a matter of course.

In an early empirical study that touched upon ethical obligations of practitioners regarding religious issues, Jaffe (1961) found that there was substantial agreement that referral to a clergyperson is appropriate and that practitioners should have a working knowledge about major religious beliefs and should know their therapeutic impact. Additionally, she found that Roman Catholics tended to respond more positively to being referred to clergy, the competency of clergy as therapists, and the connection of religious practices (such as prayer) to therapy.

In the Sheridan and Bullis study (1991), 36% of the respondents described how they addressed religious/spiritual issues in practice. Thirty-two percent reported that they only addressed such issues when they were first initiated by clients and 21% reported that if religious/spiritual issues became a major focus of therapy, they recommended referral.

This empirical survey continues with a discussion of the author's empirical research discussed in earlier chapters. Chapter 2 has already reported the study's empirical research on spiritual assessment and interventions. This section continues the reporting of this study with an examination of ethical considerations as they apply to spiritual social work practice. For each of the 25 interventions discussed in Chapter 2 (Table 2.3), corresponding ethical questions were posed. Respondents were asked whether they thought that the intervention was professionally ethical and whether they were personally comfortable with the interventions.

Table 5.1 displays the data in these areas. The interventions rated by the highest percentages of respondents as being professionally ethical and personally comfortable included exploring the client's spiritual background exploring the client's religious background and clarifying spiritual values. The interventions rated least

Table 5.1

Practitioners' Report of Professional Ethics and Personal Comfort with the Use of Religious or Spiritual Interventions in Practice

Interventions	% Reporting Professionally Ethical	% Reporting Personally Comfortable
Explore Client's Religious Background	94.7% (*n* = 108)	97.3% (*n* = 110)
Explore Client's Spiritual Background	99.1% (*n* = 112)	96.4% (*n* = 108)
Use or Recommend Religious Books	55.0% (*n* = 60)	41.3% (*n* = 45)
Use or Recommend Spiritual Books	88.6% (*n* = 101)	83.3% (*n* = 95)
Teach Spiritual Meditation to Clients	71.8% (*n* = 74)	36.7% (*n* = 40)
Meditate Spiritually with Clients	45.1% (*n* = 46)	19.3% (*n* = 21)
Pray Privately for Client	83.5% (*n* = 91)	70.5% (*n* = 79)
Pray with Client in Session	37.1% (*n* = 39)	24.5% (*n* = 27)
Use Religious Language or Metaphors	66.4% (*n* = 71)	54.1% (*n* = 59)
Use Spiritual Language Metaphors	88.4% (*n* = 99)	81.6% (*n* = 93)
Touch Client for "Healing" Purposes	13.5% (*n* = 14)	10.9% (*n* = 12)
Read Scripture with Client	32.4% (*n* = 35)	21.4% (*n* = 24)
Recommend Participation in Religious Programs (Sunday school, religious education)	72.1% (*n* = 80)	65.5% (*n* = 74)
Recommend Participation in Spiritual Programs (Meditation groups, 12-step programs, men's/women's groups)	95.4% (*n* = 104)	91.8% (*n* = 101)
Help Clients Clarify Religious Values	78.2% (*n* = 86)	72.3% (*n* = 81)
Help Clients Clarify Spiritual Values	95.6% (*n* = 108)	94.7% (*n* = 107)
Refer Clients to Religious Counselors	90.0% (*n* = 99)	87.3% (*n* = 96)
Refer Clients to Spiritual Counselors	85.2% (*n* = 92)	80.9% (*n* = 89)
Help Clients Develop Ritual as a Clinical Intervention (House blessings, visiting graves of relatives, etc.)	90.9% (*n* = 100)	86.5% (*n* = 96)
Participate in Client's Rituals as a Clinical Intervention	57.1% (*n* = 60)	38.0% (*n* = 41)
Explore Religious Elements in Dreams	82.6% (*n* = 90)	61.5% (*n* = 67)
Explore Spiritual Elements in Dreams	93.6% (*n* = 103)	82.6% (*n* = 90)
Recommend Religious/Spiritual, Forgiveness, Penance, or Amends	65.1% (*n* = 71)	57.7% (*n* = 64)
Perform Exorcism	5.7% (*n* = 6)	3.6% (*n* = 4)
Share Your Own Religious/ Spiritual Beliefs or Views	60.9% (*n* = 67)	60.2% (*n* = 68)

professionally ethical and personally comfortable were performing exorcisms, touching the client for healing purposes, and reading scripture with the client.

There is high congruence between those interventions used most frequently and those rated most ethical. There is also a correspondence between those interventions used least frequently and those rated least ethical. Table 5.1 also reveals some marked incongruence between those reporting professional ethics versus personal comfort. For example, although respondents reported that it was professionally ethical to meditate with clients, only 19.5% felt comfortable doing so and, although respondents reported that it was professionally ethical to teach meditation to clients, only 36.7% felt comfortable doing so.

Respondents also reported on a 7-point scale (1 = Very uncomfortable, 4 = Neutral, 7 = Very comfortable) their ethical comfort in discussing either religious or spiritual issues when raised by either (a) the client or (b) the clinician. These results revealed a greater degree of comfort when spiritual issues are raised by the client ($M = 5.9$, $SD = 1.7$) or by the clinician ($M = 4.3$, $SD = 1.9$) than when religious issues are raised by either the client ($M = 5.1$, $SD = 1.9$) or by the clinician ($M = 3.5$, $SD = 2.0$). It should be noted that in both categories, respondents were more comfortable when such issues were raised by the client rather than by the practitioner.

Even more revealing were the results of bivariate analyses designed to explore significant statistical relationships between the use of religious/spiritual interventions and ethical considerations. This research found that several factors, in fact, reveal such significant relationships. These results are summarized in Table 5.2.

The bivariate analyses also revealed, among others, a statistically significant relationship between the use of interventions and both the degree to which the respondents were personally comfortable with them and the degree to which respondents viewed them as professionally ethical. A strong, positive relationship exists between the degree to which the respondents were personally comfortable with the interventions and the degree to which the respondents used the interventions. This means that as the degree of personal comfort increased, so did the use of the interventions. A moderate, positive relationship was also found between the view that a given intervention was professionally ethical and the use of that religious/spiritual intervention. The more clinicians viewed the interventions as professionally ethical, the more they used the interventions.

MYSTICISM AND SOCIAL WORK PRACTICE

Mysticism and Mental Health

Beginning in Chapter 2, it is asserted that the mystical process is vitally connected to mental health (Bullis, 1992). Mysticism refers to the "the art of the

Table 5.2
Relationships Between Personal and Professional Variables and Use of
Religious/Spiritual Interventions

Variable	Use of Religious/Spiritual Factors
Religious/Spiritual Affiliation	$t(112) = 1.47$ ns
Affiliated	$M = 10.02, SD = 5.46$
Not Affiliated	$M = 7.70, SD = 4.46$
Personal Ideology	$r = .25*$
Current Religious/Spiritual Identification/Participation	$r = .35**$
Number of Credit Hours of Graduate Training in Religion/Theology	$r = .30**$
Extent of Religious/Spiritual Content in Clinical Graduate Training	$r = .22*$
Inclusion of Religious/Spiritual Factors in Assessment	$r = .54**$
Extent of Viewing Religious/Spiritual Factors as a Positive Factor	$r = .57**$
Personally Comfortable	$r = .64**$
Professionally Ethical	$r = .57**$

$*p = .01$ $**p < .001.$

union with reality" (Underhill, 1915, p.3), and is another word for spirituality. It is a more technical, and sometimes a more esoteric, term of art. Sometimes the terms mysticism or mystic scare people, as they sometimes associate mystics with harmful, dangerous, or unsavory spiritual practices.

In popular culture, mysticism is often a catchword for anything weird or supernatural. As a point of fact, some of the most profound and important religious figures have been mystics. Jallaludin Rumi, Al Halaj, Ramakrishna, Meister Eckert, Richard Rolle, Teresa of Avila, Saint John of the Cross, the Baal Shem Tov, and Abraham Issac Kook have all had major influences on their respective religious and spiritual traditions.

Given the influence of mysticism on spiritual traditions, it is surprising that so little information is available on this subject. The following section describes the typology of the mystical process and its relationship to mental health assessments. This typology and subsequent discussion can be a vital source of help in distinguishing useful from unuseful cult involvement.

Typology of the Mystical Process

There are many ways to understand the mystical process, and one typology of mysticism is discussed in this section. Understanding the typology of mysticism is important for three reasons. First, it depicts scenarios for the customary pattern of mystical or spiritual experience. The second reason is that this process can help clinicians identify both functional and dysfunctional mystical processes. Last, this process can help clinicians facilitate functional mystical processes.

Several authors have posited typologies that depict this process. Such typologies are intimately connected to changes in consciousness and opportunities for mental health. One of the first and best typologies was provided by Evelyn Underhill in her classic book *Mysticism* (1915). She formulated a series of phases or stages of mysticism including awakening of the self, purgation, illumination, penumbra, and union. These stages are graphically described in Figure 5.1. Figure 5.1 demonstrates several significant characteristics about the phases of mysticism, which are distinctive, successive, and dynamic. Each stage is distinctive in that each has its own, separate characteristics. In this sense, each phase is discrete. They are described serially below.

The Awakening of the Self. The awakening of the self is the raising of a consciousness beyond the narrow confines of oneself and one's needs, wants, inhibitions, and habitual thought. This awakening involves an encountering of the

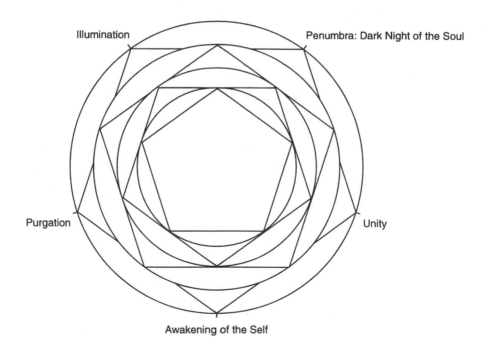

Figure 5.1 Stages of Mysticism

divine, which opens up the person to entirely new realms of experience and deeper, more expansive levels of consciousness. The individual may discover a profound sense of gratitude for life, of purposefulness, or of substantially intensified sensory perceptions. This awakening could be brought about either suddenly or gradually, and the history of spirituality records both experiences. The majority of people have gradual experiences of awakening over long periods of time, although the minority have sudden, intense, and dramatic awakening experiences. This sudden experience is illustrated by Saul of Tarsus' experience with the risen Christ on the Damascus Road (Acts 9). The Book of Acts records that Saul was riding on horseback when he was struck blind and speechless because Jesus spoke to him. Saul was struck to his very soul. With the assistance of Christians in Damascus, Saul underwent a searing self-transformation. His dramatic encounter so profoundly changed his life that he became Saint Paul.

The Stage of Purgation. An initial period of sudden or gradual awakening is often followed by a profound need to change self-defeating or harmful behavior. In the presence of the divine, all else tends to fall away. The wheat is separated from the chaff (Matthew 13). That is, the soul is purged from that which obscures it. This is a sometimes painful cleansing process. Kabir, a fifteenth century mystic and poet affected by both Moslem and Hindu influences, wrote:

> So, when I give up passion, I see that anger remains; and when I renounce anger, greed is with me still; and when greed is vanquished, pride and vainglory remain; when the mind is detached and casts Maya [illusion] away, still it clings to the letter. Kabir says, "Listen to me, dear Sadhu [wandering ascetic] the true path is rarely found." (Tagor, 1971, pp. 4-5)

The Stage of Illumination. The stage of illumination is an expanded and intensified version of the awakening. The experience feels like facing God, or the divine, in a more face-to-face manner. Illumination is the experience of the divine in an immediate and intimate way. A striking example of the stage of illumination is Moses' experience on Mount Horeb:

> And the angel of the Lord appeared to him in a flame of fire out of the midst of a bush; and he looked, and lo, the bush was burning, yet it was not consumed. And Moses said, "I will turn aside and see this great sight, why the bush is not burnt." When the Lord saw that he turned aside to see, God called to him out of the bush, "Moses, Moses!" And he said, "Here am I." Then he said, "Do not come near; put off your shoes from your feet, for the place on which you are standing is holy ground." And he said, "I am the God of your father, the God of Abraham, the God of Issac, and the God of Jacob." And Moses hid his face, for he was afraid to look at God. (Exodus 3:2-6)

This passage illustrates the illumination stage, where sensory perceptions are heightened. Colors appear more intense, sounds seem more beautiful, touch seems more sensual, tastes and smells seem more flavorful and aromatic. The sensory world is transformed. It is quite normal, under these circumstances, for people to see auras (fields of energy) around people and other living things. In this intensified state, Moses saw the aura of the tree on Mt. Horeb and heard the voice of God. His heightened consciousness initiated an intensified experience with divine reality.

In another tradition, Jalauddin Rumi, a thirteenth century Moslem mystic-poet, wrote (Whinfield, 1975):

> Through love bitter things become sweet,
> Through love bits of copper are made gold.
> Through love dregs taste like pure wine,
> Through love pains are like healing balms. (p. 80)

Rumi's poetry also testifies to the transformative nature of the illumination stage. Through divine love and the illuminative experience, everything changes. Divine love is also closely related to healing (balms). The material seems gross compared to the more subtle and gleaming spiritual consciousness.

The Stage of Penumbra. The intense experience with the light during the stage of illumination can be followed by a letdown. The penumbra is the stage of anticlimax following the ecstatic illuminative stage. This temporary period of darkness, even depression, is a natural and predictable response to the return to everyday life after such an ecstatic sensation.

There are several analogies for describing this stage. One is that of postpartum depression after childbirth; for, after a period of expectation, even euphoria, the reality of everyday living and child care settles in. The dreams of child bearing and child rearing have a very practical, routine, and even boring quality. For the mystic this period is often characterized by lethargy, doubt, and even despair.

Many have lamented personal and cultural sickness due to soullessness, but few have described the sickness related to soulfulness and contact with the divine. Far from unmitigated joy, the spiritual life is the experience of loss and grief over a former life and the confusion—even terror—of entering an unknown and strange lifestyle. Such terror is illustrated by the puzzling and dramatic Bible story of Jonah. Jonah's encounter with God was both horrific and strange. God told him to go to Nineveh to bring about that city's repentance. Instead of going to Nineveh, Jonah went the opposite direction—to Tarshish. On the way, God had a big fish (often called a whale) swallow Jonah and spit him out at Nineveh.

There Jonah sulked and pouted, but eventually carried out God's mission. It is not a pious, pie-in-the-sky story, but a story of unadorned, raw humanity and the struggle for and against the spiritual life.

The successful resolution of this stage allows the aspirant to proceed to the stage of unity. When the feelings of this stage are released and resolved, they then can flow to the next stage.

The Union Stage. The union stage is the integration or union of the deepest, divine consciousness and the individual consciousness. At the stage of unity there is no substantive distinction between the worshipper and the one who is worshipped. In his farewell message to his disciples, Jesus made several allusions to his union with God. In a final prayer to God (John 17: 11-12) he said, "And now I am no more in the world, but are in the world, and I am coming to thee. Holy Father, keep them in thy name which thou hast given me, that they may be one, even as we are one."

The analogy used most extensively to describe this state is the wedding analogy, or that of the lover and the beloved. Jean Houston uses this symbol in her book on journeys in mythology and sacred psychology. In *The Search for the Beloved* (1987), Houston integrates modern psychological insights and ancient spiritual traditions. This synthesis includes healing, the joining of the masculine and feminine, educating the imagination and creative energies, and guided imagery spiritual quests. Each of these elements can be translated into social work intervention.

The Moslem tradition shown in *The Story of Layla and Majnun* (1978) symbolizes the mystical search of the lover for his or her beloved. In this spiritual story, Prince Majnun forsakes his wealth, position, kingdom, and even his sanity for the sake of his beloved. This is yet another story of the soul's journey to God.

The following paragraphs describe how these stages are both successive and dynamic. Although the stages of mysticism are important in and of themselves, their real significance lies in how they relate to each other and their psycho dynamic significance.

The five stages described earlier are dynamically related to one another. The mystic or spiritual seeker does not simply progress through each stage routinely or systematically. Each stage dynamically impacts each other; for example, if the illuminative and penumbra stages are not successfully addressed, the unity stage is severely affected. The story of Saul of Tarsus (later St. Paul) mentioned earlier provides a good case study. Immediately after his illuminative experience on the Damascus road, he entered into the penumbra stage. The New Testament Book of Acts (Chapter 9) recounts the fuller story. Saul could neither see nor speak after his encounter. For 3 days thereafter, additionally, he neither ate nor drank.

But this was only half of the story. The Book of Acts also recounts that God sought out another disciple called Ananias to help Saul through this period. Jesus told Ananias to "Go, for he is a chosen instrument of mine to carry my name before the Gentiles and kings and the sons of Israel; for I will show him how much he must suffer for the sake of my name." Ananias left and told Saul, " . . . the Lord Jesus Christ who appeared to you on the road by which you came, has sent me that you may regain your sight and be filled with the Holy Spirit" (Acts 9:15–17).

The Book of Acts is very clear about the results of Ananias' counseling of Saul. It recounts that "immediately something like scales fell from his [Saul's] eyes and he regained his sight." This passage indicates two sets of dramas: Saul's illuminative experience, and the nurturing and the development throughout Saul's penumbra and unity stages. Without Ananias' nurturing Saul may have remained blind and deaf, and may have been overwhelmed by his initial illuminative experience. He may well have lost contact with reality, permanently or temporarily, for years to come.

The wards of psychiatric hospitals are inundated with those who have had overwhelming psychic experiences with explicit spiritual content. One such person resided in a New Jersey psychiatric hospital. The man, who was overwhelmed after taking LSD some years before, once played the author a song he had written. He pulled out his guitar and accompanied himself in a wonderfully haunting, lilting song in honor of the Virgin Mary. He and the beauty of his song will probably never leave the back wards of the hospital.

Healthy mysticism is a prominent issue in mental health. Cults provide a spiritual proving ground for the legitimate use of spirituality in social work practice.

CULTS, CULTIC BEHAVIOR, AND SOCIAL WORK PRACTICE

A discussion of mysticism is certain to include the subject of cults. At first blush, they may seem opposite in nature. Mysticism is an interior dynamic, expressed interiorly. Cultic activity, as the reader will learn, is an outward expression of an interior dynamic; religion, as noted in the introduction, is an outward expression of an outward dynamic. Mysticism and cultic behavior are opposites that attract through the inertia of spiritual dynamics. Mysticism is the germ that drives the flower of cultic behavior, which is the topic of the next section.

Cultic Activity and the Mystical Process

In present-day society, cults are becoming synonymous with disaster. Images of the 1978 mass suicide of some 900 members of Jim Jones' People's Temple in Jonestown, Guyana and the 1994 inferno at the Branch Davidian compound in Waco, Texas are seared into everyone's collective consciousness. Terrorists connected with religious fundamentalism were convicted for the bombing of the World Trade Center. *Time* magazine ran a cover story (April 3, 1995) titled "Cult of Doom," depicting a cover photograph of Shoko Asahara, the leader of the cult allegedly linked to the nerve gas attack in a Tokyo subway system. The rush hour poisoning killed 10 people.

The word cult and the phrase cultic activity have been overused and largely misunderstood, as discussed in the previous chapter. Cult simply means a work or labor and is a root of the word cultivate. It also can mean a group a people working to cultivate a worship experience or a desired state of consciousness. The term *liturgy,* which is a composite of two Greek terms transliterated *laos* and *urgos* (work of the people), means nearly the same thing. The worship liturgy is a labor of the laity. The similarities between these terms are obvious, because both connote a cultivation of worship.

Every spiritual tradition has some form of liturgy or cultic activity. In Christianity these liturgical or cultic forms surround the sacraments, which are visible, tangible signs of God's invisible graces (bread and wine being the most recognizable of them all). Different denominations and religions recognize different sacraments. By whatever name or ritual, however, all spiritual traditions have cultic forms. Thus, the issue is not whether cults are a part of spiritual life. The real issue is the nature of the client's response to cultic activity.

Today, the term cult is not used in its original and technical sense. There is no external, legitimate, consistent way to distinguish a functional cult from a dysfunctional one. In fact, clinicians can only help clients distinguish the nature of their own spiritual participation. Clinicians do not have the competency to judge the rightness or the theological propriety of cultic activity.

The early Christian church itself was cultish, a heretical splinter group of Judaism. It was only in the fourth century, after King Constantine decreed Christianity was legal in his Eastern empire, that the church gained political legitimacy. Now cult is a term used by many for any nontraditional, unrecognized, or threatening spiritual group.

As previously asserted, each of the stages of the mystical process represents a continuum in altered states of consciousness. First and foremost, cults should be seen as vehicles for entering the continuum of spiritual consciousness, at least to the extent that cults are effective and efficient means of altering spiritual consciousness. Effective and efficient means of entering spiritual consciousness are best left up to the participant to decide. However, some important questions can start the discussion. The questions related to taking a spiritual history are a good start. These questions can be focused and fine-tuned with such questions as: How did the client get involved in this group? What were (are) the emotional or spiritual attractions toward this group? How has the client's life changed since group involvement?

Having asserted that clinicians cannot deign to critique another's cultic partici-pation, though, there are tests to determine the intentionality and inner dynamics of the client's participation. The following section specifically addresses this issue.

Cultic Processes and Spiritual Discernment

As mentioned earlier, spiritual discernment is an important and longstanding spiritual practice. It is the process whereby spiritual responses, not practices, are evaluated and assessed. There is a crucial distinction between assessing spiritual responses by the client and assessing spiritual practices by spiritual organiza-tions. Spiritual responses can be assessed in the terms described below because, as a client, the spiritual participant has allowed the social worker to intrude into the client's own reactions. In limiting his or her inquiries into the client's own reactions, the social worker preserves the integrity of the client's choices and self-determination and does not judge the validity of the spiritual group. The clin-ician, however, concentrates his or her assessments on the consistency of the client's spiritual responses. In this manner, the ethical requirements of nonjudg-mentalism and self-determination are preserved as are the clinician's integrity in assessing client behaviors. Although social workers are constitutionally and pro-fessionally ill-equipped to assess the validity of spiritual groups, social workers are professionally competent to assess the internal and external consistency of client behaviors. This differentiation accounts for the difference between ethical and unethical spiritual assessment.

Social workers have begun to publish helpful material on assessments and interventions with cult behavior. It should be remembered that the author defines cult behavior by the broad and inclusive definition above that includes some behaviors in most religious conduct.

Denton (1990) asserts that social work practice is fundamentally different for religiously fundamentalistic families. He defines religious fundamentalism as including both a belief in the Bible as the literal word of God and as having author-ity over family and marital relationships. He also asserts that "non-confrontational acceptance and respect for the client are the foundation of work with the fundamen-talist family" (p. 11). This means that some fundamentalistic behaviors, including spiritual healing, speaking in tongues (glossalia), slaying of the spirit, and other cultic practices, should not only be tolerated, but also appreciated. Appreciation means that the clinician values and discerns these behaviors and how they affect both sacred and secular life. To discern such cultic behaviors not only means to intellectually appreciate them, but to stand under these behaviors as well; that is, to allow the behaviors themselves to speak to the clinician and to their own symbolism and meaning, and not to show prejudice toward these behaviors stemming from the clinician's own background, intellectual bias, treatment preference, or professional slant.

Bloch and Shor (1989) describe cults as a closed system that tends toward "intense relationships" and "authoritarian structure" (p. 232). The phenomenon of the double-bind can be a cult's way of breaking down the adherent's usual defenses. In this way the cultic behavior is made acceptable where once it may have seemed unacceptable. This is why cultic behavior, to those outside the cultic milieu, might seem weird or bizarre. The power of cultic behavior is no stranger to the American psyche or experience, if the tragic mass killings or suicides at Jonestown or the conflict between David Koresh's followers and the U.S. Division of Alcohol, Tobacco, and Firearms in Waco are any indication. It should be remembered that even the cultic behavior of Presbyterians, for example, may appear bizarre to Hinayana Buddhists and vice versa. The bizarre appearance of cultic behavior should in no way deter the social worker from delving into its deeper spiritual significance. The spiritually competent social worker delves beyond the outward expression of cultic behavior and discerns its impact on the client's psyche, soma, social, and soul contexts.

Legal and Social Work Aspects of Cult Deprogramming and Expert Witnessing in Cult Trials

There are two forensic aspects of cultic behavior that involve social workers the most. The first is when social workers help deprogram cult members or work clinically with families, and the second is when social workers testify in cult-related trials as expert witnesses. This section begins with a discussion of social work involvement with the nature of cults.

There are two broad forensic perspectives on cults that have been described by two law review articles. Fisher (1991) takes the view that cults bear the brunt of religious and spiritual prejudice. He asserts that cults have been unfairly attacked by both mainstream religions and government in derogation of their First Amendment right to freedom of religious practice. He writes:

> That which we would destroy, we must first label pejoratively. A religion is denominated a cult; proselytizing becomes brainwashing; persuasion becomes propaganda; missionaries become subversive agents; retreats, monasteries, and convents become prisons; rituals become bizarre conduct; religious observances become aberrant behavior; devotion and meditation become psychopathic trances. (p. 160)

One's spirituality is another's cult. In fact, Fisher makes the point that the terms cult and deprogramming are pejorative terms likely to create prejudice in the mind of the listener. He contends that social workers and other mental health practitioners "provide professional legitimacy for deprogramming, and in some instances, have been strident advocates of anti-cult legislation" (p. 171). What he is saying is that some social workers have become agents of spiritual correctness.

An opposing position is taken by Brown (1991). Her argument is that cults can present a danger to adherents and are not always protected by the First Amendment. Brown asserts that the tort (legal action similar to malpractice) of false imprisonment is a proper civil remedy where cult behavior unlawfully prohibits someone's liberty. She writes, "Typically, a cult will employ a definite, methodical strategy to lure a prospective recruit into the cult" (p. 414).

Brown asserts that cults use a series of brainwashing strategies including love bombing, where potential recruits are bombarded by attention and flattery. At the same time, however, they are isolated from other potential recruits and deprived of sleep, rest, and time alone. These elements, she asserts, deprive the recruit of an opportunity to reasonably consider the merits of the cult organization. These elements are combined with a heavenly deception, which is two-fold. The true name and nature of the group is disguised and the group is initially characterized by an interest in social concerns.

The recruit is then invited to a initial retreat, followed by more. At these retreats, alleges Brown, a strict regimen of sleep deprivation, continuous lectures, and continuous activity severely impairs recruits' abilities to think for themselves and to lose their volitional capacity. Her point is that cult activity that undermines the recruit's mental, if not physical, ability to escape can be legally addressed by a civil suit for false imprisonment.

The sword of false imprisonment cuts both ways. Although some parents have sued to rescue their children from cults, the rescued children have returned the favor with suits of their own. Both types of suits have yielded mixed results. An example of the latter is *Peterson v. Sorlien* (1980). Susan Peterson, a member of The Way Ministry, sued her former minister, Paul Sorlien, and her parents for false imprisonment and the intentional infliction of emotional distress. The suit arose when the defendants tried to deprogram her and disassociate her from The Way. The Supreme Court of Minnesota, affirming the trial court, again refused to hold her parents liable for false imprisonment and, although other defendants were held liable for intentional infliction of emotional distress, the Court ruled that evidence could be presented that the defendants acted in good faith in believing that Susan was acting under psychological distress by the religious group.

The second forensic connection with cult activity is when social workers testify as expert witnesses in cult activity. Expert witnesses testify in court to provide the judge or jury with social science or psychological information. An example of such expert testimony is illustrated in a case decided by the Supreme Court of California called *Molko v. Holy Spirit Association for the Unification of World Christianity* (1988). In the *Molko* case, former members of the Holy Spirit Association sued the Church for fraudulently inducing them to join through a variety of deceptive techniques. The Court allowed the testimonies of a psychologist and a psychiatrist that said that the Church's persuasion techniques rendered former Church members legally incapable of exercising their independent judgment. Essentially, the defendants claimed that the Church used brainwashing techniques. Thus, the Court recognized and accepted expert testimony on the psychosocial impact of the alleged indoctrination. The Court's overall decision was that neither federal nor state constitutions barred the fraud suit. This meant that the First Amendment's freedom of religion clause did not prevent the defendants from bringing the suit against the Church. Additionally, the Court held that the claim presented triable issues of fact which should not be prematurely precluded by a summary judgment for the Church.

At least three themes for social workers flow from these cases. First, social workers must consider the legal implications of their work with cult members, former members, or those seeking to rescue cult members. These implications include the legal jeopardy of social workers if they engage in deprogramming or rescue operations. If they engage in such activities, social workers should be prepared to defend themselves against a suit for false imprisonment, intentional infliction of emotional distress, and other torts.

Second, social workers should be mindful of ethical and legal violations of the cult members' First Amendment rights and their ethical rights of self-determination. Even though they may have joined seemingly unusual and even bizarre spiritual groups against the wishes of parents and family members, their rights to freedom of religious belief, association, and private self-determination outweigh the religious or spiritual preferences of anyone else.

Families are concerned, even traumatized, when another family member becomes involved in a spiritual group to which they object. The family may well feel that their family member is being held against his or her will or better judgment. Social workers need to remember that the ones who rescue or deprogram cult members will have to defend their actions if sued.

Social workers who counsel families of cult members should eschew any temptation to encourage family members to kidnap or to rescue them. If family members are convinced that the cult is dangerous or harmful, law enforcement officials should be contacted. They have the public authority to investigate such complaints. Private efforts on the part of family members to rescue others from cults risk the health of the members themselves and place all those involved in legal jeopardy.

Third, expert witnesses indeed need to be experts in the area about which they are testifying. They must take honest stock in their own expertise. Social workers testifying as experts need to realize, additionally, that their views and credibility will be severely challenged by the opposing attorney under cross-examination.

The previous section examined forensic implications of social work practice in rescuing adults from cults and testifying as expert witnesses in cult-related law cases. These legal implications supplement the general theme of the spiritual discernment of cult involvement. These cautions do not mean that cultic behavior should be ignored. The discernment option is designed to both value the client and to value the integrity of the spiritual process. Spiritual discernment differs from spiritual assessment in that spiritual assessments use spirituality to assess clinical behaviors. Spiritual discernment, on the other hand, assesses spirtual behavior. Social workers must have facility in both spheres. Principles of spiritual discernment are described in the following section.

Principles of Spiritual Discernment

The principles of spiritual discernment flow from the phases of mysticism described earlier. It looks for the unencumbered, graceful flow of energy among all the mystic phases.

When there are blocks or stoppages, there is something wrong. Just like the free flow of blood through veins and arteries, spiritual energy will naturally drive clients through the mystical process. However, like veins and arteries, the mystical process can become clogged—causing sclerosis of the spirit, as the late Dr. Schoenberg Setzer used to say.

The principles of spiritual discernment are designed to diagnose hardening of the spiritual arteries. Social workers thus become spiritual physicians in that they assess and treat spiritual disorders. The social work clinician is cast into the role of a theologian, psychopomp, and spiritual guide, and must be prepared for such a role.

The key question in spiritual discernment is always, "Is there more love connected with the spiritual participation?" This love cherishes both personal and community values. One specific illustration from Starhawk (1988) is the call for integrity. She writes that spirituality must match beliefs with actions—that authentic spiritual participants "cannot propose or accept solutions for someone else that we cannot propose or accept for ourselves" (p. xvi). She goes on to say that the operative assumption is to expect to get back (three-fold in the Wicca tradition) what you give out.

The Mystical Stages and Spiritual Discernment. Three spiritual discernment issues flow directly from the mystical stages. First, if the client is stuck at any one stage for too long a time, something is wrong. The natural mystical process is clogged. Many people are stuck at the illumination stage, and when this happens the client tends to identify, sometimes in an extreme way, with persons and events surrounding the illumination. The experience of illumination can be so powerful and overwhelming that the client may identify with the incidence of the experience and not with its source. The source of the illuminative experience, of course, is the divine. Some, however, make sacred persons, places, or things that the participant identifies with the experience. This is a form of idolatry.

The second issue in spiritual discrimination addresses block at the penumbra stage. The impact of the penumbra stage should not be underestimated. This is a crucial and potentially dangerous period. After the numinous, even exhilarating illuminative experience, there is an inevitable letdown that can vary in intensity from rather serious depression to minor sadness.

The spiritual dynamics of the penumbra stage follow the flow of energy. The energy generated from the illuminative stage normally propels itself into the penumbra stage. There the energy germinates in secret, like a seed before it shoots. Before proceeding to the unity stage, the energy, however, can rot like a seed in damp soil. For example, without the counsel of Ananias, it is likely that Paul would have remained in a penumbra period for much longer. Ananias' care and the nurturing of the Damascus church helped Paul overcome the blindness and deafness characteristic of the overpowering sense of confusion during this stage.

The third issue in spiritual discrimination deals with the unity stage, where the integration into the divine self is most realized. Although the fruits of this integration are visible, the fruits of the realization can be seen. They are invisible in the quality of life evidenced in their personal and community living. A spiritual life that does not invoke care and compassion for the community is an empty spirituality. A spirituality that does not tend to the personal garden of faith is stiff and embittered.

Contraindications of Spiritual Discernment. Not all spiritual discernment by social workers is necessary or even advisable. This section suggests contraindications against such spiritual discernment. Keeping in mind the important medical adage to "Do no harm," this section outlines circumstances in which serious or prolonged spiritual discussions might be harmful to clients. Although such circumstances cannot be calculated with precision, they can be described in general terms. Discernment of the spirits requires specialized skills and training, and the following paragraphs only outline the main points and issues for such discernment.

First of all, spiritual discernment must be distinguished from religious training in that it is a subspecies of religious training. All spiritual groups and orientations have some transmittable traditions. The accumulated learning is passed from generation to generation and from adherent to adherent in some fashion. This religious training consists of the rituals, *mythos,* values, and cultural *cultus* of the tradition. Further, it is the means by which the spiritual orientation is passed on and promulgated.

Spiritual discernment does not address the form and cultus of the spiritual tradition. It addresses the process of the adherent's spiritual practice and makes no value judgments on the practices themselves; spiritual discernment, rather, makes value judgements on the intentionality and the authenticity with which those practices are conducted.

The author has taken pains in the preceding chapters to emphasize the value of nonjudgmentalism. This long-standing social work value, codified in the NASW Code of Ethics, is particularly important where spiritual assessments and interventions are concerned. This section, however, makes necessary distinctions between judgmentalism and discernment of spirits.

Spiritual discernment is different from using spirituality as a factor in the assessment of, and interventions in, mental health issues. Discernment of the spirits is the assessment or diagnosis of the client's spiritual condition. It means using spiritual methods in the assessment of, or intervention in, the client's mental health condition.

Spiritual discernment is absolutely imperative to properly assess the nature and intention of the client's condition, because it enables the clinician to more accurately gauge the support attributable to the client's spiritual orientation. To reiterate, then, spiritual discernment does not discern or critique the content of spiritual orientation.

Caution must be exercised when addressing spiritual discernment with clients who have had negative or harmful experiences with spiritual practices. Clients who have been abused by clergy or other religious professionals, have felt severe distress or discomfort over conversion experiences, or have encountered severe conflict over changing spiritual orientations may be unable or unwilling to address their painful spiritual issues. Social workers, therefore, need to carefully discern the advisability and methodology of raising spiritual issues with their clients.

If the clinician decides to address spiritual issues with clients who have been hurt or spiritually traumatized, special care must be taken to not further traumatize the client. Generally, the same considerations that clinicians extend to any traumatized client—including clarity, professionalism, and authenticity—should be extended to such clients.

Additionally, clinicians addressing spiritual traumas need spiritual clarity. Acknowledging and valuing clients' spiritual tradition and their spiritual orientation within that tradition is chief among them. Judging and critiquing the client's spiritual orientation is likely to further traumatize the client. Reducing the client's spiritual trauma to some sort of infantile regression, schizophrenic episode, or other psychological reductionism is only another form of judgmentalism.

Spiritual clarity includes the willingness to "start where the client is"—a hallmark of social work practice. It means that clinicians place themselves in the emotional and spiritual shoes of the client and that they take the client's account and interpretation of their own situation seriously and respectfully. Although clinicians should not renounce their clinical judgment in favor of anyone else's, they should not impose their own judgments on the spiritual lives of their clients, either. Clinicians should, in fact, assume the role of learner at the feet of their clients while retaining their clinical skills.

It goes without saying that clients may suffer from clinical mental illness. Spiritual clarity needs to influence clinical evaluations. Two clinical contrasts, schizophrenia and depression, illustrate how spiritual sensitivity must accompany clinical assessment—particularity in assessing spiritual development and traumas. In the following section, schizophrenia is distinguished from visionary and auditory mystical experience and depression is distinguished from the "dark night of the soul."

Mysticism Clinically Distinguished from Schizophrenia. Differential diagnoses are crucial elements in distinguishing between mental illness and spiritual formation. Wapnick (1972) discusses the differences between the symptoms of schizophrenia and mysticism. Mysticism has been discussed in this chapter and clinicians have many sources for the salient elements of schizophrenia. Wapnick's distinguishing features and implications for practice are reviewed.

First, mystics can maintain meaningful inner and outer worlds whereas schizophrenics cannot maintain meaningful social relationships or boundaries. Even mystics who deliberately cloister themselves from the world maintain meaningful contact with others that is socially useful and psychologically healing. The social contact of those diagnosed with schizophrenia is marked by severe disorientation and disconnection.

Second, mystics undergo training for their spiritual experiences, but schizophrenics travel precipitously into their own inner world. Mystics generally have time and training for their spiritual experiences, and they have other spiritually trained persons to guide them through. On the other hand, the schizophrenic experience is often marked by crushing isolation and alienation with no one to guide the individual or to share the experience.

Third, the mystic has a goal of unity with divine reality, and the goal of schizophrenics is often to escape from the social world. These goals provide clear distinctions between the focus of schizophrenia and mysticism. Social escape is far removed from union with the divine.

Fourth, mystics return from their spiritual experiences to give gifts to the social world, and schizophrenics return with little to offer the social world. Mystics often become teachers and healers and take away useful experiences to bring back to the social world. Schizophrenia can offer only disorganized, often terrifying images and experiences that are not useful to others.

Fifth, schizophrenia may well be a genuine spiritual crisis. The schizophrenic break can, with the proper support and discernment, be a catalyst for reevaluation, reorientation, and reauthentication. Such suffering can generate a meaningful spiritual search if support and treatment are conducted (as in Paul's experience with Ananias).

Depression Distinguished from the Dark Night of the Soul. This section develops the clinical distinction between depression and the mystical phase of the dark night of the soul. This phrase, taken from St. John of the Cross (born 1542; died 1591), was described earlier in this chapter and is taken from his poem "Stanzas of the Soul" (Peers, 1959). The poem describes the soul's journey, "kindled in love with yearnings," through the dark night to God.

This poem symbolizes the spiritual dynamics of the dark night phase of mysticism. The story tells of the soul's journey to the beloved (or the divine). It goes forth in darkness, guided by its own inner light to reach its beloved. The goal is the transformation of the lover into the beloved. This transformation means that the lover meets someone new and becomes someone new. The lover meets the divine and is enthralled by a new state of consciousness represented by the breeze blowing from the turret and the suspension of the senses. The final stage is presaged by the lover abandoning himself or herself among the lilies.

These "stanzas of the soul" chart the essential elements of the dark night, which distinguish the dark night from depression. For the sake of variety, the distinguishing features of depression and the dark night are described below.

Diagnosis/Assessment/Discernment

Depression	*Dark Night of the Soul*
Little spiritual connection	Outgrowth of spiritual journey
Sense of worthlessness	Sense of unworthiness in presence of the divine
Few spiritual insights	Spiritual insights may be overwhelming
Sense of inappropriate guilt	Sense of appropriate guilt
Little sense of blessings	Can cultivate sense of blessings and grace
Response to emptiness, hopelessness	Response to spiritual fullness and letdown

This chart outlines the comparisons and contrasts between depression and the dark night of the soul. Depression can have several causes, both social and chemical. The dark night has but one cause—the spiritual cleansing of the self prior to a deeper, more direct experience with the divine.

These suggestions briefly offer ways in which to intervene (or not to intervene) with those who suffer symptoms of the dark night. The principles, deduced from the interventions discussed above, include the principles of authenticity, concentration, ultimate teleology, and interminability. These principles are discussed serially.

Authenticity means that the social worker accurately and unselfconsciously represents his or her spiritual knowledge and experience. Social workers should say if they have experienced such a state, but should never claim so if they have not. Neither should social workers reduce the client's experiences to their own categories. The principle of concentration means that the social worker should appreciate the intensity of the experience itself and should resist any temptation to dilute the intensity of the spiritual experience. Ultimate teleology means that there is a definite spiritual goal to this spiritual phase. This mystical phase, then, should always be seen in its total context. The principle of interminability means that this state could be of limited or unlimited duration; thus, no forecasting of the duration of the dark night is possible. The duration cannot be predicted and it should not be short-circuited or extended.

However, one important intervention consideration should be noted. Even though clinicians can do little to direct the timing, nature, or outcome of the dark night, they can become psychic guides or psychopomps. Being a psychic guide is important because it grounds clients in reality and helps them consider the consequences of their spirituality for their spouses, families, and work. The next section expands on contraindications of spiritual interventions.

Contraindications for Spiritual Interventions. The criteria for the use of spiritual interventions (described in Chapter 2) are similar to, but not the same as, the criteria for spiritual discernment. Spiritual interventions require spiritual competence, fortitude, and integrity.

They also require making clinical distinctions between spiritual concerns and mental illness. Those who suffer from mental illness, experience unwelcome hallucinations, and are not able to cope with onslaughts of unwelcome images should not be encouraged or invited to experience spiritual imagery. They might be prone to opening their psychic floodgates too much, too soon, and become overwhelmed.

Those who have been abused by clergy or religious leaders should not be encouraged or forced to participate in explicit spiritual images, because they might well induce painful memories for which the victim is unprepared to address. It is for the clinician to reasonably determine when and under what circumstances spiritual images and issues will be raised. If clients raise these issues themselves, it may mean that they are ready to address these issues. If they tolerate indirect or subtle references to spirtual images, it may also mean that they are ready to safely raise spiritual issues.

Those who have had negative spiritual experiences, are undergoing spiritual conversion, are changing spiritual orientations under family duress or other stress, or are undergoing spiritual stress compounded by other types of stress may be overwhelmed by spiritual imagery. It must be recognized, by the same token, that spiritual crises bring out spiritual imagery. Overwhelming spiritual images can confuse and frustrate clients, so the social worker should help protect clients from such overpowering images. It is up to the clinician to make reasonable determinations, from the totality of the circumstances, regarding the extent to which spiritual interventions will be conducted.

Additionally, it may be contraindicated to try spiritual interventions when the client reacts stressfully to any mention of spirituality. For example, when references to dream or prayer images evoke strong, stressful reactions, it is an indication that deliberately creating spiritual images through spirtual interventions is contraindicated at that time.

One final point must be emphasized. If the client feels that it is inappropriate to discuss spirituality or is reluctant to do so, the clinician is precluded from pressing further discussions. Clinicians should know when to cut off or to limit spiritual discussion and when to initiate or expand such discussions. Clinicians do not have to wait for clients to expressly raise such issues and can do so using their own professional discretion. However, clinicians should be equally sensitive and open to the client's desire not to engage in spiritually oriented clinical discussions.

CONCLUSION

This chapter has discussed spiritual assessment and interventions in regard to ethics, aspects of cultic behavior, and contraindications of use. Chapter 7 offers insight and suggestions as to how social workers can relate and work with spiritual leaders to the benefit of their clients.

DISCUSSION SCENARIOS AND QUESTIONS

1. You are the clinician for a young college student. He originally sought counseling because he had conflicts with his parents and has trouble concentrating on college studies. He has attended several sessions with a spiritual group and has decided to join them for a 3-year commitment, which entails quitting college and living in undisclosed locations. His parents have called you to register their extreme disapproval. You feel that he needs to continue counseling, but he will not do so if he joins this group. What is your approach to this client? Does your approach change? Would your approach change if you felt that your client was unduly influenced or induced into participation by the spiritual group?

2. You are now the clinician for the parents of the young man in the scenario above. They originally sought counseling because they had marital problems and were worried about their relationship with their son. How do you address their concerns about the son's spiritual commitment to this group while maintaining a relationship with him? How would you respond if they sought your advice about a plan to physically kidnap their son?

3. You are a clinician for an older woman who displays manic-depressive symptoms, and have been treating her as such. One day she relates that she has had a mystical or a very intense spiritual experience. She says that, because of this experience, she wants to quit her job and make pilgrimages to holy sites. How do you respond to her ideas? How do you clinically respond to her psychiatric diagnosis and her spiritual experiences? Does your therapeutic strategy change after her spiritual experiences? Do you use spiritual interventions differently?

4. A client presents you with symptoms of depression. This client also has a history of meditation and prayer. How do you distinguish depression from the ups and downs in the spiritual journey? After making such assessments, how would you use spiritual interventions with this client?

5. You are selected to represent the social service voice in a state legislative hearing that is on proposed legislation to forbid parents from suing spiritual or religious groups for false imprisonment or fraud when children join such groups. What issues would you raise either in defense of, or opposition to, such legislation? How would you counter arguments of those opposed to your position? How would you argue your side?

Chapter 6

Cross-Cultural Spiritual
Social Work Practice

Cross-cultural spirituality in social work is a prominent component of this book. Previous chapters have discussed spiritual cosmologies, spiritual anthropologies, spiritual hierarchies of need, the stages of mysticism, and assessments and interventions from a variety of cultural perspectives. A variety of spiritual perspectives has become an important part of the United States' spiritual landscape.

A *Time* magazine issue (Gray, 1995) was devoted to quantifying this landscape. It noted that Alexis de Tocqueville, a famous and astute observer of early American culture, wrote in 1835, "There is no country in the world where the Christian religion retains a greater influence over the souls of men." This influence has only intensified with the passage of time.

Observers like Gray, however, recognize that the variety of spiritual orientations has widened and dispersed since the time of de Tocqueville. In 1995, 1.1% of U.S. citizens belonged to Islam, Hindu, and Buddhist faiths. Additionally, 2% belonged to Judaism, 7.8% were black Protestants, and 23.4% were Roman Catholics. The profound news is that, in contrast to the days of de Tocqueville, the mainline Protestants (including Presbyterians, Methodists, Lutherans, and Episcopalians) are declining. On the other hand, followers of Mormons, the Southern Baptist Convention, and the Assemblies of God have increased. Religious diversity, like other species of cultural diversity, begs one's attention.

AMERICAN SPIRITUAL DEMOCRATIZATION

In discussing cross-cultural spirituality, it is necessary to note a phenomenon called spiritual democratization. This is the process of change that some spiritual traditions undergo when acculturated by the American spiritual geography. The democratization occurs when the spiritual traditions, originating and developing in their native lands, must assimilate into American values and folkways. Spiritual democratization opens up spiritual traditions to those outside its original setting. This democratization tends to change the spiritual tradition when introduced into the United States. Spiritual democratization has its most profound effect not on those who have come to the United States already practicing their spiritual traditions, but on those who want to adopt the spiritual traditions of others.

Spiritual democratization—freeing spiritual tradition from its cultural context—has opposing impacts. Some may say these are positive or negative impacts. On the one hand, spiritual democratization opens up others' traditions to those who were not raised with them. On the other, spiritual democratization may mean that the spiritual tradition itself may be compromised, altered, or even undermined. Let us examine the former proposition first.

Spiritual democratization tends to expand and extend accessibility of one spiritual tradition into other spiritual traditions. In a sense, this diffusion is entirely appropriate. After all, spiritual traditions, as divine gifts, are not the exclusive property of any single culture, time, gender, or ethnic group. They are gifts to humanity that should be shared freely, exchanged, and adapted to new times, circumstances, and new environments.

Additionally, spiritual traditions are not the exclusive property of clergy or any other group. Because of the translation of the Bible from Greek or Latin into the *lingua franca,* the common language, the monopoly of interpretation was taken from the professional religious classes. Of course, this process has continued, even accelerated, into this century. No longer are the clergy and other trained religious professionals the sole arbiters of spirituality. Today, psychiatrists, psychologists, social workers, licensed professional counselors, and other mental health professionals are writing books and lecturing on spiritual issues, as well as those who have little or no formal education whatsoever. This spiritual proliferation is both helpful and hazardous. Without professional education in theology or spirituality, comparative religion, or related topics, spirituality can be distorted. Social workers seeking spiritual competence need to acquire more than a layperson's acquaintance with spirituality.

By the same token, the wholesale absorption of a spiritual tradition into another culture and circumstance may distort important elements of the tradition. Others may assimilate the intentions and goals of other spiritual traditions into their own cultural patterns and norms. Without knowing the original nature of the spiritual tradition, and without living in the culture where the spiritual tradition originated, the more recent adherents cannot enjoy the depth of context and content of the spiritual tradition. Although this more superficial knowledge may work in favor of new and innovative trends in the spiritual tradition, they may also work to trivialize and stupefy such traditions.

Such a criticism has been leveled by Native Americans against non-Indians who purport to adhere to Native American spiritual traditions. The criticism is really two-fold. First, there is resentment that non-Indians are distorting Native American spiritual traditions. Second, there is resentment that non-Indians are seen to be preempting yet another aspect of Native American culture. Given the historic antagonism between Native American and non-Indian cultures, such a response is reasonable.

In a program on new age movements in a Christian church group, a participant was a full-blooded tribal member of an eastern Indian nation. She questioned the presence of a traditional Native American symbol on the presenter's bolo tie, and also expressed her suspicion about the contemporary vogue of non-Indians for Native American spiritualities. Words for her sentiments could be, "Anyone with a drum and rattle can claim they are shamans."

Indeed, the following section represents examples of social work practice with cross-cultural spiritual traditions. These two traditions are selected here for several reasons. They represent good examples of how social workers interact with specific spiritual traditions. They also provide examples of cross-cultural spiritualities that have influenced American spiritualities in general and mental health practices in particular. Finally, they provide examples of how some spiritualities may be changed (and some may say distorted) by their adaptation and adoption by contemporary Americans.

SHAMANISM AND SPIRITUALITY

Mircea Eliade, in his classic work *Shamanism: Archaic Techniques of Ecstasy* (1964), offers the classic definition of shamanism as a technician in an ecstatic trance in which the soul leaves the body and travels to other worlds. The shaman is a "technician of the sacred" in that he or she traditionally employs specific techniques and instruments to transform consciousness and to gain access to the other worlds.

Shamanism is a worldwide phenomena. For North American aboriginal inhabitants, the Native Americans, shamans played a prominent role. In the contemporary American sense, Native American shamans were eclectic, interdisciplinary healers. They were not just spiritual and religious leaders, but also medical doctors, herbalists, social leaders, and even military leaders. Crazy Horse and Sitting Bull were examples of shamans who employed a variety of these eclectic skills.

The traditional definition of shamanism has been changed since Eliade first proposed it in 1964. Hoppal (1987, p. 95) proposed a definition that broadened Eliade's earlier definition:

> Shamanism is a complex system of beliefs which includes the knowledge of and belief in the names of helping spirits in the shamanic pantheon, the memory of certain texts (sermons, shaman-songs, legends, myths, etc.) the rules for activities (rituals, sacrifices, the techniques for ecstasy, etc.), and the objects, tools, and paraphernalia used by shamans (drum, stick, bow, mirror, costumes, etc.). All these components are closely connected by beliefs given in the shamanic complex.

This broader definition widens the cultural complex of shamanism and includes spiritualities not traditionally associated with shamanism or shamanistic practices. Two such traditions are of concern here. In an extremely interesting article, Horwatt (1988) uncovers shamanistic behavior in the Pentecostal Church. She proposes that the rhythmic chanting, preaching, and singing evoke ecstatic trance states, "The shamanic complex in the Pentecostal church consists of the faith healer (most often the pastor), the patient, and the congregation. The faith healer claims to cure sickness of the body and of the spirit" (p. 133).

Gershom (1987) also finds shamanic practices in the Jewish tradition. He asserts that prophets and holy men and women, including Moses, Samuel, Elijah, and Elisha use traditional shamanic practices such as telepathic healing, spiritual journies, and contact of and travel to spiritual realms.

Shamanic features have also been found in ancient Celtic spiritual practices (Matthews, 1989). Druids were Celtic shamans.

> The function of the druid was to maintain what we would now call a shamanic role within the tribe. He or she—for people of either sex were druids—was the mediator, the knower, the repository of wisdom. The druids studied such abstruse matters as astrology, cosmology, physiology, theology and many other branches of learning. However, this knowledge did not make them abstract philosophers. Every part of their wisdom had to be applicable to daily life, whether it be knowing the right time for spring sowing, or the precedents of law, the prognosis of an injured limb or the nature of the gods. (Matthews, 1989, p. 36)

Matthews asserts that Druid shamanic knowledge was intimately connected with the land and trees from which they had sprung. Indeed, the word druid (The Irish is *drui;* the Welsh, *derwydd*) may have been derived from the word for oak (Gaulish, *dervo;* Irish, *daur;* Welsh, *derw*). Druids were the ones with knowledge of great trees. The trees with roots in the earth and branches in the air symbolize the facility of shamans moving from one state of consciousness to another. The woods of the Celts were the jaguars of the Maya. Both are symbols of shamanic consciousness that moves with ease and grace through altered states. The world was, once again, treated to examples of shamanic concepts and techniques with another discovery of cave paintings. Early in 1995, the French government announced the discovery of Cro-Magnon cave paintings near Avignon (Hughes, 1995), which sparked renewed interest in their spiritual purpose and their technology of altered states. Researchers assert that the spittle chewed and then blown on cave walls to make hand and animal designs was, itself, a psychoactive substance. The paint induced a trance state during which the shaman travels to the spirit world. The shaman communicates with the spirit of animals, for example, to ask for a good hunt. The researchers say, "Spitting is a way of projecting yourself onto the wall, becoming one with the horse you are painting" (p. 60). After 20,000 years, the cave paintings still stir the spiritual imagination. Today's scholars are still discovering the spiritual techniques of yesterday's shamans.

Shamanic Characteristics

The following sections describe shamanic characteristics. These characteristics have direct implications for social workers who seek spiritual compentency. Listing characteristics and criteria always involves risks. These characteristics might erroneously be considered exclusive or comprehensive, but they are neither. Some of these characteristics are outlined below in abbreviated form.

Direct Knowledge and Instructed Wisdom. Once, when a young minister was introduced to his new parish, the famous pastor Thomas Carlyle remarked, "What this country needs is a man who knows God other than by hearsay" (Wallis, n.d.). Hearsay is knowledge from an indirect source. Shamans know the spirit realms by direct, personal experience, having themselves experienced the spirit world. They have confronted the spirits themselves.

At the same time, the shaman also proceeds through a period of training under another shaman. This instruction may extend over a period of a few years or a very long period of time. The training, obviously, is all based on hearsay in that the teacher is imparting knowledge to the pupil that is neither direct nor personal. What distinguishes this instruction from being mere hearsay is that it integrates the initiant's own personal experience into the teacher's second-hand instruction. The shaman's apprenticeship consists not only of the teacher's instruction, but of experiencing, interpreting, and integrating the apprentice's own spiritual encounters. The following characteristic delves more deeply into the nature of these spiritual encounters.

Intimacy and Ecstasy. Shamanic spiritual encounters are both intimate and ecstatic. The etymology of these words bear close connections to shamanic characteristics. The word intimacy comes from a Latin word meaning to put in. The shamanic spiritual encounter places one in the divine realms. Ecstasy comes from a Greek word meaning to drive out of the body. The shamanic spiritual encounter drives the spirit from the individual body into the cosmic body.

Shamanic ecstasy is illustrated by the words of the ancient Babylonian shaman called Gilgamesh, who asked, "Where is the man who can climb to heaven?" Shamanic ecstasy propels the shaman from his or her individual consciousness into what might be called a cosmic consciousness. "Climbing to heaven" is the poetic equivalent of heightening consciousness into the ecstatic, spiritual realms. The shaman seeks experience that lies beyond the casual acquaintance of human perception. This is the intimacy that shamans seek—to put themselves into the heavens of a heightened consciousness. This intimacy requires its counterpart—ecstasy. The shaman leaves his or her body in order to be intimate.

The Essential Illness. A shattering experience breaks down barriers between the initiate and the spirit world. This devastating episode could be a physical illness, mental illness, or another kind of crisis. The crisis could come very early or later in the shaman's career, but usually it is close to the shaman's initiation or the time when the shaman realizes his or her call. This crisis is an avenue and an opportunity by which he or she accesses the spirit realm. In computer terminology, it helps the shaman "log on" to the spiritual network.

Sometimes this crisis arises spontaneously, and sometimes it is planned—even welcomed and sought after. Sometimes it is both. The vision quest of many cultures is an example of when the crisis is welcomed; yet, it may also happen in the context of an unplanned illness.

In talking about his early career, a Hidatsa medicine man in North Dakota said that, as a young man, he contracted tuberculosis. Subsequent X-rays confirmed this. He tried some medicine, but nothing seemed to help. He decided to attempt a vision quest, in which he was tied to a tree in the North Dakota wilderness. For 3 days he prayed. When he returned his illness was in remission and it has not returned since. He now is a grandfather.

Shamanic Initiations. The ultimate shamanic intimacy is the entrance into the spirit world as a profession, way of life, or raison d'etre. Really, there are two shamanic initiations. The first comes when he or she is issued the call, and the second initiation comes when the shaman responds to the call. Sometimes these two initiations cannot be precisely distinguished from one another.

An illustration of shamanic initiation has been discovered near the seashore in Provance, France. The paintings were completed in two stages. The first, consisting of hand stencils, was done between 23,000 and 20,000 B.C.; the second phase, consisting of animals and geometric signs, was done about 19,000 years ago (Clottes & Courtin, 1993). This stone age cathedral is really composed of two sections. The first section is a 450-foot long tunnel beginning at the Mediterranean Sea with a small entrance (9 feet wide and 3 feet high). When the cave was originally used, the sea level did not cover the cave entrance.

The second part of the cathedral is a 180-foot long grotto called the Cosquer Cave, which contains the animal picture and the geometric designs. Horses account for about one-third of the pictures—the remainder include portraits of ibex heads and antlers, chamois, bison, and the now-extinct Irish elk. The entrance to the stone age cathedral and cave are perfect analogies for the womb of shamanic initiation and rebirth. The long entrance is a hallway that represents a birth canal, and the cave is the womb itself. The cave is the vehicle for the initiate's spiritual birth. It is probable that initiates were brought through the long tunnel in total darkness. They were then led into the cave face-to-face with the sweeping, majestic drawings of the very animals that gave them and their tribes the sustenance of life. In fact, those animals gave much more than food to the makers of the Cosquer Cave—their skin provided cloths, their bones gave needles, their sinew gave thread, their stomachs gave cooking pots, and their antlers gave cooking utensils. Human life was intimately connected to the animals' life.

The paintings invested the initiate with eternal life. Connection with the paintings connected the shaman to the animals' energy. The paintings were the icons where the spirit could touch the spirit of life itself. Shamanic initiations require both an openness to the spirit and a will to follow the spirit's lead. Of course, these separate initiations are components of an integrated pattern of shamanic behaviors that suspend ordinary consciousness and initiate ecstatic consciousness.

The Ecstatic Intimacy. The career of the shaman is characterized by ecstatic intimacy. This is the shaman's vocation. Ecstatic intimacy drives the shaman into two directions. The first is in the direction of professional altered states, where the shaman is given instructions from the spirits on what is wrong and how to heal it. The author's poem below describes the shamanic call, the shamanic movement among the altered states of consciousness (represented by the panther), and the shamanic return to a community with blessings and a healing message (awe and glory).

Shaman Syntax

If the call comes,
it burns the ear without warning,
it snares the heart without hearing.
No voice is needed to knock at skin
and to bang the bone.

Without sound, the shaman
makes wings from words,
a call to consciousness.

The answer is a panther
moving among the elements:
teeth to earth, fur to fire.
Running water and swimming air
after the deadly prey of spirits.

The panther recites the grammars of magic
in bodies without boundaries.
Stars pray in skin languages.
Light plays tag with light.
The call crosses borders without passports,
more pilgrm than tourist.
No compass save the cunning of a contrite heart.

Only the compassionate can
quote the syllables required
in raising the dead, in shaking sleeping,
in the casual acquaintance of nightmare.

The shaman's syntax is song not theology,
is tasted not thought.

The height of the soul's technology
is not a computer, but a drum.

The drum has a mouth that calls
in decibels only the heart can hear.
Where awe is the only ethic;
and glory the only way to
respond to the beyond.

The second direction in which the shaman is driven involves service to others.
A shaman who does not conduct healing is no shaman. This healing could be
very private or very public. For every shaman, however, there is a healing
mission that can be as variable as shamans themselves. Brooke Medicine
Eagle, a contemporary shaman, speaks of her mission in this way (Halifax,
1979, p. 90):

> I feel my purpose is to help in any way I can to heal the earth. I feel that we are in a
> time when the earth is in dire need of healing. We see it everywhere, the droughts,
> earthquakes, storms, pollution. Yes, the earth itself is in need of healing. And I feel
> that any way I can help, that is my mission: to make it whole, to pay attention to
> that wholeness, not only in ourselves, but also in relation to the earth.

Healing can be conducted on many levels. Even the cloistered nuns and monks, who never went into cities or towns, welcomed those seeking healing. Others came to the monks and nuns because of who they were and what they did. Mostly, they avoided others and shunned their fame. Christian shamans, like Olga and Ambrose Worral, healed from distances (Cerutti, 1977; Worral & Worral, 1965). They received letters from troubled people and reserved a portion of every day to healing prayer.

SHAMANISM AND SOCIAL WORK PRACTICE

Cataldo (1979), Canda (1983), and Laird (1984) have all outlined the implications of shamanism for clinical social work practice. Canda outlined at least two aspects of shamanism that could inform clinical practice. First, disease and mental illness comes from an "imbalance and interruption of intrapersonal and interpersonal connections" (p. 16). This is the core of shamanic assessment. Shamans assess an individual's illness in the spiritual context's social, cultural, and cosmic symbols. Thus, although all shamans assess by spiritual means, the terms and the manner in which they make those assessments can vary widely.

Second, healing interventions include the use of healing ceremonies. These ceremonies, or rites, are myths in motion. Rites act out the healings that the myths describe. Cataldo (1979) describes several therapeutic rites including those of separation, transition, and incorporation. Healing means "restoring balance and proper connections by means of holistic therapy involving the whole person with all significant . . . others, often on a cosmic scale" (p. 16). Laird (1984, p. 125) explains the shamanic ritual:

> Rituals help define and specify family rules and also help embody and express the family's historical and cultural tradition. Through ritual, the family communicates to itself about itself, reflecting its integrating family themes. Rituals also bring order through their demand for synchrony. Although rituals may be performed in solitude, in family rituals the common experiences and behaviors of family members are synchronized and choreographed, each member dancing the steps he or she has rehearsed.

The Native American peyote ceremony is one such example of a ritual (Bullis, 1990). The participants gather to express—through songs, movement, prayers, and communal meal—the heart of their healing myths. Even the physical surroundings of the peyote ceremony are rife with rituals. As described in Chapter 4 (Figure 4.2), the interior of a tepee is used in a peyote ceremony. The fire, ashes, ceremonial altar, and other symbolic elements constitute an impressive array of ritual symbols and sacred space.

As shamans spiritually assess clients, they also conduct spiritual interventions. Again, spiritual interventions are qualitatively different from interventions based on the medical model. A variety of religious or spiritual interventions were discussed previously. Many, if not all, of these interventions are shamanic in that they involve altered states of ecstatic consciousness, ceremony, ritual, spiritual imagination, and spiritual anthropologies and cosmologies.

Social workers come in contact with shamanic activity in one of two ways. The first and most prevalent way is through the shamanic histories of their clients. As shamanism is a worldwide spiritual phenomenon, most cultures have it in their traditions. Even though clients may not label it as such, they may well acknowledge shamanic behaviors or ideas.

The second manner of contact arises from the fact that more and more social workers are using shamanic techniques of assessment and intervention. One relatively safe and simple shamanic technique is a form of guided imagery. In such a shamanic exercise, under supervision of the spiritually competent social worker, these exercises invoke the client's own healing myth. A model of guided imagery exercises is provided in Chapter 3.

Shamanism uses specialized techniques of ecstatic trance to contact spiritual dimensions, although not all spiritual techniques employ this trance. Of the religious and spiritual interventions discussed in Chapter 2, exploring a client's religious or spiritual background is not necessarily shamanic behavior, nor is helping to clarify the client's religious or spiritual values. Discussing or interpreting dreams, rituals, and ceremonies; praying with or for a client; or using religious or spiritual language or metaphors, however, are marked by shamanic characteristics.

Criteria for Using Shamanic Elements in Social Work Practice

Social workers should involve themselves in shamanic practices or cultures with the same care and grace that should accompany involvement in any professional episode involving spirituality. A list of criteria for involvement follows. The first two address working with a shaman, the next two address working in shamanic communities, and the final two address using shamanic assessments and interventions:

1. *What shamanic techniques does the shaman employ?* When working with shamans, ask exactly what techniques are used and what underlying spiritual theories support those techniques. This exploration is not meant to criticize the shaman's knowledge or experience. This investigation is conducted, rather, to protect clients. Social workers would, after all, explore the techniques used by anyone with whom they work. In legal terms, this exploration is called a "due diligence investigation." Social workers who work profes-

sionally with others may themselves be liable for harming clients, and have a duty to protect their clients from foreseeable harm. Without such due diligence explorations, even in the legal sense, social workers neither protect their clients nor themselves.

This exploration, in fact, verifies that the social worker considers the shaman a colleague and will treat him or her as such. It is proper for social workers to determine the professional skills of those with whom they work, and a shaman should be treated no differently.

This exploration need not be elaborate or intrusive, although it should be explicit. The exploration should question exactly how the shaman gets clients into ecstatic trances or altered states of consciousness, how long these trances last, what their purpose is, and (most importantly) how the shaman gets the client out of the trance. Furthermore, the exploration should determine how the information gleaned from either the shaman's own trance or the client's trance will be used. For example, if the shaman elicits images from either the shaman's or the client's trances or dream states, the social worker needs a close understanding of the manner in which the shaman will use this information therapeutically.

2. *What is the shaman's community relationship or following?* Part of the due diligence examination is an exploration of the role and status of the shaman in the shaman's own community. Clearly, it is not the role of the social worker to conduct background investigations, nor is it to evaluate the nature of shamanic techniques. It is a social worker's role to ascertain the community's evaluation of the shaman, as well as the impact of the shaman on the community. These explorations are designed to determine the consistency and reliability of the shaman's techniques and standing in his or her community.

3. *How precisely does the shamanic culture spell out a social worker's role?* Without precisely knowing their roles, how can social workers know what is expected of them? To be effective, the social worker must, in significant ways, meet the community's expectations. Frank and Frank, in their profound and influential *Persuasion and Healing* (1991), assert that there are four components of spiritual healing: (a) an emotionally charged and confiding relationship with the healing person or group, (b) a healing setting that heightens a social worker's role as healer, (c) a healing myth or concept that provides a plausible reason for the client's symptoms, and (d) a ritual or procedure for resolving those rituals in which both the healer and the client actively participate and believe (Krippner, 1992).

Interestingly, these same elements can be described in current social work practice and other practices as well. First, there is little argument that social workers have emotionally charged, confiding relationships with their clients. As a matter of fact, the NASW Code of Ethics requires that social workers maintain client confidence unless specific statutes and case law conditions dominate. Additionally, no one can seriously dispute that these emotionally charged relationships include the full complement of transferences. Indeed, these transferences must be competently handled to ensure competent clinical work. Without such competency, the client is damaged and the social worker is exposed to legal and ethical liabilities (Bullis, 1995a).

Second, social workers construct healing settings that enhance their healing role including professional clothing, demeanor, office furnishings (including fax machines and computers), evidence of professional degrees, and involvement of professional certifications and associations displayed prominently in the office. These badges of professional competency are not simply marketing or decorating techniques. They are intentionally designed to enhance the healer's role. Third, social workers use various psychodynamic theories including healing myths or concepts to provide plausible reasons for the client's symptoms.

4. *What is the relationship of the social worker to the shamanic community?* The relationship of the social worker to the shamanic community is also extremely important. When the social worker has a useful and fruitful working relationship with the shamanic community, the social worker gains its support and develops a rapport with the community. Such a relationship is of inestimable therapeutic value. If, on the other hand, the social worker has either a neutral or negative relationship with the shamanic community, therapeutic results are that much harder to achieve.

There are several ways in which to gain a beneficial relationship with the shamanic community. This relationship can be gained, first and foremost, by listening to and learning from the community. Seeking help in appropriate therapeutic situations, seeking to learn the community's rituals and traditions, and seeking to provide professionally sensitive service to the shamanic community all work toward the community's therapeutic benefit and the acceptance of the social worker.

5. *How well do the shamanic techniques match the shamanic assessments?* The social worker cannot turn a blind eye to specific interventions of the shaman. If the social worker creates a therapeutic alliance with the shaman, the social worker is obliged to take some responsibility for the shaman's actions when they work together. It is in the professional purview of the professional social worker to determine the consistency of the interventions with the assessments.

This examination of the shaman's consistency is another due diligence inquiry. When therapists lead clients into altered states, or are present when others do so, the therapists should determine for themselves whether their clients are in danger.

Specifically, social workers should assess the consistencies between their assessments and the techniques of intervention. The social worker should examine any inconsistencies and disparities between the client's situation and the intervention techniques. This connection could be based on cosmology, anthropology, spiritual traditions, or spiritual conceptualizations. Whatever the source of the connection between assessments and interventions, the connection should be clear, reasonable, and defensible.

6. *What safeguards does one employ in the use of trance states?* The phrase "to do no harm" is valuable to social workers working with shamanic techniques. Any time social workers use altered states or ecstatic states in therapy, extreme caution should be exercised. Altered states can reveal many images, some contradictory, some comforting, and some frightening. Strategies must be employed to safeguard the client from harmful results of ecstatic or trance states. The social worker should monitor such safeguards.

These protective strategies should be part of any therapeutic arsenal that uses altered states, including meditation, deep prayer, or guided imagery exercises. These strategies also include preparing the client for what to expect during the exercises, checking the client's mental status during the exercise, and debriefing the client after the exercise. These strategies were briefly discussed in Chapter 2.

Such strategies are designed to put clients on notice about what they can expect from such altered states, and thus accomplish two tasks. First, they allow the client to give an informed consent to the therapeutic procedure. Informed consent is a legal term that denotes that the one giving such consent is aware of the procedures to be conducted and any harmful effects that might reasonably be expected. Second, the strategies allow the client to prepare for the experience, which can severely diminish any negative impact such trance images may have.

Social workers should also independently monitor the client's progress during the exercise and debrief the client at the conclusion of the exercise. Careful attention to the client's demeanor, respiration, and bodily movements during the exercise can reveal major changes in the client's mental or physical state. Additionally, the client should not be allowed to leave the social worker's presence before a debriefing, which allows the client to both express any troubling experiences and to return to a normal state of consciousness. These strategies need not impede the exercises in altered states. In fact, they are designed to place the client at ease and to ensure therapeutic success.

This section has outlined characteristics of shamanism and the implications of shamanism for social work practice. The following section describes another cross-cultural spiritual orientation.

TANTRA, ECSTATIC SEXUALITY, AND SPIRITUALITY

Few authors have discussed the relationship between spirituality, religion, and sexuality in social work practice. Bullis and Harrigan (1992), however, assert that important connections exist between the religious policies of denominations and social work practice regarding sexuality.

Masters and Johnson developed an enormously helpful model of human sexuality (1966). Based on a medical model, it provides a systematic approach. Their model moves from lower excitement, to increasing excitement, to climax, and to decreased excitement. These phases are known as the excitement, plateau, orgasm, and refractory phases, respectively. While other researchers have fine-tuned this model, the basic scheme remains intact.

There is another, altogether different way to approach human sexuality. This approach, developed among Hindu, Buddhist, and Taoist thought, is often called tantra. The premise behind tantra is that sexual energy can be transformed into spiritual energy. Tantric sexuality is a kind of ecstatic sexuality.

Tantra means consciousness expansion—from the roots of *tan* (expand) and *tra* (liberates). Tantra expands consciousness through direct experience. Consciousness expansion is the vehicle for understanding both oneself and God, but tantra does not accomplish this through metaphysics or theology. In tantra, knowledge does not initiate the experience of God. The experience of God initiates theological thought. Tantra is concerned only with the reality of direct knowledge (Rawson, 1973). It trusts and values the participant's own experience and intuition in cultivating spiritual knowledge. In this sense, tantra scandalizes orthodox teachings of many religious persuasions. Tantra relies not on creeds or theological premises to communicate knowledge, but on the practitioner's own direct, personal, spiritual experience. In this sense, tantra is a spiritual, not a religious, experience.

Tantra is the set of techniques that transform the human energy of desire into spiritual drive. As one author puts it, "Sexual intercourse is the principal form of 'enjoyment' which Tantra harnesses to its spiritual ends, treating it as a paradigm of divine ecstasy" (Rawson, 1978). Tantra treats sexual intercourse, and the accompanying desire, as an act of worship. It also treats humans and sexual activity as embodiments of sacred activity. The human body reflects the divine body.

Whereas the medical model of sexual response from Masters and Johnson is based on building a momentum of excitement, the spiritual sexual response is based on a deepening sense of relaxation—even meditation. Knowledge cannot be gained in a sexually excited or aroused state. In fact, tantra asserts that excited energy is wasted energy (Rajneesh, 1975). The goal of the sexual response is the orgasmic release of the tension buildup, whereas the goal of the spiritual sexual response is deeper and deeper meditation. Only a relaxed, receptive state invites intuitive, affective, spiritual experience. Thus, the spiritual sexual response is a vehicle for prayer and spiritual energy.

This response was popularized for westerners by Chang's *The Tao of Love and Sex* (1977) and Raye's *Sexuality: The Sacred Journey* (1994). In Chang's book, the principles of Taoist tantric sexuality are explained to the Western audience and are summarized here. The principles of the spiritual energy centers are discussed in the next chapter. The fundamental principle of the spiritual sexual response is that sexual energy can be transformed into spiritual energy through two major practices. The first practice is the regulation of ejaculation, and the second is the recognition of the importance of female orgasm. Western authors such as Raye (1994), Chang (1977), and Anand (1989) have described the spirituality of sexuality.

TANTRA, ECSTATIC SEXUALITY, AND SOCIAL WORK PRACTICE

Chapter 4, in sections titled "Tantraism and Marijuanna Use" and "Constitutionally Sacred Sexuality and its Limitations with Children" introduced the concept of tantra. These sections described this concept and illustrated its application in clinical practice.

There are several ways in which social workers come into contact with tantra and ecstatic sexuality. The first is in the treatment of sexual dysfunction. The prevalence of sexual dysfunction is well documented, even though it varies considerably. The *DSM-IV* (APA, 1994) states that prevalence studies for sexual dysfunction "show extremely wide variability" (p. 495). The previous edition of the Manual (*DSM-III-R*, 1987) states that 20% of the general population suffers from hypoactive sexual desire disorder, 30% of the male population suffers from premature ejaculation, and 30% of the general female population suffers from inhibited female orgasm.

The evidence is mounting that both sexual dysfunction and sexual dissatisfaction approaches epidemic proportions. In a study reported in the *Journal of Urology* (January 1994), over half of a sample of 1,300 males in the Boston area between the ages of 40 and 70 reported a "problem maintaining or having an erection in the last six months" (Gutfeld, 1994).

In fact, sexual dissatisfaction may be even more prevalent than sexual dysfunction. In a sample representation of the U.S. population, a survey of 3,260 people (with 125 in-depth interviews) reported on several aspects of sexuality in the United States (Janus & Janus, 1993). This survey uncovered a wide variety of sexual dissatisfaction, with a total of 46% of men and 58% of women functioning at least 50% below their maximum ability. Fifty-four percent of men reported functioning 10% and 25% below maximum ability, and 42% of women reported functioning 10% and 25% below maximum ability. Any way that one views it statistically, there is a significant amount of sexual dissatisfaction among both men and women.

Given the amount of sexual dysfunction and sexual dissatisfaction, coupled with the enormous amount of spiritual seeking currently found in the United States, increased interest in spirituality through sexual means seems natural. Spiritual or ecstatic sexuality is a spiritual exercise.

Tantra and ecstatic sexuality attempt to fulfill both sexual and spiritual questions. Although many people find a sense of sacredness in religious organizations and structures, 26% experience a sense of the sacred during sex, 68% experience a sense of the sacred during the birth of a child, and 45% experience a sense of the sacred during meditation (Woodward, 1994). With one-quarter of those surveyed responding that they felt a sense of the sacred during sex, sex seems to be a major avenue for sacred experience. Tantra and ecstatic sexuality form a deliberate, disciplined focus for experiencing the sacred during sexual experiences.

Summary and Criteria for Using Tantric Elements in Social Work Practice

1. *Tantra is not comprised of just sexual techniques or technology—it is a quality of spiritual experience.* Americans are mesmerized by techniques and technologies. It is a modern distortion for tantra to be reduced to a set of techniques for enhancing sexual goals. Tantric exercises are designed to produce a spiritual quality in sexual experience that has its greatest fulfillment not in the efficiency of techniques, but in the fluency of the spiritual journey.

It is an error for social workers to rely on sexual techniques of tantra (or any other sexual techniques) to the detriment of interpersonal intimacy and spiritual ecstasy. Although techniques are designed to invite or encourage interpersonal intimacy, they are not themselves the intimacy or ecstasy nor do they guarantee that intimacy or ecstasy will come about. The mere performance of tantric sexual techniques does not equate with intimacy or ecstasy. Therefore, the spiritually sensitive social worker should take care not to confuse technology for tenderness, or techniques for spiritual authenticity.

2. *Tantric exercises should be assessed in light of their spiritual efficacy, not their sexual prowess.* Tantric sexuality means that sex is a means of prayer and meditation. As opposed to an emphasis on the technology or techniques of sexuality, tantra emphasizes the inner experience of union occasioned by the experience of deliberately focused attention to sexuality.

Spiritual efficacy means the usefulness of the spiritual exercise toward spiritual growth or development. As tantric exercises are not primarily used to cure sexual dysfunction, the standard of their utility should be spiritual, not sexual. As noted earlier in this book, spirituality refers to the intimacy or ecstasy with the sacred or divine. Thus, social workers should evaluate anyone using tantric or other sexual techniques in spirituality by the manner in which these exercises promote spiritual values, which include increasing expressions of caring, love, and charity.

3. *Sexuality is an avenue for therapeutic living.* Sexuality, in the view of tantra, has individual and social healing power. Sexuality, used properly, has the power to transform lives and society. This power of transformation is the proper province of social workers, who indeed need to be interested in any individually or socially transformative power.

The notion of sexuality has taken a beating in recent years. The politics of HIV research and government grants, the fear and stigma of HIV infection, the resurgence of sexually transmitted diseases, the current controversy over abortion, and the rate of teenage pregnancy have all contributed to a suspicious—even a threatened—attitude surrounding sexuality. This attitude is succinctly described by singer/songwriter Joni Mitchell (1994) when she sings, "Sex sells everything—sex kills."

This does not imply that morality, religion, and spirituality are hindrances to fuller—even ecstatic—functioning. It means that a morality, religion, and spirituality must be developed in a way that invites and encourages sexual expression consistent with the client's moral, religious, and spiritual orientation.

4. *Tantra exercises emphasize harmonizing couples' physical and spiritual energies.* Tantra is one of only a few spiritual disciplines that systematically and consistently utilizes spiritual practices for couples. Two tantric exercises involve breathing exercises to focus the mind and harmonize chakra energies. Muir and Muir (1989) describe individual and couples breathing exercises designed to focus the mind. During these exercises, one imagines each inhalation being drawn up through the spine, up the chakra centers, and into the crown chakra. This motion is designed to cleanse the chakras and can be adapted to couples practices.

   The "Great Gesture" is a practice that harmonizes energies between couples (Sovatsky, 1994). Partners sit facing each other and place their palms about 1 or 2 inches above and below one another. The left (receiving) palm should be face up and the right (giving) face down. They gaze into each other's eyes and concentrate on feeling the pulse of the energies between them. This and other tantric exercises combine spiritual practices such as breathing, mythic imagery, and chakra development.

Social workers who address spiritual concerns will, by the very nature of sexuality, also address sexual issues. Tantra is a means by which social workers can identify and explain spiritual issues in sexuality. This section has addressed the criteria with which social workers might use such interventions in the most appropriate, knowledgeable, professional, and safe manner.

CONCLUSION

This chapter has specifically described cross-cultural aspects of spiritual social work practice. Although this book offers a considerable number of cross-cultural examples, this chapter has described two particular examples (shamanism and tantrism) in some detail. It has also outlined suggestions for the safe and effective use of these methods.

DISCUSSION SCENARIOS AND QUESTIONS

1. You are a clinical social worker working with a family. At one point you receive a phone call requesting that you help them with a problem. The family fears that ghosts are in its home. The family describes unexplained noises, lights going on and off, and books falling from shelves. Both the

parents and children are afraid, and they ask you to help them. What do you do? Would the prior assessment that you gave for all or part of this family bear on your decision about what you response might be?

2. A couple comes to you with marital and sexual problems. After some discussion, it appears to you that the issue is an intimacy matter between the couple. One intimacy issue involves spiritual closeness because each partner seems to have different views about the religious or spiritual role of sexuality. One partner sees no connection between sexual behavior and sexual intimacy and their spiritual lives, whereas the other partner sees a strong and important connection between their sexual and spiritual lives. How do you begin to assess their counseling in a spiritual light? How do you approach this issue with the partners?

3. You are an advocate working for the legislative arm of a state or national social work organization. A bill has come before the state legislature criminalizing sexually explicit photographs. A group of social workers who work with sexual dysfunctions protest. They claim that the use of sexually explicit materials, including photographs and videos, serve therapeutic purposes. How do you approach these issues as an advocate? What is your decision?

4. What are some shamanic practices in which you have engaged? Are there shamanic practices involved in your own worshipping, religious, or spiritual traditions? Are there spiritual leaders, connected to traditions with which you are familiar, that might be willing to discuss such shamanic practices with you? What about tantric practices? How do other social workers react to colleagues who use shamanic or tantric practices?

5. How could you use shamanic practices (dreams, altered states, guided imagery exercises, etc.) in your work? Are there others in your community that might be helpful in training you to use these practices?

6. Are there communities near you that use altered states as healing techniques? Do you have any professional or personal exposure to them? How do these techniques work? What are the necessary elements for them to achieve healing?

Chapter 7

Science as Spiritual Symbolism

This chapter addresses three significant and related issues: (a) the assertion that scientific social work methodology is a symbol system of spiritual dimension; (b) the spirituality of social workers and their relationship to social work with a spiritual emphasis; and (c) the collaboration of social workers, spiritual leaders, clergy, and others with leaders of religious organizations.

Regular and careful collaboration with spiritual leaders and clergy can be of enormous help to clients and social workers alike. Such collaboration can offer the social worker additional resources and insights into the clients or communities with whom they work. It is folly to think that any single discipline or profession can effect total healing or wholeness.

This chapter outlines the probable skills of clergy with respect to clinical competence. It gives indications of such training in seminaries and other clinical training available for clergy. This chapter also provides resources for social workers to further explore the professional competence of spiritual leaders and to assess probable working relationships.

This chapter begins, however, with a general discussion of how and why social work should abandon the strictly physical cosmology in favor of a postpositive, spiritual cosmology. This new cosmology incorporates a spiritual view of the visible and invisible universe, a spiritual anthropology, a spiritual consciousness, and spiritual social work assessments and interventions.

This book provides a direct and open challenge to the current paradigm. This is a challenge to many of the current notions of cosmology, anthropology, consciousness, and therapy. In asserting a spiritual cosmology, the author challenges the cosmology introduced during the Enlightenment of the seventeenth and eighteenth centuries. Specifically, the author proposes a cosmology closer to that of the British astronomer and mathematician Sir James Jeans, who said that the universe is beginning to look more like a great thought than a great machine (Jeans,

1930). Another scientist, physicist Arthur Eddington, supports a similar theme in saying, "The stuff of the universe is mind stuff" (Rosten, 1994).

This book also asserts a spiritual anthropology that now stands in sharp contrast to the largely physical anthropology in use today. It also supports a consciousness and therapy consistent with both a spiritual cosmology and a spiritual anthropology.

The outmoded ideologies of logical positivism and determinism are the bases for scientific materialism and the outmoded medical model of disease and treatments. This new paradigm asserts that the primary datum of matter resides in the spiritual—that spiritual forces are the primary ordering energies of the universe. Thus, matter and disease are subject to spiritual forces.

THE DEMISE OF EMPIRICISM
AND THE RISE OF SYMBOLIC REALITY

In recent years, social work has searched for professional legitimacy and its own professional identity. Long in the shadow of psychoanalytic theory and professional psychology, it has searched for the validity of its own theory and intervention techniques. Such professional validity is necessary for receiving government grants, professional licensure, and public acceptance and recognition, which are legitimate goals. In so doing, social work has mimicked the epistemological standards of other disciplines—which include the dependence on empirical methods and seventeenth and eighteenth century cosmology.

Symbolic reality is a twentieth-century understanding of physical reality. This reality, underpinned by modern discoveries such as quantum physics and contemporary cosmology, understands that all reality is influenced by consciousness. This means that reality is symbolic not static. Matter has no reality of its own and is understood, ordered, and created in the observer's consciousness. There is no bright-line distinction between the observer's consciousness, or belief systems, and the subject of observation. The consciousness of a researcher affects both the data collected and the results found. To the extent that social workers recognize a spiritual cosmology and spiritual anthropology, their methodologies, models, paradigms, and results are so affected. To the extent that social workers are conscious of spiritual dimensions or elements, they play a role in the therapeutic process. Of course, the opposite is true as well.

The nature of consciousness changes the nature of reality. This is true because consciousness changes the nature and substance of the data (the experience of reality) itself. This may sound more like mysticism than science. In fact, science is beginning to sound more and more like mysticism. The nature of quazars, black holes, and interstellar worm holes is incompatible with empirical Newtownian physics. The laws of the universe, to refer back to Sir James Jeans, is starting to look more like mysticism than machinery.

Social work authors are beginning to challenge the empirical, positivistic, and deterministic hegemony. They are also recognizing the need for current and relevant cosmologies. Peile (1993) asserts a creative cosmology to replace the deterministic one. He claims the decline of positivism and determinism and says:

> The creative world view recognizes that knowledge is not just about reality, but rather is very much a part of the overall creative process of reality, where, in part, knowledge creates the very reality it seeks to understand. One implication of this approach is that there cannot be any fixed laws of the universe, and the uncovering of such laws is thus not an appropriate goal for science. (p. 133)

Simply put, the decline of determinism is the advent of a creative, holistic, healing cosmology. Social work's deterministic cosmology is in a coma, but it is still breathing. Social work's spiritual cosmology is taking its time being born. The ideology—even the consciousness—of the researcher influences what he or she discovers. Consciousness is a determining factor in the inquiry itself. Whereas Cartesian logic preaches that the mind and the object should not influence one another, quantum physics is increasingly convinced that there is no distinction between the consciousness and the object of consciousness. In other words, consciousness construes reality. Humans live in a conscious universe. Culture exerts formidable influences on the individual. The kind of data observed, the kind of conclusions drawn, the kinds of methodologies used, and the kind of research questions asked are all influenced by consciousness and culture. This book asserts that such consciousness and conclusions must be expanded to include spiritual cosmologies and anthropologies.

The scientific method itself is symbolism. It is, in fact, secular symbolism. Like some spiritual symbolism, some apply scientific theory literally, even rigidly. Scientific symbolism can become as entrenched and rigid as any religious dogma. Some view scientific theory fundamentalistically—as scientific fundamentalists! Science is a modern mythology. New science paradigms assert that everything is analogy—that theory, methodology, and data are symbolism. The new science recognizes that it does not offer reality, but only a picture of reality—and an only an impressionistic picture at that. This picture is full of symbols and signs. Indeed, art often recapitulates and originates cultural and spiritual ideas surrounding the artist. This is especially true at the close of one millennia and the opening of another. French impressionism is a case in point. One can trace, for example, the development of Cezanne from rather photographic scenes and portraits in the 1850s and 1860s to increasingly impressionistic paintings through the turn of that century.

The turn of this century and millennia has reached similar results. The Mexican photographer and artist Pedro Meyer, for example, has developed a new photography to correspond with the new millennia. Computers reform and reformulate parts of or entire photographs to make digital photographs. These new works of art capture the "digital moment" in a way similar to how unaltered photographs capture the decisive moment and look more like paintings than photographs. The images can be readily manipulated by computer to create images that are realistic and abstract at the same time. This new art reflects the new cosmology in that it suggests that there is no hard and fast reality—that reality can be manipulated and altered just like digitally manipulated photographs. Art often anticipates scientific and cultural trends.

TOWARD A NEW PARADIGM: COSMOLOGY AND CONSCIOUSNESS

The new scientific paradigm has been described as an ecological paradigm. Kafatos and Nadeau (*The Conscious Universe*, 1990, p. 183) list and describe five thematic shifts consistent with the new scientific cosmology:

1. *Shift from parts to wholes:* Characteristics of parts or components must be understood as characteristics of the whole.
2. *Shift from structure to process:* Structures are embodiments of an underlying process. This process is dynamic and relational.
3. *Shift from objective science (and knowledge) to epistemic science:* Knowledge is no longer objective and separate nor independent of the observer and the process of knowledge.
4. *Shift from building to network as a metaphor of knowledge:* Knowledge is not built upon unchanging principles, but upon an "interconnected network of relationships" founded on self-consistent and general agreement of data.
5. *Shift from truth to approximate descriptions:* The accurate description of reality ("the identification of patterns as objects") is impossible.

There is no longer a photograph of reality—only a symbol of reality is possible. All data is analogous. Thus, the true description of any object is "a web of relationships associated with concepts and models." The entire picture cannot be adequately expressed by such approximate descriptions.

Three significant themes emerge from these shifts. The first theme addresses consciousness. These shifts are not just shifts in thinking; they are shifts in consciousness itself. To think, for example, in wholes rather than in parts requires a shift in consciousness. All knowledge is relative. Epistemology is relational and is interdependent on a number of other components in the system, and consciousness is part of that system. This means that no knowledge is final knowledge.

Second, these shifts have spiritual significance. Consciousness is intimately connected to spirituality through both definition and function. Spirituality, as reviewed in this book, is tied to the nature and degree of consciousness. It is a vehicle for achieving or perceiving the presence of God or ultimate reality. Consciousness accesses spiritual or divine cosmologies. Indeed, this new scientific paradigm is a spiritual cosmology because it assigned an important role to the function of consciousness. If the consciousness is at a level where there is contact with spiritual symbols, signs, figures, or other insignia of the sacred dimensions, those insignia will influence the cosmology and consciousness itself.

Third, this new scientific cosmology has direct implications for developing a spiritual cosmology and social work practice consistent with modern epistemology. As consciousness affects scientific and spiritual cosmologies, it will affect both the clinical methodology of the clinician and the receptivity of the client. If clients see themselves as part of a spiritual cosmos, the spiritual cosmos is likely to become a crucial consideration in their therapeutic outcome.

Perhaps the most convincing evidence of both the changing scientific paradigms and methodology comes from a bastion of scientific methodology itself. In 1993 the National Institute of Health (NIH) funded 30 projects costing $30,000 each for 1 year of study. The NIH funding of research projects is not noteworthy, but the nature of those funded projects is. They all involved alternative therapies, including acupuncture, homeopathy, guided imagery, yoga, massage, macrobiotics, touch and energy healing, t'ai chi, Ayur Veda, and the effects of prayer (Tractman, 1994). This does not simply mean that new and controversial research grants are being awarded; rather, they represent a subtle shift in the scientific paradigm away from the materialistic, medical model that conforms to rigid empirical standards. They represent a shift toward a paradigm that endorses both a spiritual cosmology and a spiritual anthropology.

This new reality is more accurately described in analogical, even symbolic, language rather than descriptive and empirical. Said differently, reality is more accurately described in poetic rather than in quantitative terms. A poem describes reality more deeply than does a textbook.

The following section illustrates a spiritual cosmology that is consistent with the new scientific paradigms described earlier. It is an ancient cosmology that represents contemporary paradigms. These paradigms are briefly described in order to proffer their relevance to social work practice. This Norse cosmology appears in Chapter 3 and is discussed more fully here.

ANCIENT NORSE MYTHOLOGY, COSMOLOGY, AND SOCIAL WORK METHODOLOGY

Crossley-Holland (1980) offers both a description and a graphic representation of ancient Nordic cosmology. This description is represented by Figure 3.1. Ancient Nordic cosmology is chosen for two reasons. First, this cosmology is not well known. It is offered to demonstrate that even lesser-known cosmologies have much to offer spirituality and social work practice. Offering such a cosmology for this illustration serves to explore this cosmology in little-known and rarely used ways. Second, this cosmology has been specifically linked to shamanism and shamanic practices. The relationship between Norse shamanism and social work practice will be discussed in the following paragraphs.

The Norse cosmos is divided into three tiers and nine worlds. The highest of these three worlds is Asgard, the divine world peopled by warrior gods (aesir), fertility gods (vanir), and the land of the light elves (Alfheim). It is the location of Valhalla, where slain warriors eat and drink forever. The middle level, Midgard, is the land of human beings, including the land of the giants (Jotunheim) and the land of the dwarves (Nidavellir). The lowest level, Niflheim, is the world of the dead, which contains the realm of the dead (Hel).

These three levels of existence are connected with and undergirded by the cosmic ash tree. Yggdrasill, the center of the Nordic cosmos, is the symbol of all life and death and of all transformation. This is both the killing tree and the healing tree. Odin, the name of the great God of the Norse, is derived from the word *Yggdrasill*. *Yggdrasill* comes from *Ygg,* meaning *the terrible one.* *Drasill* means *horse.* "Odin's horse" is a play on words. A fuller explanation comes from knowing that horse was another term for the gallows. The Norse sacrificed both humans and animals. Their bodies were hung in trees and sacred groves, and their blood was sprinkled like holy water and examined for prophecies (Cohat, 1992). In an ironic twist, Odin himself hung there in a shamanic quest. Yggdrasill was the "axis of the world" (Crossley-Holland, 1980, p. 15) on which Odin rode into the sacred dimensions. The *Havamal* (sayings of the most high) has Odin describing his shamanic journey on Yggdrasill in his own words:

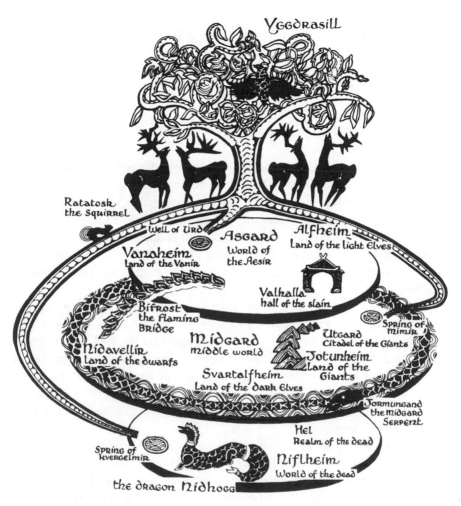

Figure 3.1 Norse Cosmology [*(From Chapter 3)*. From *The Norse Myths* by Kevin Crossley-Holland © 1980 Kevin Crossley-Holland. Reprinted by permission of Pantheon Books, a division of Random House, Inc.]

I know that I hung
On the tree lashed by
    winds
Nine full nights,
And gave to Odin,
Myself to
Myself,
On that tree
The depths of whose
    roots
No one knows.

> No bread sustained me
> Nor goblet.
> I looked down.
> I gathered the runes,
> Screaming I gathered
>   them;
> And from there I fell
>   again. (Cohat, 1992, p. 109)

Another connection between the levels and the worlds is Bifrost, meaning *the trembling roadway.* It is a flaming bridge that connects Asgard with Midgard. This connection is complemented with an additional connection, characterized by an almost cosmic, comic relief. Ironically, Yggdrasill is besieged from within and without. Deer eat its leaves. The dragon-serpent Nidhogg gnaws its roots. The squirrel Ratatosk carries insults from Nidhogg to the eagle perched in its leaves. Ratatosk represents the essential division and unity of Yggdrasill (Crossley-Holland, 1980).

The Norse shaman needed to know the secrets of both the dragon and the eagle. The eagle is a symbol of the higher states of consciousness—the consciousness closest to highest spirits. The dragon represents the depth of consciousness closest to the underworld spirits. Both kinds of consciousness are necessary in shamanic adventures. Shamanic healing requires experience in altered states consistent with any spiritual dimension. The rumors and insults carried by Ratatosk from Nidhogg to the eagle illustrate the intimate connection between the three levels of consciousness.

Norse cosmology and the mythology surrounding Odin and his shamanic journey on Yggdrasill is the Norse prototype of shamanic healing. It was the transforming tree or cross on which he learned the healing arts and the runes. Odin sacrificed himself to himself and became one with the gifts of healing, magic, prophecy, and supernatural knowledge. This is the meaning of the lines from the *Havamal* that read:

> And gave to Odin,
> Myself to
> Myself,
> On that tree

Odin became his own horse to traverse Norse cosmology and the sacred states of consciousness. Odin, the shaman, transcended the three Norse levels of their world as the shamans have always transcended the levels of consciousness—and he paid the price for his shamanic knowledge. Not only did he hang from the

Yggdrasill, but he had his side pierced. He also lost his eye in order to drink from the Spring of Mimir and receive the gift of perpetual prophesy.

The Norse horse is the equivalent of the Mayan jaguar. Both animals symbolize the means of transcendence, and even the sacred itself. Odin, the archetype of the Norse shaman, could ride his horse from Asgard across Bifrost into Midgard and even into Hel and Niflheim and back again. Norse cosmology and Odin's shamanic journey offer contemporary social workers a prototype for health, healing, and wholeness.

SHAMANIC NORSE MYTHOLOGY, CONSCIOUSNESS, AND CONTEMPORARY SOCIAL WORK PRACTICE

Norse cosmology provides ways to conceptualize consciousness in the service of social work practice. Norse shamanic cosmology and mythology have direct implications for social work practice. Five themes flow from the previous discussion, and they are discussed serially below.

First, the Norse cosmology illustrates a spiritual consciousness that is multidimensional. Consciousness has several levels, and each level has its own characteristics, environment, healing properties, and dangers. Social workers help clients find own their own Yggdrasill, or the connecting link between their own stages of consciousness. Yggdrasill connects all states of consciousness to a unified whole. The connections of consciousness extend even into social and political contexts. Social workers should thus make no distinctions between personal and collective healing. Healing on the personal level heals the whole and vice versa. Consequently, social workers should encourage clients to extrapolate their personal healing toward collective healing and vice versa.

Second, spiritual consciousness is organic, for it changes and grows. This characteristic is most evident with Yggdrasill, where this sacred axis lives and dies, grows and changes. Social workers guide their clients into a recognition of their own organic cosmology. Clients, whether or not they know it, have a cosmology. They have an idea of their world and their place in it. Clinicians guide clients into health and healing from the perspective of the clients' own cosmology. They guide clients into the avenues, symbols, and experiences, consistent with their cosmology, that are most likely to be therapeutically fruitful. They also explain where the psychic and social dangers are and guide clients away from them. Contraindications were discussed in the previous chapter, and an exercise for constructing cosmologies is included in the exercise section at the end of Chapter 2.

Third, connections between levels of consciousness are difficult and require great care and experience. The connecting links between consciousness are formidable. Bifrost is a *trembling roadway* because it is a tenuous and uncertain connection. It is a flaming bridge because only those with bravery, skill, or fool-hardiness will cross it successfully. Genesis records a similar barrier to sacred consciousness. After Adam and Eve ate of the forbidden fruit, they were banished from Eden:

> Then the Lord God said, "Behold, the man has become like one of us, knowing good and evil; and now, lest he put forth his and take also of the tree of life, and eat, and live forever"—therefore the Lord God sent him forth from the garden of Eden, to till the ground from which he was taken. He drove out the man; and at the east of the garden of Eden he placed the cherubim, and a flaming sword which turned every way, to guard the way to the tree of life. (Genesis 4:22-24)

Eden, the highest state of consciousness, is guarded against the careless and dilet-tantes. Social workers help clients pass between the flaming swords. The way to healing and the tree of life requires clients to pass through their shadows, fears, and terrors. Therapy and transformation are painful processes. Similarly, poeti-cally and practically, social workers are human bifrosts. On one hand, they are the flaming bridges that connect the levels of consciousness. Social workers pro-vide the insight, expectations, and energy to entice, invite, and encourage clients to go beyond themselves—or discover who they really are. By the same token, social workers help guide clients through the perils of Bifrost.

Fourth, cosmic knowledge is costly. Cosmic knowledge, the ability to heal or to prophecize, requires sacrifice. Odin sacrificed himself to himself, and sacri-ficed an eye at the Spring of Mimir. Social workers are witnesses and guides to the clients' own gallows. They bear witness to, and even guide and conduct, a client's own sacrifice.

Therapy and transformation requires sacrifice. Clients sacrifice parts of them-selves—even those parts they consider most sacred—for greater insight and pos-sibility of inspiration. Although clients may not necessarily donate an eye like Odin, they must sacrifice their sacred neuroses, accustomed ways of behavior, or most cherished beliefs in order to at least relieve a greater pain. The spiritually competent social worker helps make these sacrifices meaningful.

Fifth, both Norse cosmology and mythology and social work practice enjoy a teleological dimension. This means that the client's spiritual journey and accompa-nying struggle have an ultimate purpose. Therapeutic pain is in the service of greater wisdom and healing. The consciousness of both the social worker and the client matters in client outcomes. The significance of consciousness, the core of spiritual-ity, was discussed in the preceding section. The following section compares the spir-ituality of social workers and discusses implications for social work practice.

COOPERATION BETWEEN SOCIAL WORKERS AND SPIRITUAL LEADERS

Perhaps the single most important factor in describing the nature and function of cooperation between social workers and spiritual leaders is their reported differences in religiosity and spirituality. There are important differences between religious and spiritual beliefs among the general population and social workers. An overwhelming majority of Americans (94%) believe in God, pray (90%), believe that God loves them (88%), and have given a considerable amount of thought to their relationship with God over the past 2 years (78%). Conversely, only 3% believe that God does not love them (Gallup & Castelli, 1989).

Table 7.1 covers data gathered from Virginia clinical social workers (the same sample described in Chapter 3). It compares clinicians' religious upbringings with their current affiliations. It is important to note the changes in religious preferences through their lifetimes, and, by and large, social workers report less religious affiliation than the general public. For example, in none of the denominational categories do social workers affiliate as much as the general population. Indeed, while the general population reports an increased affiliation in Roman Catholicism since 1947, both social workers and LCSWs report a diminution with such affiliation. This disparity between the beliefs among social workers and the general population can cause a religious or spiritual gap between clinicians and their clients.

Table 7.1

Comparisons of Religion of Upbringing and Current Religious Affiliation

Sample	Social Workers		LCSWs[*]		(1947) General Pop.[†]	
	a	b	a	b	a	b
Roman Cath.	22.6%	17.7%	25%	12%	(20%)	28%
Protestant	54.8	41.6	60	41	(69)	57
Jewish	16.5	14.2	11	9	(5)	2
Eastern Orthodox	.9	1.8				
None	1.7	11.5	4	21	(6)	9
Other	1.7	12.4	.9	17	(1)	4
Multiple	1.7	.9				

[a] = Religion of upbringing, [b] = Current religion
[*]for LCSW's only
[†]Gallup & Castelli, 1987

SPIRITUALITY EDUCATION AND TRAINING IN RELIGIOUS ORGANIZATIONS

"Spiritual organization" is a contradiction in terms because organizations are, by their very nature, concerned with behaviors and external structures. Organizations do not have spirituality—individuals do. The extent to which organizations manifest spirituality or spiritual concerns is directly proportional to the extent that individuals in the organization manifest these same concerns. Although this chapter specifically addresses religious institutions, its main concern is the quality and quantity of such spiritual concerns. Thus, this section does not presume to offer a comprehensive description of religious education for religious leaders, nor does it presume to offer a comprehensive description of the clinical training for religious or spiritual leaders. Rather, this chapter seeks to address issues related to the cooperation between social workers and spiritual leaders.

Much of the empirical information offered in this chapter addresses, out of necessity, clergy or religious leaders. Little or no empirical data is available on the cooperation between spiritual leaders (not connected with religious organizations) and mental health practitioners. The research available is made up of reports from clergy and those religious leaders who are connected with religious organizations. This section, then, reports survey results from religious leaders and makes hypotheses about how social workers might initiate and develop therapeutic cooperation with spiritual leaders.

The following section discusses the ways in which spiritual leaders are seen by others as mental health practitioners, and how they see themselves as mental health practitioners. It will address the education, clinical training, counseling exposure, and self-reported clinical experience of these leaders.

Religious and Spiritual Leaders as Mental Health Practitioners and Healers

Ministers remain on the front line of mental health care provision and, ironically, generally see themselves as ill-prepared to provide such care (Virkler, 1979). Historically, more Americans turn to clergy than to other mental health professionals when experiencing mental or emotional difficulties. Gurin et al. (1960) reported that Americans used clergy as their primary source of mental health counseling. Forty-two percent of Americans sought help from clergy, and 29% went to general physicians, 17% went to psychiatrists, and 10% went to mental health facilities (Mollica, Streets, Boscarino & Redlich, 1986). Twenty-five years later, Veroff et al. (1976) revealed essentially the same data—that 34% of all those seeking help turned to clergy (Mollica, Streets, Boscarino & Redlich, 1986).

This trend continues to hold true. In a nationwide poll, Gallup and Castelli (1989) reported that, for those Americans suffering from depression, "prayer, meditation and Bible reading" was 97% effective in relieving depression. Additionally, talking with "pastor or religious leader" was effective for 87% of the people in relieving depression. This level of effectiveness can be compared with the 71% reported effectiveness for a "doctor or professional counselor." Additionally, the researchers reported on the methods Americans used to relieve depression. Nearly one-half (48%) of the 81% of Americans who at least occasionally felt depressed turned to "prayer, meditation, and Bible reading." Twice as many (27%) of those who at least occasionally felt depressed spoke with pastors and religious leaders as they did with doctors or professional counselors (14%). These figures suggest that Americans place more faith in spirituality than in physicians, psychiatrists, psychologists, and social workers for relief from mental health problems.

Pastor's Counseling Practices

The Virkler study also reported on the pastor's counseling practices. The average amount of counseling per week ranges from 0 to 25 hours. The usual frequency of the counseling sessions ranged from two or four sessions per month. Respondents reported that they spent an average of three or four sessions with any one particular client. This amounts to very brief interaction.

These statistics do not precisely capture the frequency with which religious and spiritual professionals and leaders are requested for spiritual healing. It is common knowledge, for example, that spiritual leaders routinely make hospital visits, nursing home visits to those residing or convalescing there, and home visits to those who have been recently discharged from medical facilities or made permanently homebound. Thus, although a counselor's experience may be limited, his or her spiritual experience in helping and healing others may be much more extensive.

Clergy Referral to Counseling Professionals

The frequency and nature of clergy referrals to other mental health care professionals has not been extensively studied. However, enough empirical information is available to make some generalizations. Regarding referral, the Virkler study (1979) is helpful in assessing the clergy's level of clinical sophistication. The study indicated that 45% of those surveyed reported that their seminary training had not addressed the criteria for professional referrals. Fifty-five percent reported that their seminary training did not contain any information about how pastors could develop referral sources. Additionally, 68% reported that they had no seminary training in how to evaluate the quality of referral sources available, and 56% reported that they had no training in assisting those being counseled in the referral process. Given this data, it not surprising that only 10% of clergy reported that they refer to other mental health practitioners. These data suggest that clergy may well be ill-prepared to choose effective referral sources, make proper referrals, or to guide an individual through a referral situation. It also indicates that clergy refer with relatively low frequency.

Sister M.V. Joseph (1988) surveyed 61 Washington, D.C. social workers and discovered referral information from the social work side. These social workers, although not strictly referring to clergy, reported that they collaborated with clergy almost twice as much as clergy did with them (18%). Additionally, these social workers reported that 31% used religious institutions for concrete social services.

Methodologies and Cooperation with Spiritual Leaders

This section offers several suggestions regarding the cooperation between spiritual leaders and social workers. They are taken from the data and information presented earlier in this chapter. These suggestions are intended to be used in a flexible manner to meet changing circumstances.

1. *Social workers will have to assert themselves with clergy and spiritual leaders.* Clergy do not receive a great deal of training in the purposes of, and procedures in, referral. Both purposes and procedures need to be specifically and affirmatively addressed by social workers. In developing cooperation with spiritual leaders, social workers have to take the lead in initiating the contact, describing the rationale for the cooperation, specifically defining the roles that each participant will play, and clearly defining and assessing the therapeutic goals.

   Establishing these procedures helps to ensure therapeutic success. The specificity with which these goals and procedures are outlined and assessed also help to ensure that the therapy is followed through to adequate completion.

2. *Social workers will have to educate spiritual leaders regarding referral procedures.* It is clear from the data provided earlier that social workers must view, with rebuttable presumption, that clergy and spiritual leaders do not have training and experience in the procedures of cooperation. This "rebuttable presumption" is like the "presumption of innocence" afforded to criminal defendants. The presumption of innocence is an assumption that a defendant is innocent until he or she is proven guilty,

and is rebuttable because it may be overruled by a showing of evidence to the contrary. In most cases, it is likely that most clergy will not have expertise in establishing and following through with therapeutic cooperation procedures.

It may be helpful, in fact, for the social worker to write a *therapeutic cooperation agreement*. This working document would memorialize the agreements, decisions, and procedures discussed between the spiritual leader and the social worker. It should include who will do what, how and when it will be done, and toward what purpose.

This therapeutic cooperation agreement might seem to be a rather complex and rigid way to spend the professional's time and energy, but it could serve several important purposes. First, it urges the social worker and the spiritual leader to discuss their procedures prior to working together. Second, it makes the two professionals discuss, with clarity and specificity, their course of action prior to cooperation. Third, the agreement provides a written reference for ascertaining whether the stated goals were achieved and whether the stated procedures were followed.

3. *Social workers should strive to educate spiritual leaders as a public service, not for self service.* Educating clergy and spiritual leaders should be done as a public service, and not as a service for self-promotion or self-aggrandizement. A public service discussion involves no self-interest and is in the primary interest of the client or clients. There are at least three reasons for providing public service education and self-service education. First, it is patronizing for spiritual leaders (or any other professional) to be lectured as to how to do their job by another professional from a different discipline. Professionals have their own ways of conducting their professionally designed roles and tasks. Social workers should not presume to tell spiritual leaders how to conduct their ministries.

Second, strict self-interest has no place in therapy. Social workers always provide therapeutic environments that benefit their clients, but are not for their own benefit. If, for example, the social workers find that a physician, psychologist, spiritual leader, or other professional is necessary or helpful to their client's progress, then they are ethically obligated to make that known to their client. This ethical obligation is for the benefit of clients. Even if social workers cannot provide such services, they are obligated to see that their clients somehow receive them.

Third, self-service undermines the social work profession. The public is in a consumer-conscious mood, and the public is increasingly critical of professional groups and their performances. When there is even an appearance of self-serving or self-dealing activity, the profession is undermined in the public eye. When the social work profession is seen by the public in a negative light, all social workers are undermined. Additionally, clients or prospective clients may suffer as well. Prospective clients who need social work help may choose not to seek such help.

4. *Social workers should define and follow clear professional boundaries.* Following clearly defined, professional boundaries is a way to avoid professional confusion and malpractice. Given that the author encourages interdisciplinary theories and methods of social work practice, it may seem strange that this author is now describing the pitfalls of "professional confusion." It may seem to the reader that a book on spirituality and social work practice is, by its very nature, fraught with professional boundary confusion. Boundary confusions, especially involving clergy, spiritual leaders, and community leaders, is an intrinsic risk associated with this undertaking. This is precisely why such care is now given to avoiding the negative aspects of blurring professional roles.

The opening up of professional roles for interdisciplinary cooperation is not the same as blurring professional boundaries. Opening up professional roles to include spiritual leaders means that social workers need to clarify their own professional role and to assess their own spiritual competencies. It also means that social workers need to articulate their professional role and the limits of their spiritual competency to their clients and to interdisciplinary colleagues. This chapter and Chapters 3 and 5 should be particularly useful to social workers who wish to clarify their professional roles relative to their spiritual competencies.

5. *Social workers should follow up in a manner consistent with their professional role.* A thorough conclusion is often as important as the interventions. It is important for at least three several reasons. First, it provides closure for all parties involved. Closure is an important element in tying up loose therapeutic ends and coming to the consensus that the therapeutic work is completed.

Second, competent follow-up is a way to decide whether the client should be referred to a counseling specialist or another professional for additional help. Third, competent follow-up, as opposed to termination, includes the invitation to return to therapy should clients require such an opportunity. Terminating is an unfortunate choice of words, but a commonly used synonym for the completion of the therapeutic process. Part of following up is referring clients to other professionals, including clergy and other spiritual leaders. The usefulness of such cooperation has already been discussed.

Contraindications for Cooperating with Spiritual Leaders

This section describes the reasons for, and circumstances under which, cooperation and coordination with spiritual leaders are contraindicated. Contraindications, here, mean situations in which the social worker should engage in the presumption of noncooperation. A rebuttable presumption of noncooperation is like the aforementioned presumption of innocence. Again, the presumption of innocence is an assumption that a defendant is innocent until he or she is proven guilty, and is rebuttable through a showing of evidence to the contrary.

Similarly, a presumption of noncooperation does not mean that no cooperation is possible. It means that this presumption may be overcome with a showing of evidence to the contrary. Thus, although contraindications are described below, they may be overcome by a showing of events or circumstances that change the outcome. All contraindications discussed below should be considered in this light:

1. *When the client feels ambivalence regarding the spiritual leader.* Clients cannot be expected to agree with everything that their spiritual leaders say or do. Such an expectation is both unnecessary and unhealthy. Most clients can be expected to disagree with suggestions from their clinicians when it is necessary. In extreme cases, clients will simply terminate therapy if such ambivalence is critical or intolerable.

   Having said this, clients who feel ambivalence or doubt about their own spiritual leader do not undermine the therapeutic relationship alone. Under most circumstances, clients can be expected to act in their own best interests, and to distinguish between those therapeutic interventions that are helpful and those that are not.

   In extreme cases, however, severe ambivalence—even suspicion—of the client toward the clinician can undermine the therapeutic process. When clients feel that their spiritual convictions are misunderstood or ignored, the therapy is undermined. Clients are unlikely to benefit from therapies with which they disagree or do not understand.

2. *When the clinician has ambivalent feelings or thoughts about the teachings or techniques of the spiritual leader.* The same dynamics are true between the clinician and the spiritual leader. Clinicians should not feel obligated to accept the teachings or techniques of the client's spiritual leader without criticism. The clinician should conduct a "spiritual due diligence inquiry" of the spiritual leader. As previously noted, such an inquiry is not intended to undermine the spiritual leader's credibility, but to determine the therapeutic fit and propriety of a professional relationship between the two.

This due diligence inquiry, described earlier in this chapter, should specifically address a number of different areas. These areas include: (a) the correspondence between the leader's cosmology and anthropology and his or her assessments and interventions, (b) the correspondence between the rationale and technique for assessments or interventions that involve placing the client in altered states, and (c) precautions and ethical considerations involved in the use of altered states and other interventions.

There need not be perfect matches between the views of the social worker and the spiritual leader on these points to produce a useful therapeutic relationship. There is no valid or reliable test for such a match. Some guidelines, however, can be suggested. First, the previously discussed areas of the due diligence inquiry should be explicitly made. Clear and forthright communication should be a hallmark of the therapeutic partnership. Second, differences should be discussed frankly. Third, if differences occur and become serious, the two professionals should consider breaking off their professional collaboration.

3. *When the social worker determines that the community has renounced or limited its support for the spiritual leader.* The social worker should assess the level of community support and trust for the spiritual leader. As already noted, spiritual leaders do not work in a vacuum. They work in an ecology of consciousness that includes social, intellectual, emotional, and spiritual dynamics. The community is but one piece of evidence for the validity and reliability of the spiritual leader's usefulness.

The community's opinion should be applied differentially with regard to the leader's validity and reliability. The spiritual leader may be effective with some people and less so with others. The social worker can make such distinctions and determine with whom the spiritual leader may be effective and with whom he or she may not be effective.

4. *When the social worker's role is not clearly defined.* Even the best social worker cannot meet unclear and unspecific expectations. Without clear and explicit definitions, the social worker cannot hope to be most effective. If social workers do not know the extent to which the client needs or wants spiritual issues to be addressed, they may inadvertently trespass on the client's most sacredly held positions.

Insisting upon clear, unambiguous communication increases the probability of therapeutic competency and success. This is particularly true in the addressing of spiritual issues. The roles of the spiritual leader and the social worker, for example, should be differentiated and specified.

Making expectations clear and explicit is especially important regarding the results expected by the client. Most likely, the client has some expectations about the nature and type of his or her return to health and wholeness. To the extent that the client's expectations are not met, the client may be disappointed and even disgruntled. Any negative or disappointed feelings can undermine therapeutic effectiveness.

5. *When the community does not recognize the social worker's role.* Confusion and lack of clarity on the part of the community undermine the social worker's role as well. The social worker, like the spiritual leader, does not work in a vacuum. The social worker's healing effectiveness are in line with the expectations of the community. This synchronicity does not mean that the social worker's effectiveness is dependent on the community's expectations, but rather that the community's expectations act as a conscious influence on the social worker and the client.

The community's consciousness can act like a support system. To the extent that the community supports the social worker, the client's healing is likely to be positively influenced. To the extent that the community supports the role of the social and the social worker's interventions, such support can literally change the client's psychic ecology.

CONCLUSION

This chapter has explored three important concepts. First, the use of spiritual assessments and interventions anticipates a quantum shift in the cosmology and anthropology under which clinicians operate. Spiritual techniques both inspire and imply a change in the models used by the clinicians. It presages a shift from the positivistic model to a spiritual, symbolic model. Second, this chapter discussed how clinicians specifically apply this new model to their clinical practices. Third, the collaboration between social workers and spiritual leaders was explored.

This book examined the exciting dynamics possible when social workers and other mental health clinicians allow their clients to give expression to their spiritual issues and questions. It also offered cross-cultural, concrete examples, resources, ideas, and illustrations of how clinicians can ethically and sensitively assess, intervene in, and approach a client's spiritual concerns.

The themes voiced in this book cross the threshold of many boundaries. This author has asserted that the great divorce between social work and spirituality is inauthentic and unsupportable. Clients who have a desire, articulated or not, to have their spiritual concerns addressed, deserve to be heard by a competent and thorough professional.

DISCUSSION SCENARIOS AND QUESTIONS

1. Cosmology and anthropology have played significant roles in this chapter. How would you define cosmology and anthropology? What is the relationship between the two? How would you get to know the cosmology and anthropology of your clients?

2. How would you describe your own cosmology and anthropology? Can you describe or draw them? Do your personal cosmology and anthropology become altered in professional situations? How? How might clinicians' cosmologies and anthropologies affect their work with their clients? What should clinicians do if their cosmologies and anthropologies clash with those of their clients?

3. What are the ethical considerations in using spiritual techniques? Do the ethical considerations vary from one technique to another? If so, how?

4. What are some of the contraindications for using some of your favorite spiritually oriented assessments and interventions? What, on the other hand, are the indications for using some of your least favorite assessments or interventions?

5. What are other spiritual assessments or interventions not discussed in this book that flow from spiritually oriented cosmologies and anthropologies? How would you assess your comfort in using them with clients?

References

Afterman, A. (1992). *Kabbalah and consciousness*. Riverdale-on-Hudson, NY: Sheep Meadow Press.

Ali, A. (1990). An approach to the Islamization of social and behavioral sciences. *American Journal of Islamic Social Science, 6* (1), 37–58.

American Psychiatric Association. (1994). *Diagnostic and statistical manual of mental disord* ers (IV). Washington, D.C.: Author.

Anand, M. (1989). *Art of sexual ecstasy*. New York: Tarcher/Perigree.

Aschrott, P.F. (1902). *The English poor law system*. London: Knight & Co.

Baring, A., & Cashford, J. (1991). *The myth of the goddess: Evolution of an image*. New York: Viking Arkana.

Berthold, S. (1989). Spiritism as a form of psychotherapy. *Social Casework, 70* (8), 502–509.

Birnbaum, J. (1995, May 15). The gospel according to Ralph. *Time, 29–35.*

Blank, W. (1991). *Tarot, torah & tantra*. Boston: Coventure.

Bloch, A., & Shor, R. (1989). From consultation to therapy in group work with parents of cultists. *Social Casework: The Journal of Contemporary Social Work, 70* (4), 231–236.

Brower, I. (1984). The 4th ear of the spiritual-sensitive social worker. (Ph.D. dissertation, Union for Experimenting Colleges and University, Microfilm International No. 8500785.)

Brown, L. (1991). He who controls the mind controls the body: False imprisonment, religious cults, and the destruction of volitional capacity. *Valparaiso University Law Review, 25,* 407–454.

Budge, E. (1895). *The Egyptian book of the dead*. New York: Dover Press.

Bullis, R. (1990). Swallowing the scroll: Legal implications of the recent Supreme Court peyote cases. *Journal of Psychoactive Drugs, 22* (3), 325–332.

Bullis, R. (1990). Spiritual genograms: Nurturing our spiritual roots. *Church Teachers. 17* (5), 174–175, 190–191.

Bullis, R. (1991). "Gag rules" and chastity clauses: Legal and ethical consequences of Title X and the AFLA for professionals in human sexuality. *Journal of Sex Education and Therapy, 17* (2), 91–102.

Bullis, R. (1992). Psychologists and the mystical process. *Journal of Contemporary Psychotherapy, 22* (1), 43–49.

Bullis, R., & Harrigan, M. (1992). Religious denominational policies on sexuality: Implications for social work practice. *Families in Society, 73* (5), 304–312.

Bullis, R. (1995a). *Clinical social worker misconduct*. Chicago: Nelson-Hall.

Bullis, R. (1995b). From gag rules to blindfolds: The pornography victims compensation act. *Journal of Sex Education and Therapy, 21* (1), 11–21.

Campbell, J. (1949). *The hero with a thousand faces*. New York: World Publishing.

Campbell, J. (Ed.). (1970). *Myths, dreams, and religion*. New York: Dutton.

Campbell, J. (1964). *The masks of God* (Vols. 1–4). New York: Penguin Books.

Canda, E. (1983). General implications of shamanism for clinical social work. *International Social Work, 26* (4), 14–22.

Canda, E. (1986). A conceptualization of spirituality for social work: Its issues and implications. The Ohio State University Ph.D. Dissertation. University Microfilms International, No. 8625190.

Canda, E. (1988). Spirituality, religious diversity, and social work practice. *Social Casework, 69* (4), 238–247.

Canda, E. (1989). Religious content in social work education: A comparative approach. *Journal of Social Work Education, 25* (1), 15–24.

Canda, E. (1990). An holistic approach to prayer for social work practice. *Social Thought, 16* (3), 3–13.

Canda, E., & Phaobtong, T. (1992). Buddhism as a support system for Southeastern Asian refugees. *Social Work, 37* (1), 61–67.

Canda, E. (1988). Spirituality, religious diversity, and social work practice. *Social Casework, 69* (4), 238–247.

Canning, R. (Tr.) (1986). *The rule of Saint Augustine.* Garden City, NY: Image Books.

Cartlidge, D., & Duncan, D. (1980). *Documents for the study of the gospels.* New York: Collins.

Cataldo, C. (1979). Wilderness Therapy: Modern Day Shamanism. (In C. Germain. Ed.). *People and environments.* New York: Columbia University Press.

Cerutti, E. (1977). *Mystic with the healing hands.* New York: Harper & Row.

Chang, J. (1977). *The Tao of love and sex.* New York: E. P. Dutton.

Chesebrough v. State, 255 So.2d 675 (Fla. 1971).

Chitty, D.J. (1966). *The desert a city.* Crestwood, NJ.: St. Vladimir's Seminary Press.

Church of the Lukumi Babalu Aye v. City of Hialeah, 113 S.Ct 2217 (1993).

Clottes, J., & Courtin, J. (1993, May/June). Stone Age Gallery by the Sea. *Archaeology,* 38–43.

21 Code of Federal Regulations § 1307.31 (1989).

Cohat, Y. (1992). *The Vikings: Lords of the sea.* New York: Harry Abrams, Inc.

Compton, B., & Galaway, B. (1979). *Social work processes.* Homewood, IL: Dorsey.

Cooper, J. (1978). *An illustrated encyclopedia of traditional symbols.* New York: Thames and Hudson.

Crossley-Holland. (1980). *The Norse myths.* New York: Pantheon.

Danielou, J. (1958). *The dead sea scrolls and primitive Christianity.* Baltimore: Helicon Press.

Davies, A. P. (1956). *The meaning of the dead sea scrolls.* New York: Signet Key Books.

Day, P. (1989). *A new history of social welfare.* Englewood Cliffs, NJ: Prentice-Hall.

Denton, R. (1990). The religiously fundamentalist family: Training for assessment and treatment. *Journal of Social Work Education, 26* (1), 6–14.

Drewal, H., Pemberton, J., & Abiodun, R. (1989). *Yoruba: Nine centuries of art and thought.* New York: Center for African Art.

Dudley, J., & Helfgott, C. (1990). Exploring a place for spirituality in the social work curriculum. *Journal of Social Work Education, 26* (3), 287–294.

Edinger, E. (1972). *Ego and archetype.* Baltimore: Penguin Books.

Eisenstadt V. Baird, 405 U.S. 438 (1972).

Employment Division, Department of Human Resources of Oregon v. Smith, 494 U.S. 872 (1990).

Epstein, P. (1988). *Kabbalah: The way of the Jewish mystic.* Boston: Shambhala.

Fisher, B. (1991). Devotion, damages and deprogrammers: Strategies and counterstrategies in the cult wars. *Journal of Law and Religion, 9,* 151–177.

Frank and Frank. (1991). *Persuasion and healing.* New York: Schocken.

Fromm, E. (1951). *The forgotten language.* New York: Grove Press.

Ehrenwald, J. (Ed.). (1991). *The history of psychotherapy.* Northvale, NJ: Jason Aronson, Inc.

Gallup, G., & Castelli, J. (1989). *The people's religion.* New York: MacMillan Publishing Co.

Gershom, Rabbi Y. (1987). Shamanism in the Jewish tradition. In S. Nicholson (Ed.), *Shamanism.* Wheaton, IL: Theosophical Publishing House.

Goetz, D., & Morley, S. (1950). *Popol vuh.* Norman, OK: University of Oklahoma Press.

Gonzalez-Wippler, M. (1987). *Santeria.* New York: Original Publications.

Gray, P. (1995, January 30). In so many gods we trust. *Time,* pp. 73–74.

Greif G., & Porembski, E. (1988). AIDS and significant others: Findings from a preliminary exploration of needs. *Health and Social Work, 13*(4), 259–265.

Griswold v. State of Connecticut, 381 U.S. 479 (1965).

Gurin, G., Veroff, J., & Feld, S. (1960). *Americans view their mental health: A nationwide interview survey.* New York: Basic Books.

Gutfeld, G. (1994, November). The prescription for male potency. *Prevention, 142,* 78–80.

Hagan, J. L. (1982). Whatever happened to 43 Elizabeth I, c.2? *Social Service Review, 56*(1), 108–119.

Hay, L. (1984). *You can heal your life.* Santa Monica, CA: Hay House.

Heikkinen, C. (1989). Reorientation from altered states: Please more carefully. *Journal of Counseling and Development, 67,* 520–521.

Helminiak, D. (1989). Self-esteem, sexual self acceptance, and spirituality. *Journal of Sex Education and Therapy, 15,* 200–210.

Hepworth, O., & Larsen, J. (1986). *Direct social work practice* (3rd Edition). Chicago: The Dorsey Press.

Hoffman, E. (1989). *The way of splendor: Jewish mysticism and modern psychology.* Northvale, NJ: Jason Aronson, Inc.

Hoppal, M. (1987). Shamanism: An archaic and/or recent belief system. In S. Nicholson (Ed.), *Shamanism.* Wheaton, IL: Theosophical Publishing House.

Horwatt, K. (1988). The shamanic complex in the Pentecostal Church. *Ethos, 16*(2), 128–145.

Hughes, R. (1995, Feb. 13). Behold the Stone Age. *Time,* 52–62.

Huxley, A. (1954). *The doors of perception.* New York: Harper & Row.

Huxley, F. (1974). *The way of the sacred.* Garden City, NY: Doubleday.

Ikenberry, J. (1975). Psi and our cosmic age. *Clinical Social Work Journal, 3* (4), 316–330.

Imre, R. (1984, Jan.-Feb.). The nature of knowledge in social work. *Social Work,* 41–45.

Jaffe, M. (1961). Opinions of caseworkers about religious issues in practice. *Smith College Studies in Social Work, 31*(3), 238–256.

Jeans, J. (1930). *The mysterious universe.* New York: MacMillan.

Jones, S. (1994, March). A constructive relationship for religion with the science and profession of psychology. *American Psychologist,* 184–199.

Joseph, M. (1988). Religion and social work practice. *Social Casework, 69,* 443–452.

Jung, C. (1965). *Memories, dreams & reflections.* New York: Vintage.

Kafatos, M., & Nadeau, R. (1990). *The conscious universe.* New York: Springer-Verlag.

Keefe, T. (1986). Meditation and social work treatment. In F. J. Turner, *Social Work Treatment* (pp. 155–180). New York: The Free Press.

Kelsey, M. (1974). *God, dreams, & revelation.* Minneapolis: Augsburg.

Kelsey, M. (1978). *Dreams: A way to listen to God.* New York: Paulist Press.

Kelsey, M. (1978). *Discernment: A study in ecstasy and evil.* New York: Paulist Press.

Krassner, M. (1986). Effective features of therapy from the healer's perspective: A study of Curanderismo. *Smith College Studies in Social Work, 56*(3), 157–183.

Krippner, S. (1992). Healing images: Contemporary shamanism in North America. (Cassette recording of title accompanies book). Irvington Publishers, Inc.

Laird, J. (1984). Sorcerers, shamans, and social workers: The use of ritual in social work practice. *Social Work, 29*(2), 123–129.

Linzer, N. (1979). A Jewish philosophy of social work practice. *Journal of Jewish Communal Service, 60*(3), 309–317.

Loewenberg, F. (1988). *Religion and social work practice in contemporary American society.* Columbia University Press: New York.

Lukoff, D., Turner, R., & Lu, F. (1992). Transpersonal psychology research review: Psychoreligious dimensions of healing. *Journal of Transpersonal Psychology, 24*(1), 41–60.

Malcolm X. *The Autobiography of Malcolm X.* New York: Grove City Press.

Mare, W. (1992). *The anchor bible dictionary,* New York: Doubleday.

Marti-Ibanez, F., (Ed.). *Tales of philosophy.* New York: Dell.

Maslow, A. (1968). *Toward of psychology of being.* New York: Van Norstrand.

Masters, W., & Johnson, V. (1966). *Human sexual response.* New York: Bantam Books.

Matthews, C. (1989). *The elements of the Celtic tradition.* Rockport, MA: Element.

Memorial Hospital v. Maricopa County, 415 U.S. 250 (1974).

Merton, T. (1960). (Tr.) *The Wisdom of the Desert.* New York: New Directions.

Meyer, M. (1987). *The ancient mysteries: A sourcebook.* San Francisco: Harper & Row.

Mitchell, J. (1994). Sex kills. On *Turbulent Indigo.* [CD]. Burbank, CA: Warner Bros.

Molko v. Holy Spirit Association for the Unification of World Christianity, 46 Cal.3d 1092, 252 Cal. Rptr. 122, 762 P.2d 46 (1988).

Mollica, R., Streets, F., Boscarino, J., & Redlich, F. (1986). A community study of formal pastoral counseling activities of the clergy. *American Journal of Psychiatry, 143*(3), 323–329.

Muir, C. & Muir, C. (1989). *Tantra.* San Francisco: Mercury House.

Muller, R. A. (1985). *Dictionary of Latin and Greek theological terms.* Grand Rapids, MI: Baker Book House.

National Association of Social Workers. (1990). *Code of Ethics.* Silver Spring, MD: Author.

Nelson, A., & Wilson, W. (1984). The ethics of sharing religious faith in psychotherapy. *Journal of Psychology and Theology, 12*(1), 15–23.

Northen, H. (1982). *Clinical social work.* New York: Columbia University Press.

Oppenheimer, J. (1957). Physics in the contemporary world. In M. Gardner (Ed.). *Great Essays in Science.* New York: Washington Square Press.

Pahnke, W. (1972). Drugs and mysticism. In White, J. *The highest states of consciousness.* Garden City, NY: Doubleday.

Peers, E. (Trans.). (1951). *Dark night of the soul.* New York: Image Books.

Peile, C. (1993). Determinism versus creativity: Which way for social work. *Social Work, 38*(2), 127–134.

Peterson v. Sorlien, 299 N.W.2d 123 (1980).

Popple, P., & Leighninger, L. (1991). *Social work, social welfare, American society.* Boston: Allyn & Bacon.

Pritchard, J. (1975). *The ancient near East* (Vol. 2). Princeton, NJ: Princeton University Press.

Quasten, J. (1960). *Patrology* (Vol. VIII). Westminster, MD: Newman Press.

Rajneesh, B. (1975). Tantric sex: Going all the way. *New Age Journal, 1*(4), 20–27.

Rawson, P. (1973). *Tantra.* New York: Thames and Hudson.

Rawson, P. (1978). *The art of tantra.* New York: Thames and Hudson.

Raye, M. (1994). *Sexuality: The sacred journey.* Colorado Springs, CO: Action Press.

Ray, S. (1976). *I deserve love.* Berkeley, CA: Celestial Arts.

Religious Freedom Restoration Act, 42 U.S.C 2000bb (a)(4) (1993).

Ritter, K., & O'Neil, C. (1989). Moving through loss: Spiritual journey of gay men and women. *Journal of Counseling and Development, 68,* 9–15.

Roof, W. (1993). *A generation of seekers.* New York: HarperSanFrancisco.

Sanford, J. (1978). *Dreams and healing.* New York: Paulist Press.

Sanville, J. (1975). Therapists in competition and cooperation with exorcists: The spirit world clinically revisited. *Clinical Social Work Journal, 3*(4), 286–297.

Schodde, G. H. (1885). The rules of Pachomius. *Presbyterian Review, 6,* 678–689.

Scholem, G. (1991). *On the mystical shape of the godhead.* New York: Schocken.

Setzer, J.S. (1973). Figure presented in class at Hartwick College, Onconto, NY. Adapted from J. Silva (1977) *The Silva Mind Control Method.* New York: Poclat Books.

Shapiro v. Thompson, 394 U.S. 618 (1969).

Sherbert v. Verner, 374 U.S. 398 (1963).

Sheridan, M., & Bullis, R. (1991). Practitioner's views on religion and spirituality: A qualitative review. *Spirituality and Social Work Journal, 2*(2), 2–10.

Sheridan, M., Bullis, R., Adcock, C., Berlin, S., & Miller, P. (1992). Serving diverse religious client populations: Issues for social work education and practice. *Journal of Social Work Education, 28*(2), 190–203.

Shinn, F. (1925). *The game of life.* Marina del Ray, CA: DeVoss.

Silva, J. (1977). *The Silva mind control method.* New York: Poclat Books.

Singer, J. (1972). *Boundaries of the soul.* Garden City, NY: Doubleday/Anchor Press.

Sovatsky, S. (1994). *Passions of innocense.* Rochester, VT: Destiny Books.

Specter, M. (1989, November 15). Dead sea scrolls: Open to whom? *The Washington Post,* p. A3.

Spencer, S. (1956). Religious and spiritual values in social casework practice. *Social Casework, 57,* 519–526.

Spencer, S. (1957). Religion and social work. *Social Work, 1,* 19–26.

Spencer, S. (1961). What place has religion in social work education? *Social Service Review, 35,* 161–170.

State v. Blake, 695 P.2d 336 (Hawaii App. 1985).

State v. Rocheleau, 451 A.2d. 1144 (1982).

Stenfels, P. (1994, February 10). Psychiatrists' manual shifts stance on religious and spiritual problems. *New York Times.*

Stroup, H. (1986). *Social work pioneers*. Chicago: Nelson-Hall.

Tagore, R. (Tr.) (1971). *One Hundred Poems of Tagore*. Delhi: Macmillan Co. of India.

Tart, C. (1972). En-trancing is the word. In Muses and Young (Eds.). *Consciousness and reality*. New York: Outerbridge & Lazard.

Towle, C. (1957). *Common human needs*. New York: National Association of Social Workers.

Tractman, P. (1994). NIH looks at the implausible and the imexplicale. *Smithsonian, 26* (6), 110–123.

Trattner, W.I. (1984). *From poor law to welfare state*. New York: The Free Press.

Underhill, E. (1911). *Mysticism*. New York: E. P. Hutton.

Underhill, E. (1915). *Practical mysticism*. New York: E. P. Hutton.

Vermaseren, M. (1977). *Cybele and Attis*. (Tr. Lemmers). London: Thames & Hudson found in Baring & Cashford (1991) *The myth of the goddess*. New York: Viking Arkana, p. 403.

Vermes, G. (1968). *The dead sea scrolls in English*. Baltimore: Penguin Books.

Veroff, J., Kulka, R., & Douvan, E. (1976). *Mental health in America*. New York: Basic Books.

Virkler, H. (1979). Counseling demands, procedures, and preparation of parish ministers: A descriptive study. *Journal of Psychology and Theology, 7*(4), 271–280.

Wapnick, K. (1972). Mysticism and schizophrenia. *The highest states of consciousness*. Garden City, NY: Doubleday.

Wigner, E. (1972). The place of consciousness in modern physics. In Muses and Young (Eds.). *Consciousness and reality*. New York: Outerbridge & Lazard.

Wilkinson, R. (1992). *Reading Egyptian art* . New York: Thames & Hudson.

Woodward, K. (1994, November 28). On the road again. *Newsweek*, 61–62.

Worral, A., & Worral, O. (1965). *The gift of healing*. Columbus, OH: Ariel Press.

Appendix A

Available Resources

This bibliography offers a sampling of the books available concerning a number of different religious or spiritual traditions. This bibliogprahy does not claim comphrehensiveness either in the spiritual groups listed nor in the books offered under each section. Scriptures of each spiritual tradition, such as the Bible, Koran, or Bhagadvad-Gita, are not always listed due to their obvious necessity and the many English translations available.

AFRICAN-AMERICAN & CARIBBEAN

Drewal, H., & Pemberton, J. (1989). *Yoruba: Nine centuries of African art and thought.* New York: Center for African Art.
Gonzalez-Wipper, M. (1987). *Santeria.* Bronx, NY: Original Products.
Owens, J. (1976). *Dread: The Rastafarians of Jamaica.* Kinston, Jamaica: Sangster.

ASTROLOGY

Berg, P. (1986). *Astrology: The star connection.* New York: Research Centre of Kabbalah International.
Elwell, D. (1987). *Cosmic loom: The new science of astrology.* London: Unwin Hyman.
Nesle, S. (1981). *Astrology: History, symbols and signs.* Leon Amiel.

AUTOBIOGRAPHIES (SPIRITUAL)

Dass, Ram. (1971). *Be here now.* San Cristobal, NM: Lama Foundation.
Jung, C. (1965). *Memories, dreams and reflections.* New York: Vintage.
Merton, T. (1965). *The seven story mountain.* Pope John Paul XXIII.
(1964) *Journal of a soul.* New York: Signet.
X, Malcolm. (1965). *The autobiography of Malcolm X.* New York: Grove City Press.

BIBLICAL LITERATURE (VERSIONS)

The Holy Bible, Revised Standard Version (1952, 1946). New York: Thomas Nelson & Sons.

BUDDHISM

Blythe, R. (1960). *Zen in English literature and oriental classics.* New York: Dutton.
De Project, Y. (1987). *Art of enlightenment.* Berkeley: Dharma Publishing.
Kapleau, P. (Ed.) (1965). *The three pillars of zen.* Boston: Beacon Press. (Ed.).
Kapleau, P. (1971). *The wheel of death.* New York: Harper Collins.
Merton, T. (1968). *Zen and the birds of appetite.* New York: New Directions.
Merton, T. (1965). *The way of Chuang Tzu.* New York: New Directions.
Pal, P. (1991). *Art of the Himalayas.* New York: Hudson Hills Press.
Reps, P. (n.d.). *Zen flesh, zen bones.* Garden City, NY: Doubleday.

CELTIC MYSTERIES

Bedier, J. (1965). *The romance of Tristan and Iseult.* New York: Random House.
Bord, J. & C. (1990). *Atlas of magical Britain.* Seacaucus, NJ: Chartwell Books.
Carmichael, A. (1972). *Celtic invocations.* Noroton, CT: Vineyard.
Lang, L. & J. (1992). *Art of the Celts.* New York: Thames and Hudson.
Layard, J. (1975). *A Celtic quest: Sexuality and soul in individuation.* Dallas: Spring Publications.
Matthews, C. (1989). *The elements of the Celtic tradition.* Rockport, MA: Element Books.
Moscati, S., Frey, O., Kruta, V., Raferty, B., & Szabo, M. (1991). *The Celts.* New York: Rizzoli.
Rutherford, W. (1987). *Celtic mythology.* New York: Sterling Publishing.
Scherman, K. (1981). *The flowering of Ireland: Saints, scholars & kings.* Boston: Little, Brown & Co.
Van deWeyer, R. (Ed.) (1990). *Celtic fire.* New York: Doubleday.

COMPARATIVE RELIGION

Campbell, J. (1988). *Historical Atlas of World Mythology* (5 vols.) New York: Harper & Row.
Campbell, J. (1974). *The mythic image.* Princeton: Princeton University Press.
Campbell, J. (1969). *The masks of God* (Vols. 1-4). New York: Penguin Books.
Campbell, J. (1949). *The hero with a thousand faces.* New York: Meridian Books.
Eliade, M. (1963). *Myth and reality.* New York: Harper Torchbooks.
Eliade, M. (1959). *Cosmos and history.* New York: Harper & Row.
Eliade, M. (1959). *The sacred and the profane.* New York: Harcourt, Brace & Jovanovich.
Eliade, M. (1957). *Myths, dreams, and mysteries.* New York: Harper Torchbooks.
Smith, H. (1976). *Forgotten truth: The primordial tradition.* New York: Harper Colophon.
Smith, H. (1958). *The religions of man.* New York: Harper & Row.

CHRISTIANITY

Dechanet, J. M. (1960). *Christian yoga.* New York: Harper & Row.

Cerutti, E. (1977). *Mystic with the healing hands: The life story of Olga Worrall.* New York: Harper & Row.

Kelsey, M. (1976). *The other side of silence: A guide to Christian meditation.* New York: Paulist Press.

Leech, K. (1985). *Experiencing God.* New York: Harper & Row.

Leech, K. (1977). *Soul friend: A study of spirituality.* London: Sheldon Press.

MacNutt, F. (1981). *The prayer that heals.* Notre Dame, IN: Ave Maria Press.

Merton, T. (1971). *Contemplation in a world of action.* Garden City, NY: Image Books.

Merton, T. (1971). *Contemplative prayer.* Garden City, NY: Image Books.

Merton, T. (1960). *The wisdom of the desert.* New York: New Directions.

Metford, J. (1983). *Dictionary of Christian lore and legend.* New York: Thames and Hudson.

Neff, H. (1971). *Psychic phenomena and religion.* Philadelphia: The Westminster Press.

Shinn, F. (1925). *The game of life and how to play it.* Marina del Ray, CA: DeVorss & Co.

Strong, M. (Ed.). (1948). *Letters of the scattered brotherhood.* New York: Harper & Row.

Waddell, H. (Trans). (1977). *The desert fathers.* Ann Arbor: University of Michigan Press.

HINDUISM

Bhattacharya, D. (1969). *Love songs of Chandidas.* New York: Grove Press.

Collis, M. (1947). *Quest for Sita.* New York: Capricorn Books.

Dass, B. (1973). *The yellow book: The saying of Baba Hari Dass.* San Cristobal, NM: The Lama Foundation.

Dimock, E., & Levertov, D. (1967). *In praise of Krishna.* Garden City, NY: Anchor.

Narayan, R. (1972). *The Ramayana.* New York: Penguin Books.

Prabhavananda, S., & Isherwood, C. (1953). *How to know God: The yoga aphorisms of Patanjali.* New York: New American Library.

Tagore, R. (n.d.). *Gitanjali.* New York: Collier/Macmillan.

ISLAM

Glasse, C. (1989). *The concise encyclopedia of Islam.* New York: HarperSanFrancisco.

Khan, V. (1974). *Toward the one.* New York: Harper Colophon.

Shah, I. (1967). *Tales of the dervishes.* New York: Dutton.

Shah, I. (1971). *Caravan of dreams.* Baltimore: Penguin.

Shah, I. (1970). *The way of the Sufi.* New York: Dutton.

Shah, I. (1971). *Thinkers of the East.* Baltimore: Penguin.

Shakir, M. (Trans.) (n.d.). *The Qurán.* Elmhurst, NY: Tahrike Tarsile Qur'an, Inc.

Whinfield, E. (Trans.) (1975). *Teachings of Rumi.* New York: Dutton.

JUDAISM

Buber, M. (1948). *Tales of the Hasidim.* New York: Schocken Books.
Epstein, P. (1988). *Kabbalah: The way of the Jewish mystic.* Boston: Shambhala.
Frankel, E., & Teutsch, B. (1992). *The encyclopedia of Jewish symbols.* Northvale, NJ: Jason Aronson, Inc.
Graves, R., & Patai, R. (1964). *Hebrew myths.* New York: Doubleday.
Halevi, Z. (1985). *The work of the Kabbalist.* York Beach, ME: Samuel Weiser.
Kaplan, A. (Trans.) (1995). *The Bahir.* Northvale, NJ: Jason Aronson, Inc.
Kaplan, A. (1995). *Meditation and the Bible.* Northvale, NJ: Jason Aronson, Inc.
Kaplan, A. (1995). *Meditation and the Kabbalah.* Northvale, NJ: Jason Aronson, Inc.
Kushner, L. (1990). *The river of light.* Woodstock, VT: Jewish Lights Books.
Kushner, L. (1977). *Honey from the rock.* New York: Harper & Row.
Kushner, L. (1975). *The book of letters.* New York: Harper & Row.
Schachter-Shalomi, Z. (1991). *Spiritual intimacy: A study of counseling in Hasidim.* Northvale, NJ: Jason Aronson, Inc.
Schutz, A. (1988). *Call Adonai.* Goleta, CA: Quantal Publishing.
Sperling, H., & Simon, M. (Trans.) (1984). *The Zohar* (Vols. 1-4). New York: The Soncino Press.
Unterman, A. (1991). *Dictionary of Jewish lore and legend.* New York: Thames and Hudson.

LAW REPORTERS

The Entheogen law reporter. Subscriptions can be made by contacting the Reporter at P.O. Box 73481, Davis, CA 95617-3481.

NATIVE AMERICAN

Brown, J. (1990). *The spiritual legacy of the American Indian.* New York: Crossroad.
Castaneda, C. (1987). *The power of silence.* New York: Simon & Shuster.
Castaneda, C. (1974). *Tales of power.* New York: Simon & Shuster.
Castaneda, C. (1972). *Journey to Ixtlan: The lessons of Don Juan.* Middlesex, England: Penguin Books.
Feldman, S. (Ed.). (1965). *The storytelling stone.* Dell: New York.
McLuhan, T. (Ed.). (1971). *Touch the Earth.* New York: Touchstone.
Rothenberg, J. (Ed.). (1972). *Shaking the pumpkin: Traditional poetry of the Indian North Americas.* Garden City, NY: Doubleday.
Tooker, E. (1979). *Native North American spirituality of the Eastern Woodlands.* New York: Paulist Press.

PSYCHOLOGY AND SPIRITUALITY

Assagioli, R. (1965). *Psychosynthesis*. New York: Penguin Books.

Coster, G. (1972). *Yoga and western psychology*. New York: Harper & Row.

Ebin, D. (Ed.). (1961). *The drug experience*. New York: Grove Press.

Edinger, E. (1972). *Ego and archetype*. Baltimore: Penguin.

Ehrenwald, J. (Ed.). (1991). *The history of psychotherapy*. Northvale, NJ: Jason Aronson, Inc.

Frank, J. (1973). *Persuasion and healing*. New York: Schocken Books.

Fromm, E. (1951). *The forgotten language*. New York: Grove Press.

Gould, R. (1978). *Transformations*. New York: Simon & Shuster.

Houston, J. (1987). *The search for the beloved*. New York: J. P. Tarcher.

Houston, J. (1982). *The possible human*. Los Angeles: J. P. Tarcher.

Jacobi, J. (1973). *The psychology of C. G. Jung*. New Haven: Yale University Press.

Jung, C. (1964). *Man and his symbols*. New York: Dell.

Kelsey, M. (1978). *Dreams: A way to listen to God*. New York: Paulist Press.

Krieger, D. (1979). *The therapeutic touch*. Englewood Cliffs, NJ: Prentice-Hall, Inc.

Krippner, S., & Welch, P. (1992). *Spiritual dimensions of healing*. New York: Irving Publishers.

Masters, R., & Houston. (1966). *The varieties of psychedelic experience*. New York: Dell.

Masters, R., & Houston. (1972). *Mind games*. New York: Dell.

Murdock, M. (1987). *Spinning inward: Using guided imagery with children for learning, creativity & relaxation*. Boston: Shambhala.

Singer, J. (1972). *Boundaries of the soul: The practice of Jung's psychology*. Garden City, NY: Anchor Press.

Tart, C. (Ed.). (1975). *Transpersonal psychologies*. New York: Harper Colophon.

Ward, C. (Ed.). (1989). *Altered states of consciousness and mental health*. Newbury Park, NJ: Sage.

White, J. (Ed.). (1972). *The highest state of consciousness*. Garden City, NY: Anchor Books.

Whitmore, C. (1985). *Alcoholism and spirituality*. East Rutherford, NJ: Thomas W. Perrin, Inc.

SHAMANISM

Ashe, G. (1992). *Dawn behind the dawn*. New York: John Macrae/Henry Holt.

Doore, G. (1988). *Shaman's path*. Boston: Shambhala.

Fortune, R. (1963). *Sorcerers of Dobu*. New York: Dutton.

Halifax, J. (1979). *Shamanic voices: A survey of visionary narratives*. New York: Dutton.

Kakar, S. (1982). *Shamans, mystics and doctors*. Boston: Beacon Press.

Kalweit, H. (1988). *Dreamtime and inner space*. Boston: Beacon Press.

Krippner, S. (Ed.). *Spiritual dimensions of healing*. New York: Irvington Publishers.

Torrey, E. (1986). *Witchdoctors and psychiatrists*. New York: Harper & Row.

WICCA (WITCHCRAFT)

Adler, M. (1979). *Drawing down the moon: Witches, druids, goddess-worshippers, and other pagans in America today.* Boston: Beacon Press.
Budapest, Z. (1979). *The holy book of women's mysteries* (Parts 1 & 2). Los Angeles: Susan B. Anthony Coven No. 1.
Starhawk. (1988). *Dreaming the dark.* Boston: Beacon Press.
Starhawk. (1979). *The spiral dance.* New York: Harper & Row.

WOMEN'S SPIRITUALITY

Andrews, L. (1985). *Jaguar woman.* New York: Harper & Row.
Baring, A., & Cashford, J. (1991). *The myth of the goddess.* New York: Viking.
Kramer, R. (1988). *Maenads, martyrs, matrons, monastics: A sourcebook on women's religions in the Greco-Roman world.* Philadelphia: Fortress.
Spretnak, C. (1978). *Lost goddesses of early Greece.* Boston: Beacon Press.

VIDEO

Campbell, J. (1989). *The world of Joseph Campbell: Transformations of myth through time* (13 volumes-9 tapes). Public Media Video.

AUDIO TAPES

Krippner, S. (1992). *Healing images: Contemporary shamanism in North America.* Irving Publishers. This cassette accompanies the book *Spiritual dimensions of healing.*

Appendix B

A Spiritual History

PARENTS OR CUSTODIANS

1. What was the religious or spiritual faith of your parents?
2. Were they strict or lenient (casual) in their beliefs?
3. Does this strictness or leniency have a bearing on you today? How so?
4. What do you think were the most important spiritual beliefs that they held? Did they pass these on to you? How?

SPOUSES OR SIGNIFICANT OTHERS

1. What is their main religious or spiritual identity?
2. In what religious/spiritual orientation were they raised? Have they remained with this orientation? Why or why not?
3. What religious/spiritual issues, if any, have caused problems in your relationship? If they are resolved, how did you resolve them? If they are not resolved, how do they affect your relationship?
4. If you have children, do you and your spouse (or significant other) agree or disagree on the spiritual orientation with which they are being raised? What are the principle spiritual values that you both wish to impart to your child(ren)?

YOURSELF

1. In what religious/spiritual orientation were you raised?
2. Was your instruction strict or lenient? What values and ideas have stayed with you?
3. What is your current religious or spiritual affiliation? What are its major tenets? What are its major values and principles?
4. How has your spiritual orientation changed since your upbringing? Why has it changed? What events or experiences helped to change you?

Appendix C

Text of Guided Meditation or Deep Prayer

The following text is taken from an actual guided meditation or deep prayer. The goal of the prayer was healing. The text is artificially divided into the following categories to illustrate the phases of this kind of prayer.

RELAXATION

Let us begin by sitting and breathing right. Sit in your chair with your feet flat on the floor. Place your bottom flush against the backrest so that your spine is straight. Place your hands comfortably in your lap. Close your eyes; now, breathe deeply a couple of times. As you breathe in, imagine breathing in warmth and light and rest. As you breathe out, imagine breathing out any stress or anxiety you may feel right now. Continue breathing like this for a few moments.

Now, in your mind's eye, see your feet resting on a pillow of light. Your feet feel warm and good resting there. Imagine that the light now moves up through the rest of your body. Where the light is—there is no anxiety, just comfort. Imagine that the light is moving up your ankles, into your knees and thighs. All these muscles relax as they feel the light around them. The light moves up into your thighs and into your pelvis and bottom.

The light continues throughout your body. It moves up into your torso, moving now up into your shoulders and neck. The light warms and soothes the muscles. You can feel the stress ooze out of them. Now the light proceeds up your neck and into the back of your head, and the light loosens any tension there. And the light envelops the rest of your body, going down your arms and into your hands. You see the light enveloping your entire body—bathing it in its soothing warmth.

VISUALIZATION

Your body is now full of the pulsing, radiant light. Now this light takes a form and a figure. Light comes in a way known best to us—a light reaching into our light, and into our darkness. It comes in a form special to us, in a way that is useful to ourselves and others. The form it takes may be a man or woman, it may not be human, it may be a feeling or an object. But this radiance can now speak with you and can touch you. This form comes to you and holds out its hands.

And now we see a place in our bodies where the stress and tension has settled. A place where the pain is buried, where the wound lies unresolved. You may see that place in your body as a dim or distorted place. Or this place may be a dark place or it may feel heavy or uncomfortable. When you have found that place, you know that is the place that we have neglected, where we are unloved—where we are unloving.

AFFIRMATION

You also see the light, in whatever form, surrounding the wound. And the holy form of light comes and touches that part of us—lays its hand into our hurt, lays its wisdom into our wound, lays its light into our darkness. And in that place where your pain or hurt is kept, the holy light opens up its cage and lets the pain go. The light infuses it with an overflowing love, washes it with living water. The holy light can speak as well and the light says:

> In my light there is nothing but health . . .
> In my light there is nothing but love . . .
> and all are as loved as they can be.
>
> This light works to release, resolve and expose
> any anger of fear or disappointment
> now in your bodies and in your spirits.
> It can reveal your hurts and your healing.
> It can show the love of God for you,
>
> You lay your own wounds at the well
> of God, they can receive the healing of
> the Holy One.

We feel the light in that wounded part of us growing—and healing and wholeness takes place, a release of tension and contention, a release of energy as we feel the light radiating from our wound. The light there now soothes and comforts.

CONFIRMATION

When we feel that enough light has come into that part, we confirm that gift. We thank that form with touch, a word, or a wave. We feel the health radiate from our whole body. We feel healthy, whole, and holy. Our healing is being perfected and we resolve to help our own healing. As our healing is perfected, we let the Holy One go, knowing that we will take the healing with us.

CONCLUSION

We now can return to this time and place. We begin to feel our body on the chair. We can start to feel our feet on the floor and wiggle your toes. [The clinician's voice should become louder.] You can hear the noises outside and you can feel your hands folded in your lap. When you are ready to return fully, you can open your eyes and look at me. [At least 10 minutes should be devoted to debriefing after this exercise.]

Appendix D

Biblical Resources

The following resources were used in putting together this book:

The holy bible. (1952). (Revised Standard Version). New York: Thomas Nelson and Sons.
The HarperCollins study bible. (1989). (New Revised Standard Version). New York: HarperCollins.
The Oxford annotated bible with the apocrypha. (1965). (Revised Standard Version). New York: Oxford University Press.
The Jerusalem bible. Garden City, NY: Doubleday & Company.

Appendix E

Religious Organizations and Counseling Organizations with Spiritual Components

Below is a list of counseling organizations that have members who are interested in spirituality. This list is not comprehensive and, in some cases, the organization itself does not have a specific committee related to spirituality. The inclusion of these organizations does not necessarily denote an endorsement.

American Association of Pastoral Counselors
9508a Lee Highway
Fairfax, VA 22031
This association helps to publish the *Journal of Pastoral Care*.

American Association of Sex Educators Counselors and Therapists
435 N. Michigan, Suite 1717
Chicago, IL 60611-4067

American Counseling Association
5999 Stevenson Avenue
Alexandria, VA 22304
This association has both national and state committees named Association for spirituality, religion, and values in counseling which, as the name implies, addresses spiritual issues in counseling. The national ASERVIC committee publishes a journal titled *Counseling and Values*.

American Protestant Correctional Chaplains Association
P.O. Box 1441
Huntsville, TX 77342
This Association helps to publish the *Journal of Pastoral Care*.

Association for Clinical Pastoral Education
1549 Clairmont Road, Suite 103
Decatur, GA 30033
This association helps to publish the *Journal of Pastoral Care*.

Association of Mental Health Clergy
12320 River Oaks Point
Knoxville, TN 37922
This association helps to publish the *Journal of Pastoral Care*.

Canadian Association for Pastoral Education
P.O. Box 96
Roxbury, P.Q., H8Y 3E8, Canada
This association helps to publish the *Journal of Pastoral Care.*

Christian Association for Psychological Studies
P.O. Box 890279
Temecula, CA 92589-0279
This association publishes the *Journal of Psychology and Christianity.*

College of Chaplains of the American Protestant Health Association
1701 East Woodfield Rd., Suite 311
Schaumburg, IL 60173
This association helps to publish the *Journal of Pastoral Care.*

International Religious Foundation
GPO Box 1311
New York, NY 10116
The Foundation publishes the journal *Dialogue & Alliance.*

National Academy of Certified Clinical Mental Health Counselors
5999 Stevenson Avenue
Alexandria, VA 22304
703-823-9800

National Association of Catholic Chaplains
3501 South Lake Dr., P.O. Box 07473
Milwaukee, WI 53207-0473
This association helps to publish the *Journal of Pastoral Care.*

Dr. Edward Canda, Professor
School of Social Work
University of Kansas
Lawrence, KS 66045
Professor Canda produces a journal dealing directly with the connection between spirituality and social work.

National Institute of Business and Industrial Chaplains, Inc.
Wesley Medical Center
550 North Hillside
Wichita, KS 67214
This association helps to publish the *Journal of Pastoral Care.*

Index